RECONSTRUCTING SCHIZOPHRENIA

Despite nearly one hundred years of research, very little progress has been achieved in the understanding of schizophrenic behaviour. Although it is widely believed that schizophrenic symptoms reflect an underlying biological disorder, the evidence for such a disorder remains disputed and many different biological defects have been implicated. There remains considerable uncertainty even about the fundamental features of the hypothesized illness.

Reconstructing Schizophrenia subjects the difficult concept of schizophrenia to rigorous scientific, historical, and sociological scrutiny. The contributors, who are all psychologists with considerable research and clinical experience in the field of adult psychopathology, examine the concept of schizophrenia and ask how it attained its present position as the cornerstone of modern psychiatric theory. They ask why a biological defect has been assumed in the absence of hard evidence, and look at what can be done psychologically to alleviate schizophrenic symptoms. Finally they explore what new models and research strategies are required in order to understand schizophrenic behaviour. The result is a book that provides a distinctive and critical perspective on modern psychiatric theories and which demonstrates the severe limitations of an exclusively medical approach to understanding madness.

Reconstructing Schizophrenia will appeal to any one with an interest in mental health, but will be of particular relevance to students and practitioners in the disciplines of psychology, psychiatry, social work, and psychiatric nursing.

The editor: Richard Bentall is Lecturer in Clinical Psychology at the University of Liverpool.

RECONSTRUCTING SCHIZOPHRENIA

EDITED BY RICHARD P. BENTALL

London and New York

First published 1990
by Routledge
11 New Fetter Lane, London EC4P 4EE

First published in paperback in 1992
Reprinted 1995

Simultaneously published in the USA and Canada
by Routledge
29 West 35th Street, New York, NY 10001

Printed and bound in Great Britain
by Biddles Ltd, Guildford and King's Lynn

British Library Cataloguing in Publication Data
A catalogue record for this book is available from the British Library

Library of Congress Cataloguing-in-Publication Data
A catalogue record for this book is available from the Library of Congress

ISBN 0–415–01574–X (hbk)
ISBN 0–415–07524–6 (pbk)

CONTENTS

FIGURES AND TABLES

FIGURES

TABLES

ABBREVIATIONS

CFI	Camberwell Family Interview
DAS	Danish Adoption Studies
ECT	Electroconvulsive therapy
EE	Expressed emotion
EEG	Electroencephalogram
EPQ	Eysenck Personality Questionnaire
MIND	National Association for Mental Health
NSF	National Schizophrenia Fellowship
PBC	Perinatal birth complication
PSE	Present State Examination
RDC	Research Diagnostic Criteria
TLE	Temporal lobe epilepsy
VBR	Ventricular/brain ratio

CONTRIBUTORS

Peter Barham The Hamlet Trust and The Centre for Community Mental Health in Europe, Goldsmiths' College, University of London

Richard P. Bentall Department of Clinical Psychology, University of Liverpool

Mary Boyle Department of Psychology, Polytechnic of East London

Gordon Claridge Department of Experimental Psychology, Oxford University

Robert Hayward The Hamlet Trust and The Centre for Community Mental Health in Europe, Goldsmiths' College, University of London

Howard F. Jackson Department of Clinical Psychology, Moss Side Hospital, Maghull, Merseyside

Richard Marshall Nottingham Psychological Service, Nottingham

David Pilgrim The Roehampton Institute, London

Peter D. Slade Sub-department of Clinical Psychology, Liverpool University Medical School

Nicholas Tarrier Department of Psychiatry, University of Manchester

Peter H. Venables Department of Psychology, University of York.

To Sally
(and Hairy of course)

PREFACE

If in life we are surrounded by death, so too in the health of our intellect we are surrounded by madness.

Ludwig Wittgenstein
Notebook on Culture and Value, 1944

It is tempting, on opening a book of this sort, to proceed immediately to those chapters which are of interest, and to skip the preface, or at least to give it only a cursory glance. It is hoped that in this case the reader will make an exception. The purpose of this preface is to provide a rationale for what might otherwise seem just another collection of chapters on the subject of 'schizophrenia' and, at the same time, to draw to the reader's attention the main issues which will be debated in the following pages. These issues relate to questions that have received all too little consideration in the literature on schizophrenia; it is the focus on these issues which makes the present book somewhat different from other contributions to the field.

The concept of 'dementia preacox', later renamed 'schizophrenia' by Bleuler, was first outlined by Kraepelin in an edition of his famous textbook of psychiatry dated 1896. At the time of writing, therefore, the diagnosis of schizophrenia approaches its one hundredth birthday. According to most accounts, schizophrenia is an illness which is characterized by various symptoms, including auditory hallucinations, bizarre and irrational beliefs, disordered thought as manifest in incoherent speech, poverty of affect, and social withdrawal. A contemporary attempt to define the salient characteristics of the disorder – the definition of schizophrenia contained in the Revised Third Edition of the American Psychiatric Association's Diagnostic and Statistical Manual of Mental Disorders – is given in Table p.1.

Table P.1 DSM-III R diagnostic criteria for schizophrenia

For a diagnosis of schizophrenia the following are required:

(A) Presence of characteristic psychotic symptoms in active phase: either (1), (2), or (3) for at least one week (unless the symptoms are successfully treated).

  (1) Two of the following:
      (a) delusions;
      (b) prominent hallucinations (throughout the day for several days or several times a week, each hallucinatory experience not being limited to a few brief moments);
      (c) incoherence or marked loosening of associations;
      (d) catatonic behaviour;
      (e) flat or grossly inappropriate affect.
  (2) Bizarre delusions (i.e. involving a phenomenon that the person's culture would regard as totally implausible, for example thought broadcasting, being controlled by a dead person).
  (3) Prominent hallucinations (as defined in 1(b) above) of a voice with content having no apparent relation to depression or elation, or a voice keeping a running commentary on the person's behaviour or thoughts, or two or more voices conversing with each other.

(B) During the course of the disturbance, functioning in such areas as work, social relations, and self-care is markedly below the highest level achieved before onset of the disturbance (or, when the onset is in childhood or adolescence, failure to achieve expected level of social development).

(C) Schizoaffective Disorder and Mood Disorder with Psychotic Features (defined elsewhere in the manual) have been ruled out, i.e. if a Major Depressive or Manic Syndrome has ever been present during an active phase of the disturbance, the total duration of all episodes of a mood syndrome has been brief relative to the total duration of the active and residual phases of the disturbance.

(D) Continuous signs of the disturbance for at least six months. The six-month period must include an active phase (of at least one week, or less if the symptoms have been successfully treated) during which there were symptoms characteristic of schizophrenia (symptoms in A), with or without a prodromal or residual phases, as defined below:

Prodromal phase: A clear deterioration in functioning before the active phase of the disturbance that is not due to a disturbance in mood or to a Psychoactive Substance Use Disorder (defined elsewhere in the manual) and that involves at least two of the symptoms listed below.

Residual phase: Following the active phase of the disturbance, persistence of at least two of the symptoms noted below, these not being due to a disturbance in mood or to a Psychoactive Substance Use Disorder.

Prodromal or residual symptoms:
  (1) marked social isolation or withdrawal;
  (2) marked impairment in role-functioning as wage-earner, student, or home-maker;

(3) marked peculiar behaviour (for example collecting garbage, talking to self in public, hoarding food);

(4) marked impairment in personal hygiene and grooming;

(5) blunted or inappropriate affect;

(6) digressive, vague, overelaborate, or circumstantial speech, or poverty of speech, or poverty of content of speech;

(7) odd beliefs or magical thinking, influencing behaviour and inconsistent with cultural norms, for example superstitiousness, belief in clairvoyance, telepathy, 'sixth sense', 'others can feel my feelings', overvalued ideas, ideas of reference;

(8) unusual perceptual experiences, for example recurrent illusions, sensing the presence of a force or a person not actually present;

(9) marked lack of initiative, interests, or energy.

Examples: Six months of prodromal symptoms with one week of symptoms from A; no prodromal symptoms with six months of symptoms of A; no prodromal symptoms with one week of symptoms from A and six months of residual symptoms.

(E) It cannot be established that an organic factor initiated and maintained the disturbance.

(F) If there is a history of Autistic Disorder (defined elsewhere in the manual) the additional diagnosis of schizophrenia is made only if prominent delusions or hallucinations are also present.

Source: *Diagnostic and Statistical Manual of Mental Disorders (third edition – revised),* Washington: American Psychiatric Association (1987).

Despite the apparent certainty of such definitions, schizophrenia alone among all the concepts of modern medicine continues to provoke considerable philosophical and scientific controversy. Serious questions remain about whether schizophrenia can be considered an illness; about whether it is one condition or several, about whether clear dividing lines can be found between schizophrenia and normal functioning or even between schizophrenia and other kinds of mental disorder. On the assumption that a scientifically meaningful schizophrenia illness entity has been identified, vast amounts of money are spent every year in many countries in order to find out what causes it. Perhaps every variable known to affect human conduct has been implicated as a possible cause of schizophrenia. Neural organization, brain biochemistry, viral agents, season of birth, genetic endowment, birth complications, life stresses, early childhood experiences, family structure, and the reactions of others to deviant conduct are but some of the possibilities that have been investigated. In the face of persisting uncertainty about the nature of schizophrenia, researchers continue to insist that the answer lies just around the corner and demand more funding for their activities. As most of the research that is carried out is biological in nature, these demands often amount to requests for larger and more expensive forms of hardwear – bigger and better PET or CT scanners, for example. The sceptical observer may be inclined to ask what progress has been made in the understanding of schizophrenia as a result of all this effort. Such scepticism is reinforced, in particular, when the achievements of schizophrenia research are compared with the scientific progress made in difficult areas of medicine such as oncology. Unlike the case of cancer, 'hard facts' or discoveries about schizophrenia are difficult to identify. The multiplicity of theories proposed to account for schizophrenic behaviour itself suggests a substantial degree of uncertainty about the nature of the hypothesized disorder.

The proposition behind this book is that it is time to try and look at the concept of schizophrenia afresh, without preconceptions. This may not seem like an original proposition; after all was this not precisely what Laing, Szasz, Scheff, and others were suggesting in the 1960s and early 1970s? Unfortunately, much of the critical literature about psychiatry published at that time failed because it was built on soft philosophical ground. Those critics of traditional psychiatry argued often contradictory positions and did so with little concern for the requirement to provide evidence for their assertions. Some appeared to be rejecting scientific method or rational argument altogether. It is not surprising, therefore, that their ideas failed to convince many people working in the domain of mental health. As a result, arguments about the nature of psychiatric disturbance have become polarized and bogged down in the rhetoric of competing ideologies. This has led to the illusion that one is required to take one of two possible positions: either to accept the traditional account of psychiatric disorder (together with the forms of crude biological reductionism that inform it) or to reject an empirical approach to understanding madness altogether (throwing scientific reasoning out with the psychiatric bathwater in the process). Of course this is a false choice, and those who insist that it must be made – whether they be biologically orientated researchers or their opponents – do a serious disservice both to the scientific community and to those individuals who are the unfortunate consumers of existing psychiatric services.

The alternative to this kind of sterile debate is to subject psychiatric concepts, in the case of this book the concept of schizophrenia, to rigorous philosophical, historical, and scientific scrutiny, using all the relevant evidence that is available – and much evidence has been collected since the 1960s. New investigations in the history of psychiatry, for example, have shed much light on the origins of the concept of schizophrenia. New work by phenomenologically inclined investigators has yielded important data about the relationships between the different symptoms of mental disorder. Much is now known about the life course of patients diagnosed as schizophrenic and developments in the neurosciences and cognitive psychology have yielded powerful models that suggest new ways of looking at abnormal conduct. Finally, and of great importance to those diagnosed as schizophrenic and their relatives, new ideas about psychological treatment suggest new ways in which psychiatric patients and those who suffer with them might be helped.

Several interlocking themes are therefore represented in this book. First, a number of the contributors, Boyle, Marshall, and Pilgrim in particular, address questions concerning the history of psychiatric ideas in general and the development of the schizophrenia concept in particular. A common argument of these contributors is that what might be called the traditional history of psychiatric ideas – the view that the history of psychiatry has consisted of a gradual unravelling of scientific truths about naturally occurring kinds of mental disorder – does not bear up under close examination. Second, many of the contributors question whether the concept of 'schizophrenia' represents a scientifically valid and naturally occurring entity that can serve as a useful object of research. It is fair to say that there is a certain amount of disagreement among the contributors on this point. Relating to this question is the further problem of how research into madness should proceed if the traditional model of schizophrenia is rejected. In my own chapter I argue the value of studying specific symptoms of madness, rather than hypothetical syndromes. Barham and Hayward, on the other hand, argue for the importance of studying the life histories of people diagnosed as schizophrenic, whereas Claridge emphasizes the benefits of studying those who exist on the borderline between schizophrenic and normal functioning. Venables demonstrates the value of studying those who appear to be at risk of later breakdown.

A third theme concerns the role of biological variables in the understanding of abnormal behaviour. It is fair to say that the controlling role of medical practitioners in the domain of mental health has led to an almost exclusive concern with biological variables as potential causes of psychiatric disorder. Marshall describes how genetic investigators have systematically exaggerated the case for the inheritance of schizophrenia, whereas Jackson argues that the range of biological abnormalities apparently linked to schizophrenia is itself evidence that there is not just one disorder.

The final theme represented in this book concerns the potential usefulness of psychological methods of treatment for persons diagnosed as schizophrenic. Following Kraepelin's view that dementia praecox inevitably leads to feeble-mindedness, it has become widely accepted (even by those who have disagreed with Kraepelin about the inevitability of mental degeneration in schizophrenia) that the outcome of the disorder is generally poor. The life-history data described by Barham and Hayward suggest that this view is false. However, because the pessimistic view of schizophrenia has persisted, it has usually been assumed that what little that can be done for schizophrenic persons must be in the form of medical treatments (usually phenothiazine medication). Psychologists have probably not helped in this regard as they have been, until recently, happy to accept a division of labour between themselves working with 'neurotics' and psychiatrists working with 'psychotics' (the 'real mentally ill'). The chapters by Tarrier and Slade in the present volume, however, give some grounds for optimism about the potential efficacy of psychological interventions.

A few words about the origins of this book are appropriate at this point. The present volume was first mooted following a symposium on 'Contrasting models of schizophrenia' held at the British Psychological Society Annual Conference at Sheffield University in April 1986. All the contributors with the exception of Tarrier presented papers at that symposium. The symposium, like this book, was convened because a number of psychologists had expressed the view, during informal discussions, that the time had come to 'rethink' the schizophrenia concept. There was also the feeling abroad that psychologists in particular ought to have something fresh to say about the nature of schizophrenic behaviour. The contributors to this book, therefore, share the common attributes of being both psychologists and British citizens. It is hoped that this will not prevent the book from being relevant to members of other professions or to people who may be working in other countries. None the less, it is clear that much (but not all) of what is in this book is best thought of as psychological. As already indicated, not all of the contributors to the book are in complete agreement with each other. What they share is a willingness to think critically about the schizophrenia concept. No doubt there will be some readers who react negatively to this exercise; in doing so, however, they will demonstrate the need for such an approach. This book has been compiled with the conviction that it is only by the combination of sound research and critical enquiry that progress (in any domain of knowledge) can be achieved.

Richard Bentall,
Liverpool, June 1989.

Part One

THE CONCEPT OF SCHIZOPHRENIA – PROBLEMS AND PROSPECTS

Chapter One

THE NON-DISCOVERY OF SCHIZOPHRENIA?

Kraepelin and Bleuler reconsidered
MARY BOYLE

It might appear that the history of the concept of schizophrenia has been well documented: a number of texts (for example, Leigh 1961; Hunter and MacAlpine 1963; Jones 1972) describe the historical background against which concepts like schizophrenia were to emerge, while texts or articles which discuss 'schizophrenia', whether academic (for example, Lewis 1966; Neale and Oltmanns 1980; Strauss and Carpenter 1981) or aimed at a wider audience (for example, Wing 1978; Clare 1980) give due consideration to Kraepelin's introduction and elaboration of the concept of dementia praecox in the fifth and subsequent editions of his textbook, to his disagreements with Bleuler, and to Bleuler's introduction of the concept of schizophrenia. It will be argued here, however, that these accounts, which are usually couched in terms of Kraepelin and Bleuler having described or differentiated a form of mental illness, are best thought of as received wisdom about 'schizophrenia', and that an analysis of what Kraepelin and Bleuler actually *did* (as distinct from what they are said to have done) not only casts considerable doubt on the accuracy of traditional accounts but also helps us to understand some of the problems facing the modern concept of schizophrenia.

In a separate chapter of this volume, Pilgrim describes the ways in which traditional accounts of the development of psychiatry as a scientific and humanitarian enterprise have been seriously questioned. One of the most detailed and able of these critiques has been provided by Scull (1979). A number of important points arise from his and others' work, but two are of particular interest here. The first is that, in Great Britain at least, humane asylum provision was originally conceived of as a lay and not a medical enterprise and that medical dominance in asylums was achieved only after protracted political struggle. The second point is that medical dominance was won in the absence of any scientific evidence as to the efficacy of medicine in theorizing about and intervening in deviant behaviour. Taken together, these points emphasize the back-to-front nature of traditional histories of psychiatry: it was not that psychiatry developed more humane ways of dealing with the 'mentally ill' or more scientific ways of understanding 'mental illness' but that medical dominance over deviant behaviour contributed to the later widespread adoption of the idea that it should be viewed as illness. The lack of evidence for the efficacy of medical theories and practice meant that Kraepelin and Bleuler arrived at the study of deviant behaviour remarkably ill-equipped for the task: as far as can be seen, they had little awareness of the problems of describing, observing, and recording behaviour. They also approached their task with strong *a priori* beliefs about the kinds of patterns they would find in the behaviour of asylum inmates and the variables which controlled such behaviour. Before their work is discussed, it will be helpful to describe in more detail the theoretical models which guided them (particularly Kraepelin) and the ways in which these relate to the activities of medical and scientific researchers in general.

'SCHIZOPHRENIA' AS DISEASE ENTITY – SYNDROME – HYPOTHETICAL CONSTRUCT

Like all scientific research, medical research is concerned with the valid description of patterns or regularities. When patterns are suggested, it is usual for researchers to infer unobservables from them (electricity, atoms, intelligence, learning, and so on). Of particular interest here is the type of unobservable usually known in psychology as a hypothetical construct, and two conditions must be met if it is to be claimed as valid. First, it must be derived from an observed pattern; this pattern or set of events then becomes the criterion for inferring the construct. Second, the construct must lead to new observations (the construct of Down's syndrome, for example, eventually led to the observation of chromosome abnormalities). These two conditions are sometimes referred to as the necessary and sufficient conditions for claiming a construct's validity, to reflect the fact that the

4

necessary, but not sufficient, condition for asserting the validity of a hypothetical construct is that it be derived from a pattern; the sufficient condition for claiming validity is that the construct leads to new observations. If the necessary condition is not fulfilled, i.e. if the construct is not derived from a pattern, then obviously the sufficient condition cannot be either. It is unfortunate that the language of medicine tends to obscure the process of concept formation: when new patterns are suggested, we are apt to talk of 'a new disease being discovered'. Constructs inferred from the patterns (for example, multiple sclerosis, AIDS, diabetes) then become, misleadingly, the 'name of diseases' which people are said to 'have'.

In medical research, a favoured way of demonstrating that certain events 'go together' is to show that a proposed cluster is reliably associated with (an)other independently and reliably measurable event(s), known as signs. In turn, this new cluster may be shown to be associated with other events so that an originally sparse cluster may become elaborated as research findings accumulate. As Engle and Davis (1963) have pointed out, medical classification systems contain different types of patterns which vary both in terms of the type of events they include (structural damage, presence of micro-organisms, abnormal processes, and so on) and in terms of their 'richness' – some, for example, include events thought to be antecedents; others are little more than descriptive labels. Engle and Davis have divided these proposed patterns into higher and lower 'orders of certainty' (i.e. the certainty with which new exemplars may be recognized) to reflect the fact that some of the patterns are more clearly described than others and/or show less variability across exemplars. People bitten by rattlesnakes, for example, will show a less variable picture than those said to 'have multiple sclerosis'. At the bottom of Engle and Davis's list – at the lowest order of certainty – is that pattern known as a 'syndrome', or a proposed cluster of signs and symptoms whose antecedents are unknown. This type of cluster is the very least that is required in order to claim that a pattern has been observed and it is this status which is claimed for the cluster from which the modern hypothetical construct of schizophrenia is derived.

Kraepelin, however, did not set out to describe a syndrome. Instead, he believed that his task was to discover 'disease entities'.

In this, he was reflecting medical thinking of the day: the idea that there existed 'out there' natural (?God given) and discrete groupings or clusters, each with its own antecedent both necessary and sufficient to produce the cluster. Although this idea had been strongly criticized, it received, as can be imagined, strong support from Pasteur's work on infectious micro-organisms. It would be unfair, however, to judge Kraepelin's work by asking whether he described a disease entity: neither he nor anyone else has ever claimed that he did so. The important question, and that which will be addressed here, is whether he described any kind of pattern. In other words, were the necessary conditions for inferring the hypothetical construct of dementia praecox ever fulfilled?

THE PROBLEM OF PATTERN RECOGNITION

The sophistication of modern medical theory and research techniques is such that some new patterns are identified and elaborated relatively quickly. Perhaps because of this, because success stories are well publicized and we will never know how many patterns are missed, it is easy for us to lose sight of just how difficult is the process of identifying patterns amongst seemingly similar and overdetermined phenomena. Should we, for example, group together all instances of chest pains, coughing blood, and emaciation?; or 'wasting' of the limbs and loss of power in them? If negative answers to these seem obvious, it is only so with hindsight. It can be argued that the whole scientific enterprise is an attempt to reduce errors in this process, to impose criteria whereby putative patterns can be shown not to be chance co-occurrences. In medicine, this concern is reflected in the demand that complaints, or symptoms, be reliably associated with an independently and reliably measurable event before a new pattern is (tentatively) said to have been described.

Kraepelin was well aware of the fact that he was required to demonstrate that certain phenomena 'went together' in order to justify his concept of dementia praecox, but he faced major problems in his choice of criteria for making this demonstration. The history of the medical study of deviant behaviour in asylums had been marked by repeated failures to demonstrate reliable associations between disturbing behaviour and particular biochemical processes, i.e. a relationship between so-called symptoms and signs. Nevertheless, rapid progress in medical research, particularly the descriptions of the 'infectious diseases' and the demonstration of the link between earlier syphilitic infection and later madness, encouraged asylum doctors to believe that results were just round the corner; in the meantime, other criteria had to be used to support the claim to have observed patterns. It was, of course, important to claim that patterns had been observed, that new forms of mental illness were being discovered, lest the public begin to question the wisdom of medical dominance in asylums, or lest physicians question the validity of their alienist colleagues' claim to be part of the medical profession.

Kraepelin's chosen criterion for claiming to have observed a pattern which justified inferring dementia praecox was similarities in onset course and outcome. Thus, he suggested that the phenomena from which he had previously inferred catatonia belonged to the same cluster as did those from which he inferred dementia praecox because 'both in their development and in their origins and prognosis we find an extensive correspondence between the two forms of illness' (Kraepelin 1896: 461). He also suggested that the phenomena from which he inferred dementia paranoides should be kept separate because 'Not only does [dementia paranoides] develop on average at a rather higher age, it has a course and an outcome which is considerably different.' (ibid.: 469) Kraepelin did not favour this criterion in general; it appears to have been chosen for want of anything more satisfactory. In choosing this criterion, Kraepelin was claiming that if he could identify a group of people whose behaviour changed in a similar way at one point (onset), showed further similarity in development over time (course), and reached a similar end-point (outcome), he would be entitled to conclude that he had observed a meaningful cluster of events and to infer a new hypothetical construct.

There are, however, a number of serious problems with this criterion for imputing meaningfulness. First, although the terms 'onset', 'course', and 'outcome' are often used as if they refer to simple, discrete events, in practice they are usually summary terms for a set of complex and continuous processes, particularly when they are applied to behaviour. Thus, what is actually recorded under these headings may be quite arbitrary and will differ across researchers. Second, and more important, these criteria offer no guidance in specifying *important* similarities: is sudden weight loss an important similarity?; or persistent joint swelling?; or eventual paralysis? If this method is applied to a heterogeneous population, showing a wide range of both similarities and differences (as did Kraepelin's population), the likely result is unstable and ever-changing groupings as different investigators, or the same investigator at different times, apply varying criteria for deciding whether a superficial similarity is important. This is exactly the situation found in Kraepelin's writings. A third problem of this criterion is that the inclusion of 'outcome' requires that nothing be concluded about the population of interest until all members of it have reached a point where no further change is possible. Even if this were achieved – say all had died – it would still not be possible to identify new exemplars of the proposed pattern until they too had reached an agreed end-point. Thus, diagnosis and research would be seriously obstructed.

It is thus highly unlikely that Kraepelin, using the criterion of similarities in onset, course, and outcome, would have been able to demonstrate satisfactorily that he had observed a pattern which justified inferring dementia praecox. It might reasonably be argued, however, that if he did describe a cluster which showed such similarities then it would at least be a starting-point for research, for attempts to demonstrate that the grouping of these similarities enabled predictions of new observations. As will be described below, however, there is no evidence that Kraepelin reached even this starting-point.

KRAEPELIN'S EARLY WRITINGS – 1896 AND 1899

Given Kraepelin's adoption of the criterion of similarities of onset, course, and outcome, it might be thought that he would introduce his concept of dementia praecox by first presenting evidence that he had observed similar initial behaviour changes, similar development, and similar outcome and then conclude by offering a construct derived from these. In fact, he started where he should have ended: he took the concept for granted, and proceeded to talk, in a rather haphazard way, about 'cases of dementia praecox'. In other words, he wrote as if he had earlier or elsewhere presented evidence to justify his inference when in fact he had not. All the reader can therefore do is to extract what appears to be relevant information from the global accounts provided.

Similarities in onset, course, and outcome?

Initial changes in behaviour (onset)

Kraepelin appears to have paid little attention to two fundamental problems of discussing 'onset' in this context. The first is that of knowing what behaviour changes were important within his framework, i.e. which were indicative of an assumed common biological process; and the second that of the reliability of information collected retrospectively. Kraepelin does not even say from what source or how he obtained the reports of alleged behaviour changes. The problem is highlighted by his claim that: 'The whole upheaval can take place so imperceptibly and with such indefinite indications that those around imagine they are confronted simply with the outcome of an unhappy development, perhaps even some character fault' (1896: 426); and 'In more than half the cases, the upheaval occurs so imperceptibly and with such indefinite indications that its actual beginning cannot be determined in retrospect' (1899: 149). It is difficult to understand how Kraepelin could have made use of the criterion of similarities in onset, course, and outcome when he believed that onset could not be observed in more than half of those said to be suffering from dementia praecox.

The problem is compounded by the fact that Kraepelin provided no clear information about the extent of within-group similarities and between-group differences in what were claimed to be important initial changes, in spite of the fact that such data are crucial to his arguments. It is clear, however, that he included a wide variety of initial changes in his supposed similarities in onset, with no indication of why these apparently diverse phenomena should belong together: 'One often notices, particularly at the beginning, hypochondriacal complaints, self-recriminations, fears for the future...' (1896: 427); 'Very often, sensory delusions also occur' (ibid.: 431); 'In the patient's behaviour, either a marked inertia and lassitude or very childish characteristics make themselves apparent' (ibid.: 428).

Kraepelin also appeared to use the *age* at which some change in behaviour occurred, rather than any specific changes, as one criterion for inferring dementia praecox. This use of age of onset, of course, begs the question of how Kraepelin could know that an alleged change marked the onset of dementia praecox as well as that of why age should be considered a valid criterion for assigning importance to changes in behaviour.

Changes in behaviour over time (course)

Given that Kraepelin stressed the importance of within-group similarities in onset, course, and outcome, is it surprising to see explicit references to the large amount of variability he observed in the supposed course of dementia praecox: 'The course of this process of illness can take the most varied forms (1896: 426); 'The further course of the illness in these cases is a varied one insofar as the imbecility sometimes develops more rapidly, sometimes more slowly and can in fact stop progressing at very different stages' (ibid.: 429). The problem is compounded by the fact that groups of asylum inmates who had initially been 'joined together' by Kraepelin (i.e. had the same construct inferred from their behaviour) on the grounds that the course of their illnesses was the same, were later to be described as showing quite different behaviour changes over time. However, they were not, apparently, then separated. Similarly, groups who had been separated on the grounds that they showed quite different courses were later to be joined together but without any indication of how what had been 'considerably different courses' in 1896 came to be similar ones in 1899.

Thus, for neither 'onset' nor 'course' did Kraepelin provide evidence that he had observed within-group similarities in behaviour, far less that he had observed important similarities.

End-point behaviour (outcome)

In his attempts to identify regularities in the behaviour of asylum inmates, Kraepelin appeared to place more emphasis on outcome than on onset or course. There is, however, no justification within his framework for doing so and he never tried to provide any. However, the problems with his descriptions of outcome are similar to those already discussed with respect to onset and course: they are often vague, are highly varied, and give no indication of the extent of within-group similarity or the justification for considering such similarities to be important. To add to the confusion, Kraepelin apparently used different criteria to infer 'feeble-mindedness' (the alleged outcome of dementia praecox) depending on the inmate's past behaviour. 'so that often enough we must remain in doubt as to the meaning of a particular final condition, should we be without the preceeding history' (1905: 205).

Kraepelin also used present behaviour to reconstruct the past when no information was available:

> Still, even now, in a considerable number of cases, the careful observation of clinical symptoms makes it possible for us to trace out at least a rough outline of what has gone before from the final stages of the malady.
>
> (ibid.: 205)

It is, incidentally, difficult to know how Kraepelin felt able to do this, given his earlier, and never contradicted, statement that: 'Unfortunately, I have not yet been able to discover particular indicators for drawing conclusions about the likely outcome of the illness in individual cases.' (1899: 180)

Thus, Kraepelin failed to avoid the trap of interpreting present observations to fit the past and of reconstructing an unknown past to fit present observations; in other words, he failed to keep onset, course, and outcome independent. The tendency to indulge in this dubious practice is yet another reason for the disfavour with which similarities in onset, course, and outcome are viewed as criteria for claiming that a cluster of events is meaningful.

KRAEPELIN'S LATER WRITINGS: 1913/1919

By 1913, Kraepelin's claim that dementia praecox ended in feeble-mindedness had been challenged, particularly by Bleuler. Kraepelin appeared to accept these criticisms and, perhaps because of this, placed less emphasis on similarities in onset, course, and outcome in his later writings. Instead, he introduced the new idea of 'disorders which characterize the malady':

'Dementia praecox consists of a series of states the common characteristic of which is a peculiar destruction of the internal connections of the psychic personality' (1919:3).

In adopting this idea, however, Kraepelin overlooked two fundamental problems. The first was that his use of similarities in onset, course, and outcome to justify his original inference to dementia praecox meant that it was nonsensical to talk of some cases having a favourable outcome. If Kraepelin wished to abandon his original criterion, then he should have abandoned his construct and started all over again the search for a pattern amongst asylum inmates' behaviour. There is no indication that Kraepelin, or any of his contemporaries, ever did this or, indeed, that they even recognized the problem. The second, and related problem was that of knowing what was meant by 'characterize the malady'. Kraepelin may have meant disorders shared by every inmate from whose behaviour dementia praecox has been inferred; but in order to seek such disorders, there must first be available a valid and independent set of criteria for inferring dementia praecox, i.e. a pattern must previously have been observed. There is no indication in Kraepelin's writings that this was ever achieved. Alternatively, Kraepelin may have meant criteria for inferring dementia praecox, but this leads to the same problem: such criteria could only result from the prior observation of patterns. Given this state of affairs, it is not surprising that Kraepelin never made clear what he meant by 'characterize the malady'. Nor did he describe how he came to discover what these 'disorders' were; he claimed only to have found them. The fact that his descriptions of the supposed disorders are extremely vague is of secondary importance beside these basic conceptual problems.

Kraepelin was, perhaps, not unaware of the difficult position into which he had manoeuvred himself by introducing and retaining a construct in the absence of any supporting evidence. However, rather than abandon the construct and re-start his search for patterns, Kraepelin chose the questionable escape route of relying on personal experience:

we have therefore even yet to rely purely on the valuation of clinical experience. The result is, as it appears to me, that we are with great probability justified in connecting the great majority of the cases up to the present brought together under the name dementia praecox with the same morbid process, and therefore in regarding it as a single form of disease.

(1919: 255)

THE WORK OF EUGEN BLEULER

Bleuler's work will be described more briefly than Kraepelin's, because he made very similar errors. He began, first, by taking it for granted that Kraepelin had been justified in originally inferring dementia praecox and that any subsequent debate would be on matters of detail. A major detail on which he disagreed with Kraepelin was that of the outcome of dementia praecox: Bleuler claimed that it was not always unfavourable, hence the change of name. Unfortunately, he, like Kraepelin, overlooked the necessity of demonstrating that his construct was derived from an observed pattern. Bleuler also emphasized 'characteristic' or 'fundamental' symptoms which he said were 'present in every case and at every period' (1911/1950: 13). However, he failed to specify how he could recognize a case of schizophrenia or to demonstrate that he had identified a group of people in each of whom certain characteristics were always present; instead, he simply asserted that 'it was proven that there exist certain constant symptoms' (ibid.: 284). However, he also made the apparently contradictory claim that 'at....times [the accessory symptoms] alone may permanently determine the clinical picture' (ibid.: 13).

Neither Bleuler nor Kraepelin made any attempt to explain how they could possibly know that any given behaviour should be interpreted as a symptom of dementia praecox or schizophrenia. If a pattern *had* been observed, then 'symptoms' would be those complaints which reliably co-occurred with and had theoretical links with, particular signs. In the absence of such a pattern as the source of dementia praecox/ schizophrenia, Kraepelin and Bleuler were, in effect, free to call any phenomena they pleased 'symptoms'. In doing so, Bleuler appears to have used both his authority and his beliefs about how 'normal' people behaved:

It should also need no proof that the disturbances of the complex functions of intelligence...ellipsis the impaired synthesis of the total personality, the disordered strivings and efforts of the patients...the altered relations to reality...are comprehensible only in connection with the already mentioned secondary symptoms; therefore they themselves are secondary manifestations for the most part.

(1950: 354)

Just how prominent the various symptoms have to be in order to permit a diagnosis can hardly be described.

(ibid.: 298)

it is easier to sense [the symptom of affective disturbance] than to describe it.

(ibid.: 42)

All the nuances of sexual pleasure, embarrassment, pain or jealousy may emerge in all their vividness which we never find in the healthy when it is a question of recollecting the past.

(ibid.: 46)

during celebrations one can observe how much longer it takes the schizophrenic to get into the party mood than it does the healthy person.

(ibid.: 45)

It is worth mentioning here that the work of Kurt Schneider, which has been influential in European psychiatry, provides no more support for the concept of schizophrenia than does that of Kraepelin or Bleuler. Schneider (1959) made very similar mistakes: he took for granted, without providing evidence, the validity of 'schizophrenia' and then claimed, in a tautological fashion, that symptoms of schizophrenia were phenomena 'frequently found and therefore a prominent feature of schizophrenia'. Like Kraepelin and Bleuler, he overlooked the fact that such a statement made sense only if there existed valid and independent criteria for inferring schizophrenia in the first place.

WHAT *DID* KRAEPELIN AND BLEULER DO?

If neither Kraepelin nor Bleuler presented evidence to justify introducing 'dementia praecox' or 'schizophrenia', is there any indication from their writings of what they might have been doing? One clue comes from the observation (see, for example, Strauss and Carpenter 1981; Cutting 1985; Hare 1986) that the 'kinds of cases' seen by Kraepelin and Bleuler are apparently almost never seen today. It is interesting that no systematic attempt has been made to explain this anomaly, apart from brief references to the possibility of tranquillizing drugs 'halting the progress of schizophrenia' or of its becoming less severe with time. A much more likely explanation is that Kraepelin and Bleuler were in fact describing a totally different population from that called schizophrenic today, and one, moreover, which would not now be called schizophrenic. This idea is supported by the fact that Kraepelin's and Bleuler's descriptions of alleged cases of dementia praecox/schizophrenia are virtually identical to descriptions of the infectious disorder called encephalitis lethargica and its Parkinsonian sequelae. It is important to note that von Economo did not observe the pattern from which encephalitis lethargica was inferred, and the link between that and later motor and affective disorders, until 1917, some years after Kraepelin and Bleuler had completed their major writings. Just how similar these descriptions are, and how different from descriptions of those called schizophrenic today, can be seen from Table 1.1.

As well as the phenomena listed there, Kraepelin, Bleuler, and von Economo provided descriptions of marked peculiarities of gait (indeed, Bleuler claimed that he could distinguish schizophrenic patients from other inmates simply by watching them walk); excess production of saliva and urine; dramatic weight fluctuations; tremor; cyanosis of the hands and feet; constraint of movement and the inability, in spite of effort, to complete 'willed' acts. In addition, all of them described delusions and hallucinations of many sensory modalities while both Kraepelin and von Economo provided details of the severe structural brain damage which was revealed microscopically at post-mortem. Both stressed the great damage to nerve tissue and the proliferation and 'infiltration' of abnormal glia cells. Given

Table 1.1 Descriptions of dementia praecox, schizophrenia and encephalitis lethargica/post-encephalitic Parkinsonism

---

'The spasmodic phenomena in the musculature of the face and speech which often appear, are extremely peculiar.' (Kraepelin 1913/1919: 83)

'Fibrillary contractions are particularly noticeable in the facial muscles and "sheet lightning" has long been known as a sign of a chronically developing [schizophrenic] illness.' (Bleuler 1911/1950: 170)

'As a rule, other spontaneous movements are associated with the choreic movements of Encephalitis Lethargica, the myclonic and fasciscular twitches of the disease: an important point with regard to differential diagnosis....These myclonic movements are more or less rhythmical and symmetrical flash-like short twitches of separate muscles or groups of muscles.' (von Economo 1931: 39)

'Dufour has described disorders of equilibrium, staggering, adiadochokinesia and tremor which he regards as the expression of a "cerebellar" form of dementia praecox.' (Kraepelin 1913/1919: 79)

'Constraint is also noticeable in the *gait* of the patients. Often indeed it is quite impossible to succeed in experiments with walking. The patients simply let themselves fall down stiffly, as soon as one tries to place them on their feet.' (ibid.: 148, original emphasis)

'In some cases the ataxia attains such a degree that the instability of gait, the deviation towards one side, the tendency to fall backwards on standing, the tremor, the giddiness and the nystagmus can only be ascribed to an involvement of the cerebellum in the inflammatory process.' (von Economo 1931: 32)

'[Ermes] found that a fall of the leg held horizontally only began after 205 seconds [in cases of dementia praecox], while in healthy persons it made its appearance on an average after 38 seconds, at latest after 80 seconds. There followed then [in dementia praecox] either a repeated jerky falling off with tremor or a gradual sinking.' (Kraepelin 1913/1919: 79)

'if...one lifts up the forearm of a patient [suffering from the amyostatic-akinetic form of encephalitis lethargica] the arm remains raised for quite a time after having been released, and is only gradually brought back in jerks and with tremors' (von Economo 1931: 44).

'During acute thrusts [of schizophrenia], though rarely in the chronic conditions, we often encounter somnolence. Patients are asleep all night and most of the day. Indeed, they often fall asleep at work. Frequently, this somnolence is the only sign of a new thrust of the malady.' (Bleuler 1911/1950: 169)

'In the now increasing somnolence [of the acute phase of the somnolent opthalmoplegic form of encephalitis lethargica] one often observes that the patients, left to themselves, fall asleep in the act of sitting or standing or even while walking...[somnolence] is repeatedly found in quite slight cases as the only well marked symptom.' (von Economo 1931: 27)

'Hoche also mentions the markedly increased secretion of the *sebaceous glands* [in schizophrenic patients].' (Bleuler 1911/1919: 167, original emphasis)

'A hypersecretion of the sebaceous glands (probably centrally caused) causes the peculiar shining of the faces of these patients.' (von Economo 1931: 46, parentheses in original)

'The tendency to edema *(sic)* is usually ascribed to poor circulation, but it may have other causes....In a physically strong female patient with a beginning mild schizophrenia, edemas were noted in the thigh area....At times more severe edemas may make movement painful.' (Bleuler 1911/1950: 166)

'Oedema of hands and feet...are...more frequent in the amyostatic than in the other forms of encephalitis lethargica' (von Economo 1931: 46).

'In the most varied [schizophrenic] conditions, [the pupils] are often found to be unequal without having lost their ability to react...this pupilliary inequality is rarely persistent; it often varies within a few hours, becoming equal or reversed.' (Bleuler 1911/1950: 173)

'[The] behaviour of the pupils is of great significance. They are frequently in the earlier stages [of dementia praecox] and in conditions of excitement conspicuously wide...here and there one observes a distinct difference in the pupils. The light reaction of the pupils often appears sluggish or slight' (Kraepelin 1913/1919: 77).

'pupillary disturbances are very common. In patients [with the hyperkinetic form of encephalitis lethargica] one generally finds unequal and myopic pupils with a diminished and sluggish reaction but sometimes also one-sided or double or complete absence of reaction or an absence of light reaction only. These pupilliary disturbances often vary considerably [in the same patient]' (von Economo 1931: 38).

'A differential diagnosis between [encephalitis lethargica and chorea] must necessarily be very difficult except where there exist for our guidance pupilliary disturbances or other objective signs of encephalitis lethargica.' (ibid.: 39)

---

that Kraepelin and Bleuler are credited with having first described schizophrenia 'so thoroughly and sensitively' (Gottesman and Shields 1982) it is remarkable that, apart from delusions and hallucinations, not one of the phenomena described above and in Table 1.1, appears in the index of a comprehensive academic text on 'schizophrenia' (Neale and Oltmanns 1980).

This apparent mistake on the part of Kraepelin and Bleuler, and its persistence, can perhaps be better understood by considering some aspects of their work and its context. The first is that in Germany, the distinction between psychiatry and neurology was almost non-existent; Kraepelin saw himself as a neurologist. This, and the fact that neurology in any case was in its infancy, meant that asylums were populated with people who, today, would come under the province of neurologists. Second, although some of the singular phenomena which von Economo later attributed to viral infection (somnolence, motor disorders, and so on) had been repeatedly described, the *pattern* was not recognized. Sacks (1971) has suggested that each generation apparently 'forgot' the observations of the previous one and that von Economo was considerably aided in 'seeing' the pattern by the devastating European epidemic of 1917-27 and by his mother's recollection of the Italian epidemic of the 1890s. (Von Economo himself acknowledges this.) He was no doubt helped also by the fact that neurology had made considerable strides in the mean time. A third important aspect of the work of Kraepelin and Bleuler is their apparent disregard for the necessity to provide good empirical evidence in support of their constructs. They were not alone in this: psychiatric texts of the day, and classification systems, abounded with constructs which lacked any obvious empirical support.

However, it did not escape the notice of neurologists of the time that what von Economo described as the short and long-term results of infection were very similar to what they had been used to calling dementia praecox or schizophrenia. Von Economo declared that some people said to be suffering from dementia praecox were in fact cases of encephalitis lethargica, while Hendrick (1928) pointed to cases, some apparently of dementia praecox, in which the diagnosis of encephalitis lethargica was confirmed at post-mortem examination. The problem here, however, was that by the first decades of the twentieth century the concept of dementia praecox/schizophrenia appeared to have taken on a life of its own, quite detached from any consideration of its origins. Thus, it was taken for granted, though without any evidence ever being provided in support, that Kraepelin and Bleuler had described a different disorder from von Economo, but that it could be very difficult to tell the difference between them. As would be expected, the criteria suggested for doing so were both vague and varied. Hendrick (1928:1007) suggested that:

> the [encephalitis lethargica] patient...can be shown much
> more easily than the schizophrenic to be highly sensitive

and his withdrawal from contact with others is a motivated defence rather than a product of preoccupation and dulling of external interests;

while von Economo claimed that:

Stransky in 1903 established the fundamental thesis that in the schizophrenic diseases an intra-psychic ataxia (that is a dissociation of the 'noö- and thymo-psyche') exists as a basic symptom. In this division he meant 'noö-psyche' to be the representative of the purely intellectual functions, while 'thymo-psyche' embraced the urges, emotions, and volition....In encephalitis lethargica, though no genuine dissociation as in dementia praecox occurs, an isolated disturbance of the thymo-psyche takes place, leaving the noö-psyche intact.

(von Economo 1931: 163, parenthesis in original)

Hauptman (cited in Jelliffe 1927) considered that schizophrenics were unable to relate their psychomotor disorders to the soul life. To add to the confusion, papers appeared on 'organic aspects of schizophrenia' (for example, Hoskins 1933; Hoskins and Sleeper 1933), describing phenomena such as oedema, pupilliary disturbances, cyanosis, and polyuria clearly described by von Economo as consequences of the infection. Since then, what appears to have happened is that, as the incidence of 'encephalitis lethargica' and its Parkinsonian sequelae declined, the referents of 'schizophrenia' changed in an idiosyncratic way, until the term came to be applied to people who bore only a slight and probably superficial resemblance to Kraepelin's and Bleuler's population, perhaps in much the same way as people with headaches might be said to resemble people with brain tumours. The transformation from a construct derived from neurological, physiological, and behavioural phenomena to one derived from behaviour, was, of course, facilitated by the fact that the application of medical theoretical frameworks to deviant behaviour was well-established by the beginning of the twentieth century. And the mistake of assuming that Kraepelin and Bleuler described a separate pattern which justified inferring dementia praecox/schizophrenia, continues today: Torrey and Peterson (1973), Tyrrell et al. (1979), and Crow (1984) talk of 'schizophrenic symptoms' being found in association with a number of other disorders including viral encephalitis. The nature of this persistent error can perhaps be clarified by using an analogy with the now outmoded idea of humoral disorders or, indeed, with 'systematic insanity' or any defunct construct. It has now been demonstrated that a variety of more useful constructs can be inferred from the phenomena which used to lead to the inference of humoral pathology. We do not argue, however, that symptoms of humoral disorder are found in a variety of conditions, including, say, kidney failure, cancer, and so on, although, of course, what were *assumed* to be symptoms of humoral disorder are found. Nor do we argue that humoral pathology is difficult to distinguish from cancer, and so on, and seek criteria for doing so. Rather, we point out that the idea of humoral pathology was simply an erroneous interpretation of the available data, and was eventually superseded by more useful constructions. It can thus be argued that Kraepelin's and Bleuler's ideas and constructs stand in the same relationship to the modern study of deviant behaviour as does the idea of humoral pathology to modern medicine. It is difficult to know where claims (for example, Tyrrell et al. 1979; Crow 1984) to have identified a virus-like agent in the cerebrospinal fluid (CSF) of a minority of 'schizophrenics' – and in control groups – fit this picture. What can be said is that those behaviours now claimed to be symptoms of schizophrenia are likely to be under the control of a number of different antecedents and maintaining factors (as were the 'symptoms of humoral disorders') and that our knowledge of these will not be advanced by retaining the concept of schizophrenia. It is worth emphasizing that the concept is as obstructive to attempts to describe links between biological variables and behaviour as it is to attempts to describe links between social/psychological variables and behaviour.

It is not being suggested here that Kraepelin or Bleuler 'discovered' encephalitis lethargica and its Parkinsonian sequelae or that all of their cases were suffering from this disorder. It hardly makes sense to claim on the one hand that they provided no evidence of having observed a pattern to justify inferring dementia praecox/schizophrenia, and, on the other, that they described a pattern to justify inferring encephalitis lethargica. There are, too, good reasons for supposing that their cases may have been suffering from a variety of physical disorders. What is claimed is that a considerable number of those from whom the construct of dementia praecox/schizophrenia was derived should probably have been diagnosed as cases of encephalitis lethargica, and that the antecedents of the bizarre behaviour of any who should not, remain uncertain or unknown.

Ultimately, however, the case against the concept of schizophrenia does not rest on whether Kraepelin and Bleuler described encephalitis lethargica. It rests on their failure to provide evidence of having observed *any* pattern to justify their constructs and on the predictable failure, to be described in subsequent chapters, to find valid diagnostic criteria or reliable support for predictions from these constructs. Those who wish to continue using the concept of schizophrenia or any of its variants as independent variables should perhaps first address themselves to this question: if neither Kraepelin nor Bleuler nor Schneider discovered or described schizophrenia, then who did?

REFERENCES

Bleuler, E. (1950) *Dementia Praecox or the Group of Schizophrenias*, New York: International Universities Press (translated from the German edn, 1911).

Clare, A. (1980) *Psychiatry in Dissent: Controversial Issues in Thought and Practice*, 2nd edn, London: Tavistock Publications.

Crow, T.J. (1984) 'A re-evaluation of the viral hypothesis: is psychosis the result of retroviral integration at a site close to the cerebral dominance gene?', *British Journal of Psychiatry* 145: 243–53.

Cutting, J. (1985) *The Psychology of Schizophrenia*, Edinburgh: Churchill Livingstone.

Engle, R.L. and Davis, B.J. (1963) 'Medical diagnosis: past present and future. I. Present concepts of the meaning and limitations of medical diagnosis', *Archives of Internal Medicine* 112: 512–19.

Gottesman, I.I. and Shields, J. (1982) *Schizophrenia: the Epigenic Puzzle*, Cambridge: Cambridge University Press.

Hare, E.H. (1986) 'Schizophrenia as an infectious disease', in A. Kerr and P. Snaith (eds) *Contemporary Issues in Schizophrenia*, London: Royal College of Psychiatrists/Gaskell.

Hendrick, I. (1928) 'Encephalitis lethargica and the interpretation of mental disease', *American Journal of Psychiatry* 7: 989–1014.

Hoskins, R.G. (1933) 'Schizophrenia from the physiological point of view', *Annals of Internal Medicine* 7: 445–56.

— and Sleeper, F.H. (1933) 'Organic factors in schizophrenia, *Archives of Neurology and Psychiatry* 30: 123–32.

Hunter, R.A. and MacAlpine, I. (1963) *Three Hundred Years of Psychiatry*, Oxford: Oxford University Press.

Jelliffe, S.E. (1927) 'The mental pictures in schizophrenia and in epidemic encephalitis. Their alliances, differences and a point of view', *American Journal of Psychiatry* 6: 413–65.

Jones, K. (1972) *A History of the Mental Health Services*, London: Routledge & Kegan Paul.

Kraepelin, E. (1896) *Psychiatrie*, 5th Aufl., Leipzig: Barth.

— (1899) *Psychiatrie*, 6th Aufl., Leipzig: Barth.

— (1905) *Lectures on Clinical Psychiatry*, London: Ballière Tindall (translated from 2nd German edn, 1905).

— (1919) *Dementia Praecox and Paraphrenia*, Edinburgh: Livingstone (translated from 8th edn of *Psychiatrie*, 1913).

Leigh, D. (1961) *The Historical Development of British Psychiatry. Vol. 1: The Eighteenth and Nineteenth Centuries*, Oxford: Pergamon.

Lewis, N. D. C. (1966) 'History of the nosology and the evolution of the concept of schizophrenia', in P.H. Hoch and J. Zubin (eds) *Psychopathology of Schizophrenia*, New York: Grune & Stratton.

Neale, J.M. and Oltmanns, T.F. (1980) *Schizophrenia*, New York: Wiley.

Sacks, O. (1971) 'Parkinsonism – a so-called new disease', *British Medical Journal* 9 October: 111.

Schneider, K. (1959) *Clinical Psychopathology*, 5th edn, New York: Grune & Stratton.

Scull, A.T. (1979) *Museums of Madness: The Social Organisation of Insanity in Nineteenth Century England*, London: Allen Lane.

Strauss, J.S. and Carpenter, W.T. (1981) *Schizophrenia*, New York: Plenum Medical.

Torrey, E.F. and Peterson, M.R. (1973) 'Slow and latent viruses in schizophrenia', *The Lancet* 7 July: 22–4.

Tyrrell, D.A.J., Crow, J.J., Parry, R.P., Johnson, E., and Ferrier, I.N. (1979) 'Possible virus in schizophrenia and some neurological disorders', *The Lancet* 21 April: 839–41.

Von Economo, C. (1931) *Encephalitis Lethargica: Its Sequelae and Treatment*, Oxford: Oxford University Press.

Wing, J.K. (1978) *Reasoning about Madness*, Oxford: Oxford University Press.

Chapter Two

THE SYNDROMES AND SYMPTOMS OF PSYCHOSIS

Or why you can't play 'twenty questions' with the concept of schizophrenia and hope to win

RICHARD P. BENTALL

INTRODUCTION

Since first given life by Kraepelin and Bleuler almost 100 years ago (see Chapter 1 by Boyle in this volume), the concept of 'schizophrenia' has become so pervasive that approximately 1 per cent of individuals in western countries can be expected to be labelled 'schizophrenic' at some time in their lives (Torrey 1987). Many of these people will spend a considerable portion of their adult lives in psychiatric hospitals, will be treated with powerful medications, and will live impoverished, marginalized existences (see Chapters 8 and 3 by Pilgrim, and Barham and Hayward respectively, in this volume). Because of the economic, social, and personal costs of the hypothesized disorder, research continues to be carried out into schizophrenia on a massive scale and numerous theories have been proposed by scientists to account for schizophrenic behaviour. Hypothesized causes of schizophrenia include genetic endowment (for example, Gottesman and Shields 1982; see Chapter 4 by Marshall in this volume), abnormalities of brain structure or brain biochemistry (Pincus and Tucker 1978; Green and Costain 1981; see Chapter 5 by Jackson in this volume), diet (Singh and Kay 1976), season of birth (Watson et al. 1982) linked to hypothetical viral agents (Crow 1984), social stress (Faris and Dunham 1939), life events (Brown and Birley 1968) and family structure (Bateson et al. 1956). Indeed, almost every variable known to affect human behaviour has, at one time or another, been held to be important in the aetiology of schizophrenia. Although it is not possible within the confines of the present chapter to review the evidence pertaining to these hypotheses, it is fair to say that each of the theories is favoured by some researchers yet rejected by others. Thus, despite the fact that there has been a tendency in recent years to talk about schizophrenia as if it were a neurological condition (Eccleston 1986), few would wish to claim that the causes of schizophrenia are known. Indeed, the sceptic may be inclined to ask whether nearly 100 years of multidisciplinary research into the aetiology of schizophrenia has yielded any substantial progress. (Compare, for example, the rapid progress that has been made in AIDS research in just a few years; cf. Connor and Kingman 1988.) Why, then, has schizophrenia proved so resistant to scientific effort?

NO
CURE

One answer that a traditional schizophrenia researcher might give to this question would be to claim that the disorder is simply a very complex one and thus intrinsically much more difficult to understand than all the other disorders (for example, AIDS, cancer, the dementias) for which substantial advances have been achieved in recent years. It is difficult to refute this claim directly; indeed, it is not impossible *a priori* that schizophrenia will suddenly yield up its secrets to some kind of medical or technological breakthrough. However, before persisting for another hundred years of research, the committed student of schizophrenia might consider another possibility (which is open to empirical examination), namely that for all these years researchers have been chasing a ghost within the body-politic of psychiatry. As Boyle has demonstrated in the previous chapter, the concept of schizophrenia was full of contradictions at birth; perhaps it remains full of contradictions now. Put simply, it is possible that schizophrenia is not a meaningful scientific concept and that it should therefore be abandoned along with all the other meaningless concepts (for example, the four humors, phlogyston, the luminiferous ether) which have been cast aside by scientists during crucial periods of scientific progress. If this second possibility is correct, the current state of schizophrenia research (many variables implicated, none conclusively) is precisely what would be expected to result from the traditional schizophrenia researcher's strategy of comparing heterogeneous groups of 'normals' with equally heterogeneous samples of 'schizophrenics'.

contra-
dictions

The present chapter, then, has two purposes. The first will be to determine whether schizophrenia is a useful scientific concept. By the examination of relevant data, mainly collected by distinguished psychiatrists, it will be argued that the faith placed in the concept by clinicians and researchers is largely unjustified. If this argument is accepted it follows that the traditional research strategy of playing 'Twenty Questions' with the concept of schizophrenia is doomed to failure. The second purpose of the present chapter will therefore be to suggest alternative methods of carrying out research into psychotic phenomena. To reject schizophrenia as a useful concept is not to deny that people suffer from distressing psychiatric symptoms that clinicians and students of human behaviour should take these symptoms seriously, or even that these symptoms have, at least in part, a biological component. There is therefore a pressing need to develop research strategies in psychopathology which do not depend on the validity of traditional psychiatric diagnoses. Several such strategies are in fact available but the one which will receive particular attention within the present context involves studying specific symptoms of psychosis. An attempt will be made to show how this approach can lead quite rapidly to interesting results.

ISSUES OF RELIABILITY AND VALIDITY

For a diagnostic system to be of either scientific or clinical utility it has to be both reliable and valid. The reliability of a diagnostic system refers to the consistency with which patients are diagnosed – one psychiatrist's schizophrenic must be another psychiatrist's schizophrenic. Validity, on the other hand, refers to the meaningfulness or usefulness of the diagnostic categories as judged by other criteria. Thus, for example, the symptoms of a hypothesized disorder should correlate with each other – a patient having one symptom of schizophrenia should have a high probability of experiencing other symptoms of the alleged disorder. Moreover, on the basis of a diagnosis the clinician should be able to predict the course and outcome of the disorder, and whether or not it is likely to respond to particular treatments. Also, there should ideally be some relationship between diagnosis and aetiology. (Of course, any particular diagnosis might not meet all of these tests but if we are to admit that a diagnosis is meaningful if must meet some of them.)

In this context it is important to recognize that reliability is a necessary but insufficient condition for validity. In other words, as Spitzer and Fliess (1974) remark, 'There is no guarantee that a reliable system is valid but assuredly an unreliable system must be invalid.' This is because any combination of symptoms can be made reliable simply by specifying them clearly enough. (Consider a 'disease' characterized by red hair, foot size greater than size 10, and a preference for vanilla ice-cream over other flavours: the diagnosis of such an entity might be made reliable but would none the less be scientifically meaningless.) The demonstration of validity therefore requires further tests. The present author has reviewed the evidence on the reliability and validity of the schizophrenia concept elsewhere (Bentall 1986; Bentall et al. 1988) but a further outline of these issues will be useful in the present context.

Reliability

Given the inauspicious beginnings of the schizophrenia concept it is not surprising that there have been frequent disagreements about the symptoms of the hypothesized disorder. Eugen Bleuler (1911) held that the loosening of associations is the essential feature of schizophrenia. Schneider (1959), on the other hand, argued that delusions and hallucinations are the symptoms that are the most important for making a diagnosis and that only a proportion of schizophrenics are thought-disordered. Even among followers of Schneider, differences of opinion about the relative importance of particular symptoms have persisted (Koehler 1979). Because of these disagreements, the differential diagnosis of schizophrenia from other hypothesized psychiatric disorders has remained difficult.

Early studies of this problem found that psychiatrists were often inconsistent in assigning individuals to diagnostic categories (Beck et al. 1962; Blashfield 1973; Kuriansky et al. 1974; Sandifer et al. 1964). Psychiatrists have responded to these findings in two ways: by developing operational (i.e. precisely defined) criteria for different psychiatric diagnoses and by developing structured interview schedules which ensure that patients are questioned about their symptoms in a consistent fashion. The former approach is exemplified by the Research Diagnostic Criteria

(RDC) of Spitzer et al. (1978) and by the third edition of the American Psychiatric Association's *Diagnostic and Statistical Manual of Mental Disorders* (DSM-III; APA 1980 – see the preface for these criteria). The latter approach is exemplified by the widely used Present State Examination (PSE) developed by Wing et al. (1974). In practice the two approaches tend to be used together – data collected using the PSE, for example, can be used to yield a diagnosis using a set of operational criteria in the form of a computer program. There can be no doubt that by using clearly defined diagnostic criteria and a structured approach to illiciting information from patients, a high degree of agreement can be achieved when psychiatrists attempt to diagnose patients.

Unfortunately, however, there are good reasons for doubting whether this increase in reliability is all that it appears. In practice, many sets of operational criteria for schizophrenia have been proposed. Presumably, if they are all designed to identify the same type of mental disorder, a high degree of agreement should be observed when these different criteria are compared. In a test of this prediction, Brockington et al. (1978) applied ten sets of criteria to 322 patients in a large psychiatric hospital. The concordance between the different diagnostic systems was very low indeed (an average kappa value of 0·29 for the statistically minded; a value of 0·70 or above is usually considered acceptable), although a slightly better level of agreement was achieved when fewer criteria were used to diagnose a smaller sample of patients from a second hospital. Reasonable levels of concordance were only observed between diagnostic criteria which were historically related to each other: for example, a kappa value of 0·72 between Schneider's criteria and a PSE diagnosis of schizophrenia is not surprising when it is remembered that the PSE criteria were devised with Schneider's view of schizophrenia in mind.

Thus, the problems of diagnostic classification which led to the development of operational criteria for making diagnoses have not been solved by them. Whereas, in the past, psychiatrists using their own idiosyncratic approaches to diagnosis often disagreed about whether or not particular patients suffered from schizophrenia, at least an equivalent degree of disagreement now exists between the diagnostic criteria available to psychiatrists. A patient may or may not be schizophrenic, for example, depending on whether Schneider's criteria or DSM-III criteria are used to make the diagnosis. If schizophrenia is a valid scientific concept, then, at the very least psychiatrists will need to answer the question: Which sets of criteria are the right ones?

Construct validity

In their efforts to solve the problem of the reliability of psychiatric diagnoses, psychiatrists have almost completely ignored problems of validity. Yet, as already indicated, even if the reliability of the diagnosis could be assured (which seems doubtful), this would not be sufficient to guarantee that schizophrenia is a useful scientific concept.

Various tests of validity are possible. One type of test concerns the 'construct validity' of the concept – whether or not the concept is internally consistent. As Wing (1978) has noted, if schizophrenia is a valid concept the disorder should manifest itself in the form of a set of symptoms that tend to go together – in other words, there should be an identifiable syndrome of schizophrenia. By similar reasoning, as Kendell (1975) has pointed out, if psychiatric disorders are discrete entities, there should be few individuals suffering from the symptoms of more than one disorder.

The poor correlations observed between symptoms and diagnoses have long been a source of embarrassment to psychiatrists (Zigler and Phillips 1961) and many of the symptoms of schizophrenia have also been associated with other diagnoses. Thus, for example, delusions and hallucinations are often found in patients diagnosed as suffering from affective disorders (Winters and Neale 1983; Asaad and Shapiro 1986) and thought disorder is often found in patients diagnosed as manic (Andreasen 1979). In recognition of this problem, sophisticated statistical techniques have been used to address the question of whether or not identifiable syndromes of mental disorder can be identified.

Factor analysis (Child 1970) has been used to assess the correlations observed between symptoms in order to see whether certain symptoms tend to occur together. In practice, the results achieved by this method have been inconsistent (Blashfield 1984). Moreover, Slade and Cooper (1979) have identified an important flaw in much of the research using this kind of approach. As individuals with few psychotic symptoms are less likely to be hospitalized than those suffering from many symptoms, groups of patients found in hospitals are likely to give an inflated impression of the association between symptoms. Slade and Cooper were able to devise a method of mathematically correcting for this possibility. Applying their procedure to data collected by Trouton and Maxwell (1956) they were unable to find evidence that psychotic symptoms are other than randomly associated.

A second statistical technique which has been applied to this problem is cluster analysis (Everitt 1980). Instead of looking at correlations between symptoms (as in factor analysis), cluster analysis looks at the similarities between persons and attempts to assign patients to groups according to simple rules. Thus, for example, a cluster analysis program might search through a database of patients and their symptoms and begin by placing together those patients with the most similar symptoms; during subsequent sweeps through the database the computer program will add patients to different groups according to their similarities to the patients already assigned to those groups. If patients fall into natural groups which correspond to traditional psychiatric diagnoses, this would suggest that those diagnoses reflect true 'cleavages in nature' and would be powerful evidence of their validity. Unfortunately, the results achieved by this method have been no more convincing than those achieved using factor analysis. The World Health Organization (1975), for example, carried out a cluster analysis of symptom data obtained from patients in eight different countries using the PSE: patients diagnosed as schizophrenic were spread across the ten clusters generated in the analysis. In a slightly more sophisticated study Everitt et al. (1971) applied two methods of cluster analysis to symptom data collected from patients from two hospitals. Everitt et al. claimed to identify clusters corresponding to the depressive and manic phases of manic depression, and to the diagnosis of paranoid schizophrenia. However, over 60 per cent of their patients fell into two or three 'dustbin' clusters containing patients with almost every kind of diagnosis.

Further statistical techniques have been used to test Kendell's observation that patients with symptoms of more than one psychiatric disorder should be relatively few in number. As already noted, the differential diagnosis of schizophrenia has proved to be problematic and patients presenting with 'mixed' symptoms are quite common. This has been particularly the case with respect to the distinction between schizophrenia and the affective disorders, first made by Kraepelin and described by Kendell and Gourlay (1970) as 'one of the cornerstones of modern psychiatry'. Some have suggested that patients with a mixture of affective and schizophrenic symptoms suffer from a third kind of psychosis – 'schizo-affective disorder' (Kasanin 1933). Others have suggested that schizophrenia and the affective disorders are at opposite ends of a spectrum of psychopathology (Beck 1967), that schizophrenia and mania are essentially identical (Ollerenshaw 1973), that depression may be a side-effect of the treatment of schizophrenia (Hirsch 1982) or that depression is a hidden feature of schizophrenia unmasked during remission (Johnson 1986). Discriminant-function analysis has been used to investigate this problem: using this method, data from patients already diagnosed as schizophrenic or affective is assessed to determine whether an efficient mathematical rule based on the weighting of symptoms can be constructed for assigning patients to the diagnostic groups. Research using this technique has generally failed to generate efficient classification rules, suggesting that no clear borderline exists between affective and schizophrenic disorders (Kendell and Gourlay 1970; Kendell and Brockington 1980; Brockington and Wainright 1980).

It is worth noting, in this context, that the dividing line between psychotic and neurotic (fear and anxiety) disorders has proved equally difficult to determine and that large numbers of schizophrenic patients have been found also to suffer from neurotic symptoms (Foulds and Bedford 1975; McPherson et al. 1977; Bagshaw and McPherson 1978; Sturt 1981). Moreover, it has recently become apparent that the dividing line between schizophrenia and normal functioning is also difficult to specify and that many psychotic symptoms are related to normal mental states. This has led to an interest in 'schizotypal' traits in otherwise normal individuals (see Chapter 6 by Claridge in this volume for a detailed discussion of research in this area).

Predictive validity

Internal consistency is obviously important if the schizophrenia concept is to be taken seriously. However, if the concept is going to be useful it must also be predictive: it is on the basis of a diagnosis that the clinician wants to know what kinds of outcomes are to be expected and which kinds of treatments are likely to be successful.

It will be recalled that Kraepelin believed that schizophrenia invariably has a chronic, deteriorating course. However, recent long-term studies carried out in Switzerland and Germany, including one carried out by the son of Eugen Bleuler, have established that outcome is enormously variable, with roughly one-third of patients recovering completely, one-third experiencing repeated episodes of psychosis, and one-third deteriorating into the chronic 'defect' state (M. Bleuler 1978; Ciompi 1980, 1984; Huber et al. 1980). Such was the variability in the course of recovery from schizophrenia observed by Ciompi that he felt compelled to reject the idea of a unitary schizophrenia disease entity on these grounds alone. (For a more detailed account of these studies see Chapter 3 by Barham and Hayward in this volume.)

Shorter-term studies carried out in Britain and the United States have yielded similar findings. Thus, for example, Strauss and his colleagues in Washington (Strauss and Carpenter 1974a, 1974b, 1977; Hawke et al. 1975) found that symptoms were poor predictors of functioning 5 years after admission to hospital, and that a group of schizophrenic patients had only a marginally worse outcome than a mixed group of patients with other diagnoses. Similarly, Kendell and Brockington (1980) found that symptoms were poor predictors of outcome at 6 years in a group of British patients with mixed schizophrenic and affective symptoms, although patients with exclusively schizophrenic symptoms tended to fare marginally worse than those with exclusively affective symptoms.

Response to treatment has also proved equally difficult to predict on the basis of diagnosis. Thus, for example, although neuroleptic drugs are usually considered the treatment of choice for patients diagnosed as schizophrenic, controlled studies suggest that only a small proportion of patients benefit from these drugs (Crow et al. 1986) and that minimal differences in outcome are observed between patients given these medications and those on low dosages or no medication at all (Carpenter et al. 1977; Manos et al. 1977; Nair 1977; Lonowski et al. 1978; Warner 1985).

On the other hand the effective treatment with neuroleptics of patients diagnosed as suffering with affective disorders has been reported (Naylor and Scott 1980), as has the successful treatment of patients diagnosed as schizophrenic with lithium, usually considered the treatment of choice for those suffering from bipolar affective disorders (Delva and Letemendia 1982). Benzodiazepines, commonly used in the treatment of anxiety, have also been found to be effective in the treatment of specific psychotic symptoms such as hallucinations (Beckman and Haas 1980; Lingjaerde 1982).

Although psychological methods of treatment are widely held to be particularly ineffective with patients diagnosed as schizophrenic, and find little place in large psychiatric institutions in Britain and the United States, it is becoming increasingly clear that such pessimism is not warranted. A wide range of behavioural approaches has been found to be effective in changing psychotic behaviour (see Chapter 9 by Slade in this volume), as have interventions aimed at changing the patterns of relationships within the families of those diagnosed as schizophrenic (see Chapter 10 by Tarrier in this volume). Even traditional forms of psychotherapy, long abandoned by most clinicians interested in schizophrenia (Stanton et al. 1984), may have their place. Interestingly, the interaction between medical and psychological treatments may be crucial in determining outcome, and it is probably naïve to believe that the effects of these two modes of therapy are simply additive. Karon and VandenBos (1981), for example, have attributed the success of their controlled trial of psychotherapy with patients diagnosed schizophrenic to the fact that the patients given psychotherapy received no medication. Similarly, the results of a large study in Finland suggest that a combination of low-dose neuroleptics and psychotherapy is more likely to be effective than either treatment alone or treatments involving higher dosages of medication (Alenen et al. 1986)

ALTERNATIVE APPROACHES

If the foregoing analysis of the relevant data is correct, current faith in the scientific meaningfulness of the schizophrenia diagnosis cannot be justified. Patients do not fall into discrete types of psychiatric disorder as is commonly assumed and those experiencing a mixture of schizophrenic and non-schizophrenic symptoms are the norm. Nor is there a clear dividing line between schizophrenia and normal functioning. The schizophrenia diagnosis does not predict outcome or response to treatment. Given that schizophrenia appears to be a disorder with no particular symptoms, no particular course, no particular outcome, and which responds to no particular treatment, it is unsurprising that 100 years of research has failed to establish that it has any particular cause. Indeed, it is difficult to see how any findings of substance could be made by comparing heterogeneous groups of 'normals' with equally heterogeneous groups of 'schizophrenics'. Given these considerations it is obviously important that psychopathologists develop strategies of research which do not depend on the validity of existing methods of psychiatric classification.

One approach that investigators might take involves looking at the process of classification afresh. Just because existing diagnostic systems have little scientific value it does not follow that all potential diagnostic systems will be worthless. Indeed, a number of investigators have already proposed that there may be several independent schizophrenic syndromes. Crow (1980), for example, has speculated that the negative and positive symptoms of psychosis result from different pathologies of the central nervous system although the evidence for this hypothesis is equivocal (Mackay 1980; Lewine 1985). The statistical techniques described above might be used in an attempt to construct or evaluate more useful diagnostic systems. In constructing such systems it is likely that psychopathologists will have to abandon the notion that patients fall into discrete types (Eysenck et al. 1983) and the idea that a clear dividing line can be found between sanity and madness. Indeed, all the data that have already been outlined tend to point towards a dimensional rather than a categorical model of mental disorder. Recent advances in the detection of borderline states have led to considerable interest in individuals who exhibit schizophrenic characteristics to a degree insufficient to qualify for a full diagnosis of schizophrenia (Claridge 1987). Interestingly, there is increasing evidence that a multidimensional model is required to account for individual variations in such schizotypal traits (see Chapter 6 by Claridge in this volume for a detailed account of these developments).

33

A further approach that might be taken is to abandon diagnosis altogether. As a number of authors have pointed out (Bannister 1968; Slade and Cooper 1979; Harvey and Neale 1983; Persons 1986; Bentall et al. 1988), instead of investigating hypothetical *syndromes* psychopathologists could make particular *symptoms* the objects of their enquiries. Although there may remain problems in defining and detecting symptoms (which will presumably not be nearly as severe as the problems involved in validating syndromes), the virtue of this approach is that it avoids the problem of diagnosis altogether.

THE SYMPTOM APPROACH TO PSYCHOPATHOLOGY

In fact, there have been a number of advances in the understanding of psychotic symptoms in recent years. In part, these developments follow advances in 'normal' cognitive psychology, which provides a useful language for understanding abnormal experiences and behaviour. For reasons of space it is not possible to describe these advances in great detail but an attempt will be made to indicate some of the more salient findings.

Hallucinations

Since the early 1970s a steady trickle of research on hallucinations has appeared in the literature on psychopathology (Asaad and Shapiro 1986; Slade and Bentall 1988) and a number of variables have been found to affect the probability that a person will hallucinate (Slade 1976a). Clinical evidence suggests that hallucinations in psychotic patients and those previously mentally well follow periods of stress (for example, Reese 1971; Siegel 1984; Slade 1972, 1973) and are accompanied by abnormal arousal (Toone et al. 1981; Cooklin et al. 1983). There also appears to be a relationship between the onset of hallucinations and environmental stimulation, with hallucinations more likely to occur during periods of relative sensory deprivation or during periods of unpatterned stimulation (such as white noise or traffic noise). Progressive sensory loss seems to make elderly people in particular vulnerable to hallucinations (for example, Hammeke et al. 1983). On the other hand, it seems clear that hallucinations are less likely to occur when the individual is successfully attending to meaningful stimuli such as speech (Slade 1974; Margo et al. 1981). Hallucinations also seem to be related to contextual cues and the individual's expectations about what kind of events are likely to occur (Alpert 1985), a finding which may help explain the considerable cultural and geographical variation in the prevalence and type (modality) of hallucinatory experiences (Bourguignon 1970; Al-Issa 1978).

Obviously, not everyone hallucinates so there must be cognitive factors (perhaps biological in origin, perhaps environmentally determined) that predispose the individual to these kinds of experiences. Despite claims that hallucinators experience abnormally vivid mental imagery, research in this area is contradictory and generally does not support this suggestion (for example, Slade 1976b; Brett and Starker 1977; Catts et al. 1980); in any case, this hypothesis may be unsound on theoretical grounds (Neisser 1967; Bentall 1990). On the other hand there is evidence that hallucinating patients and normal subjects are more likely to respond to suggestions to hear voices than non-hallucinating psychiatric or normal controls (Mintz and Alpert 1972; Young et al. 1987). There is also evidence that intellectual deficits, particularly with respect to descriptive language skills, are associated with vulnerability to hallucinations (Johnson and Miller 1965; Miller et al. 1965; Heilbrun and Blum 1984). An interesting finding is that auditory hallucinations tend to be accompanied by small movements of the speech muscles, known as 'subvocalization' (McGuigan 1966; Inouye and Shimizu 1970). On the other hand there is no evidence that the majority of hallucinators suffer from perceptual deficits, although they do tend to respond rapidly (Schneider and Wilson 1983) and over-confidently (Alpert 1985) on perceptual tasks.

A number of theories have been proposed to account for hallucinations. Frith (1979) suggested that hallucinations might result from a disorder of the selection processes believed to underlie normal speech perception. On this view perception involves the generation of a series of 'unconscious hypotheses' which are steadily filtered out until only the 'correct' hypothesis reaches consciousness; hallucinations are said to result from a failure of this filtering process. This leads to the prediction that patients will hallucinate when attempting to attend to what others are saying, whereas the contrary appears to be the case. More recently, Hoffman (1986) has suggested that hallucinations result from a deficit in speech production also hypothesized to underlie thought disorder (see below), causing hallucinators to experience their own thoughts as unintended and thus alien. One problem with this hypothesis is that it suggests that there should be an association between the symptoms of thought disorder and hallucination, which does not appear to be the case in practice (Bentall and Slade 1986). Another problem with this hypothesis is that it fails to account for hallucinations that are occasionally experienced by normal subjects (Posey 1986) or in non-verbal modalities (for example, visual hallucinations). An alternative but in some ways similar hypothesis proposed by the present author (Bentall 1990) leans on recent research in metacognition (see Figure 2.1). 'Metacognition' is a term that has been used by experimental psychologists to denote those mental processes involved in knowledge about mental processes: such processes are clearly important not only in introspection but also in the human being's ability to direct and control his or her thinking (Flavell 1979). Some research in this area (Johnson and Raye 1981) suggests that the ability to discriminate between the 'real' and the 'imaginary' is an inferential skill. In other words, people do not automatically know whether a perceived event is self-generated (as in mental imagery) or generated by the external world, and must guess between these two possibilities on the basis of the available evidence. On this view, persons hallucinate when they wrongly infer that internally generated cognitive events (for example, verbal thoughts) are externally generated 'real' stimuli. Experimental evidence that supports this hypothesis has been provided by Heilbrun (1980), who found that hallucinators are relatively poor at identifying their own previously recorded thoughts, and by Bentall and Slade (1985), who used a signal-detection task to show that hallucinators have a relative bias towards attributing experiences to an external source in conditions of uncertainty. The hypothesis is also consistent with the observation that auditory hallucinations are accompanied by subvocalization as small movements of the speech muscles have also been observed in healthy people during ordinary verbal thinking (McGuigan 1978). This theoretical framework also has the advantage of explaining the effects on hallucinations of the

36

Figure 2.1 A cognitive model of normal reality discrimination and psychotic hallucinations after Bentall (1990) and Slade and Bentall (1988). In normal reality discrimination, individuals determine the source (internal or external) of a perceived stimulus (which may be either internally or externally generated) by unconsciously applying a set of criteria. Factors which may be taken into account include properties of the stimulus, contextual cues, and expectations. Other variables which may affect the criteria include environmental stimulation (under conditions of sensory deprivation, or unpatterned stimulation, the individual will more readily attribute a stimulus to an external source) and style of information processing (stress causing shallow processing and hence poor accuracy). It is also hypothesized that the criteria may be affected by reinforcement (for example, anxiety reduction following misattribution of hostile thoughts to non-self). Hallucinations result when the criteria fail to distinguish between internally and externally generated events (see text).

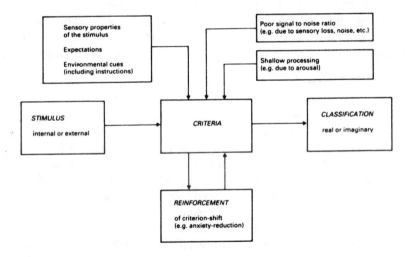

variables outlined above. It is not surprising, for example, that it is most difficult to discriminate imaginary from real events under conditions of unpatterned or degraded sensory input. As stress-induced arousal has been shown to lead to the rapid but 'shallow' processing of sensory information (Schwartz 1975; Eysenck 1976) it is also not surprising that reality-discrimination skills fail in stressful circumstances.

Delusions

In contrast to hallucinations, very little empirical research has been carried out into delusions (Winters and Neale 1983). This is surprising because psychologists have for many years studied the processes involved in the acquisition and maintenance of normal beliefs and it might therefore be expected that they would have something to say about the abnormal beliefs observed within the psychiatric clinic. Within the psychiatric literature there has been considerable debate about the extent to which paranoid disorders are related to other forms of schizophrenia. Zigler and Glick (1988), noting that paranoid and affective patients tend to have a similar premorbid status, have made the interesting suggestion that paranoia is a defence against depression and should therefore be classified as an affective syndrome.

An all too crude outline of factors which might be implicated in the acquisition of a belief is shown in Figure 2.2. Most beliefs are presumably formed on the basis of data in the world. This data has to be perceived and inferences drawn before a belief can be generated and it is this latter stage of inference that has most interested social and experimental psychologists studying normal cognition. Finally, of course, some kind of search for further data either to corroborate or refute beliefs that have been established might occur, although the available evidence on normal reasoning suggests that most people proceed less than logically in this regard (Nisbett and Ross 1980). It is likely that delusions will reflect abnormalities at one or more of these stages, although an abnormality at any particular stage may be neither necessary nor sufficient for a delusion to be formed.

The bizarreness of many delusional beliefs can lead both the clinician and the researcher to neglect the possibility that such beliefs may be rational descriptions of unusual events. As the old

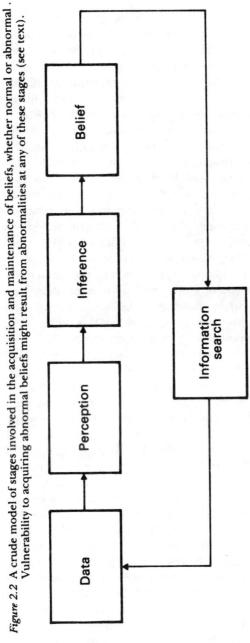

Figure 2.2 A crude model of stages involved in the acquisition and maintenance of beliefs, whether normal or abnormal. Vulnerability to acquiring abnormal beliefs might result from abnormalities at any of these stages (see text).

joke goes: Just because people are paranoid does not mean that they are not being persecuted. At the very least it is doubtful whether delusions spring out of the minds of patients at random and have no connection with the real world, and the possibility that delusional beliefs have metaphorical significance has been suggested by a number of existentialist investigators and psychotherapists (Laing 1967; Arieti 1974; Bannister 1986).

The view that delusions might result from perceptual abnormalities has been most vigorously promoted by Maher (1974), who argued that they are often rational interpretations of abnormal experiences. Much of the evidence cited to support this claim is negative in the sense that it consists of data demonstrating that patients diagnosed as schizophrenic (and therefore presumably deluded) perform normally on tasks of formal reasoning (for example, Williams 1964). However, Maher and Ross (1984) have also presented a number of case-studies of delusions which apparently begin with abnormal perceptions, and a further case-study of a patient who attributed unrecognized sexual arousal to molestation by 'warm forms' (Johnson et al. 1977) can also be interpreted in this light. Consistent with Maher's hypothesis, it has been found that deafness is a vulnerability factor in paranoia (Kay et al. 1976; Zimbardo et al. 1981) and that paranoid patients have an enhanced ability to discriminate between genuine and sham facial emotions (LaRusso 1978). Furthermore, prosopagnosia (damage to the areas of the brain implicated in facial recognition) has been suggested as a possible causal factor in the Capgras syndrome – the belief that a loved one has been replaced by a doppelgänger (Hayman and Abrams 1977). It is not difficult to see, for example, how an inability to hear what people are saying might predispose an individual to believe that he or she is being talked about, or how the perception that there is something not quite right about the appearance of a familiar person might lead to the Capgras syndrome. It should be noted in this regard that the clear distinction made between perception and inference in the described model is in reality oversimplistic and perception is to some extent belief-driven (Wilding 1982). In this regard it is interesting to note that paranoid patients have an abnormally strong tendency to organize ambiguous information in a meaningful way (McCormick and Broekma 1978).

In contrast to theories of delusional beliefs that implicate perception some authors have argued that abnormal reasoning may play a role. It is important to recognize that the kind of evidence cited by Maher in this regard is arguably irrelevant as it concerns formal reasoning tasks and persons selected according to broad diagnostic criteria rather than specific symptoms. A more appropriate perspective from which abnormal beliefs might be considered concerns social judgement, which has been much studied by social psychologists interested in the attributions (explanations) that people make for the behaviour of other people (Hewstone 1985). This kind of perspective is particularly appropriate because many of the delusions encountered in clinical practice (for example, persecution, grandiosity) concern the patient's position in the social universe.

Recently, Kaney and Bentall (1989) investigated the 'attributional style' of patients suffering from persecutory delusions. Abramson et al. (1978) had previously hypothesized that depressed people tend to make 'internal, global and stable' attributions for negative events (i.e. they judge the cause of those events to be internal to themselves, affecting all areas of their lives and beyond their control – an example of such an attribution would be 'my own lack of intelligence' to explain exam failure). Kaney and Bentall found that paranoids, in contrast, made external, global, and stable attributions for such events. Thus, like depressed patients they attributed bad events to causes which would affect their entire lives and which were beyond their control, but unlike depressed patients they felt that these causes were external to themselves. Interestingly, paranoids also tended to make excessively *internal* attributions for positive events (i.e. they credited themselves for such events), indicating why both persecutory and grandiose delusions might result from the same cognitive traits. In a further study, Bentall et al. (1991) investigated the attributions that persecuted patients made for social events that did not involve themselves. The subjects were asked to make judgements about the causes of interactions between an actor and a victim (for example, 'Fred hits Jim') and were presented with contextual information which had previously been shown to determine normal individuals' tendencies to make person attributions (i.e. blame the actor) or stimulus attributions (i.e. blame the victim). Not surprisingly, the persecuted patients

41

tended to make more person attributions than the controls, particularly when the actor's behaviour was socially undesirable. However, they were no less sensitive to the contextual information than the controls, although they were relatively over-confident in their judgements.

The final set of factors involved in belief acquisition outlined in Figure 2.2 concerns the search for further information. Hemsley and Garety (1986) have argued that the inability to weigh up new evidence and adjust beliefs accordingly may lead to delusional beliefs. Traditionally, of course, delusions have been described as beliefs that are resistant to counter-arguments. However, a number of studies have shown that this is not in fact the case and that delusions may be given up in the face of evidence, particularly if presented in a non-confrontational manner (Watts et al. 1973; Hole et al. 1979; Hartman and Cashman 1983; Chadwick and Lowe 1990). None the less, Brennan and Hemsley (1984) found evidence that paranoid patients, more than normal and psychiatric controls, tend to perceive illusory correlations between randomly associated items (subjects were presented with words paired together in random sequence), particularly if relating to their delusions, suggesting that they are insensitive to evidence about the covariation between events. In a subsequent study of probabilistic judgement, Huq et al. (1988) went on to show that deluded subjects, in comparison with controls, make over-confident decisions when presented with limited evidence and make less effort than controls to seek out further evidence.

It is unlikely that delusions have one cause. Within the context of the admittedly oversimple model outlined, it can be seen that a range of deficits might make persons vulnerable to delusions given appropriate circumstances. The kind of model outlined here may have particular relevance to coherent sets of delusions such as those found in patients described as paranoid, but may be less relevant to the understanding of some of the more bizarre delusional perceptions observed in some psychotic patients (Hamilton 1984). In this regard, however, psychopathologists should be aware that the attributions they make about psychiatric symptoms may be as much subject to non-rational biases as the symptoms of the patients themselves. Thus, Shoham-Salomon (1985) found that medically qualified clinicians attributed less freedom of choice and purposefulness to the behaviour of schizophrenics than psychosocial therapists rating the same behaviours. Clearly, the beliefs and assumptions of both patients and psychopathologists warrant further investigation.

Disordered discourse

Of all the psychotic symptoms, thought disorder has perhaps received most attention from cognitive psychologists, perhaps because the loosening of associations was identified as the core feature of schizophrenia by Eugen Bleuler (1911). Unfortunately, much of this research has been based on broad diagnostic categories on the assumption that a cognitive deficit specific to the diagnosis of schizophrenia might be identified. It is only recently that researchers have attempted to relate their measures to formal assessments of thought disorder (Harvey and Neale 1983).

Thought disorder in reality amounts to disordered discourse: the thought disordered patient's difficulties are manifest in bizarre and sometimes incoherent attempts to communicate with others. In practice, a range of discourse abnormalities are observed, and are found not only in patients diagnosed as schizophrenic but also typically in those labelled manic (Andreasen, 1979; Harrow et al. 1986). Confusingly, there has been a tendency to talk about negative thought disorder (poverty of speech) and positive thought disorder (incoherent speech) as if they exist at either end of a dimension of pathology, although there is evidence that these are independent characteristics of psychotic speech (Pohue-Geile and Harrow 1984). There is some evidence that patients diagnosed as manic tend to show more severe thought disorder of the positive kind whereas those diagnosed as schizophrenic tend to show more poverty of speech, although both groups of patients exhibit both types of disorder to some degree (Harvey et al. 1984). Of course this does not mean that 'mania' and 'schizophrenia' cause different types of speech pathologies: it is more likely that psychiatrists make their diagnoses partly on the basis of their patients' speech characteristics.

Considerable research has been directed towards identifying key features of positively disordered discourse. An influential account was given by Rochester and Martin (1979), who suggested that the speech of thought-disordered schizophrenic patients typically exhibits referential failures, so that there are few clear links between clauses and few clear references to previously presented ideas. As a result, listeners find it very hard to follow the thread of the thought-disordered person's speech. Durbin and Marshall (1977) subsequently demonstrated just these kinds of deficits in the speech of thought-disordered patients diagnosed as manic. In a particularly well-controlled study along the same lines, Harvey (1983) compared thought-disordered patients diagnosed as schizophrenic and manic with non-thought-disordered patients with the same diagnoses: cohesion and reference failures were generally found in the thought-disordered segments of patients with both diagnoses but not in the speech of the non-thought-disordered patients.

A number of explanations have been offered for the disordered discourse of psychotic patients. Hoffman et al. (1982) suggested that thought-disordered schizophrenics have inadequate discourse plans (according to some theories of language production, discourse planning is a pre-verbal stage in which speech is planned in the mind prior to being uttered). Hoffman et al. inferred ineffective planning on the basis of a structural analysis of thought-disordered speech, but as Harvey (1985) has pointed out, no direct cognitive evidence of ineffective planning was provided. Moreover, Hoffman et al.'s method of analysing speech has been criticized for being unreliable and subjective (Beveridge and Brown 1985).

A rather different approach to explaining disordered discourse has been promoted by a number of researchers who have emphasized the role of executive or metacognitive processes in the regulation of speech (it will be recalled that it has already been suggested that metacognitive deficits may be implicated in hallucinations). Harrow and Prosen (1978) found that the intermingling of associations from the past is a common feature of disordered speech, suggesting that thought-disordered patients suffer from an impairment of perspective which prevents them from deciding whether their speech is appropriate to the circumstances.

Consistent with this hypothesis, Harrow and Prosen (1979) demonstrated that thought-disordered patients were able to provide rationales for their bizarre speech in terms of their past experiences, and Harrow and Miller (1980) found that they showed a selective failure to appreciate when their own speech (but not the speech of other thought-disordered patients) was inappropriate.

A slightly different approach to thought disorder in terms of metacognitive functions has been taken by Harvey (1985), who hypothesized that disordered discourse might result from a failure of reality monitoring (the ability to recall whether a remembered stimulus was self-generated or perceived). Harvey suggested that reference failures in discourse might result from a patient's inability to discriminate speech that has already been said from discourse plans – i.e. the patient cannot work out what has already been said and what remains to be stated. In a study of thought-disordered and non-thought-disordered patients diagnosed as schizophrenic and manic, Harvey found that thought disorder was associated with deficits on a reality-monitoring task.

Disordered discourse has not only stimulated the interest of cognitive psychologists but also those with different concerns. In the only attempt to investigate genetic factors involved in a particular symptom, Berenbaum et al. (1985) found no evidence for the inheritance of disordered discourse. However, a factor analysis revealed two separate components of thought disorder of verbosity and speech discontinuities and there was evidence that the former was familial but non-genetic. As Berenbaum et al. point out, this finding is reminiscent of previous research by Wynne and his associates (Singer and Wynne 1965; Wynne et al. 1976) which showed that both biological and adoptive parents of psychotic patients could be identified blind on the basis of verbosity. Taken together, these results therefore suggest that at least some aspects of disordered discourse are acquired by learning.

Negative symptoms

Following Crow's (1980) hypothesis of two separate schizophrenia syndromes, it has become increasingly common for researchers to distinguish between positive symptoms (hallucinations, delusions, and thought disorder) and negative symptoms (poverty of speech and speech content, apathy, anhedonia, attentional impairment) of psychosis. According to Crow, the positive symptoms reflect a disorder of the dopamine system in the brain whereas the negative symptoms reflect neurological impairment (see Chapter 5 by Jackson in this volume for a discussion of the role of neurological and biochemical variables in psychosis). Crow's hypothesis was based on claims that the negative symptoms are resistant to neuroleptic medications (which act by blocking dopamine receptors), that amphetamine (a dopamine agonist) exacerbates positive but not negative symptoms, and that ventricular enlargement is observed in association with negative symptoms. Each of these claims has not gone unchallenged (Lewine 1985). It has been reported, for example, that negative symptoms do sometimes respond to neuroleptics (Sommers 1985), that patients with predominantly positive symptoms are unresponsive to the amphetamine (Kornetsky 1976), and that ventricular enlargement is not uniquely associated with negative symptoms (Luchins et al. 1984).

Comparatively little progress has been made in the understanding of negative symptoms compared with the progress which has been made in the understanding of other psychotic phenomena. Traditionally, these symptoms have been viewed as part of the schizophrenia disease process and/or a side-effect of medication and/or the result of institutionalization. Following Crow's hypothesis, most experimental research has been directed towards finding neurological or neuropsychological correlates of negative symptoms. Johnstone et al. (1976) reported that patients with predominantly negative symptoms were worse than other patients on tests measuring reverse-digit span (repeating a series of numbers backwards – often regarded as an index of attention), learning of paired associates, and facial recognition. More recently, Green and Walker (1985) administered a variety of neuropsychological tests to patients with mainly positive, mainly negative, or mixed symptoms: negative symptoms tended to be associated with visual-motor and visual-spatial deficits whereas positive symptoms tended to be associated with an impairment of short-term verbal memory. In an interesting study which focused on one particular negative symptom, Mayer et al. (1985) found that flat affect was associated with right-hemisphere impairment as measured by neuropsychological tests, the extra-pyramidal side-effects of medication, and hospitalization. Mayer et al. therefore reached the conclusion that flat affect is the final common pathway for the behavioural expression of 'multiple independent underlying processes'.

This finding raises the possibility that environmental variables might contribute to negative symptoms, as has often been supposed (Wing and Brown 1970). This would be consistent with the data on outcome in psychosis, and with the observation that recovery from breakdown is related to socio-economic conditions (Warner 1985). Moreover, as some authors have observed, similar features are found in the behaviour and attitudes of other severely marginalized individuals such as concentration-camp victims (see Chapter 3 by Barham and Hayward in this volume). The finding that some negative symptoms are responsive to behaviour-modification programs (Paul and Lentz 1977; see also Chapter 9 by Slade in this volume) has been interpreted as evidence that they are environmentally determined, although there is in fact no reason why disorders with a biological aetiology should be resistant to psychological therapy. A study by Johnstone et al. (1981) failed to find much in the way of differences in negative symptomatology between hospitalized and non-hospitalized patients diagnosed as schizophrenic, but this result may not be decisive as most long-term psychiatric patients in the community lead very impoverished lives, often in extremely depressing conditions.

Part of the problem in explaining negative symptoms would seem to be the lack of a clear understanding of what these symptoms are and how they are related. Thus, although Andreasen (1982) has published reliable scales for their assessment, a factor analysis by Gibbons et al. (1985) indicated that they have three separate components: apathy, psychomotor retardation, and loss of goal orientation. Andreasen (1985) herself noted that there was some confusion about whether there really is an identifiable negative syndrome and suggested that this should be regarded as at best a tentative hypothesis. Progress in this area is likely to result from a better description of these phenomena, together with more imaginative strategies for investigating aetiology. For example it would be interesting to know the extent to which negative symptoms occur in the long-term unemployed or the chronically depressed. It would also be interesting to know whether patients exhibiting negative symptoms have any of the cognitive features of depression (such as feelings of lack of control).

47

RICHARD P. BENTALL

CONCLUSIONS: SYMPTOMS OR SYNDROMES OF INSANITY?

It is hoped that this brief outline of research into the symptoms of psychosis will be sufficient to convince the reader of the value of this approach. In general, the approach seems to offer a way in which the enquiring psychopathologist can be scientific about mental disorder without accepting the traditional Kraepelinian model and the almost certainly meaningless concept of schizophrenia. It is an approach which is 'neutral' with respect to the roles of environment and biology in determining abnormal behaviour, and has the additional virtue of relating explanations to what is actually observed in the clinic – i.e. the actual experiences and conduct of patients. As there is nothing illogical in the idea that there are valid syndromes of madness waiting to be discovered (given the correct application of appropriate empirical techniques), it might also be expected that the strategy of research on classification and the strategy of researching symptoms will eventually converge. On this view, it could be hoped that another hundred years of research will lead to the reconstruction of a medical model of mental disorder with a substantially different system of psychiatric classification.

Yet it is possible that the symptom-orientated approach offers a more radical restructuring of the tenets of psychopathology. The key issue in this regard concerns what is to be inferred from a syndrome. Although syndromes are mere statistical associations between symptoms there is the tendency to believe that they carry greater implications. Thus, traditional theorists tend to assume that a syndrome implies some kind of hidden cause as if, for example, labels like 'schizophrenia' or 'the positive syndrome' are more than descriptors of groups of behaviours and have potential explanatory power. This is a way of thinking that is deeply confused: it involves the kind of 'category error' rightly lampooned by the philosopher Gilbert Ryle (1949) in his celebrated critique of 'ghost in the machine' models of mental functioning. Its consequence is the fruitless search for occult entities of psychopathology and the kind of convoluted thinking that is all too frequently used to account for patients who show symptoms of more than one diagnostic prototype (for example, disputes about which symptoms belong to which disorders, the argument that some patients are doubly unfortunate and suffer from more than one kind of mental disorder, and so on).

Figure 2.3 A schematic 'cognitive table' (analogous to the periodic table in chemi____
relating some symptoms of mental disorder to specific abnormalities of the
perceptual, cognitive, and metacognitive systems. All abnormalities shown are in
comparison with the functioning of 'normal' individuals. Evidence for the
abnormalities indicated is available from a number of sources including the
following: (1) Hammeke et al. (1983); (2) Kay et al. (1976); (3) Alpert (1985)
and Schneider and Wilson (1983); (4) McCormick and Broekma (1978); (5)
Brennan and Hemsley (1984); (6) Alloy and Abramson (1979); (7) Kaney and
Bentall (1989); (8) Abramson et al. (1978); (9) Alpert (1985); (10) Huq et al.
(1988) and Bentall and Kaney (1989); (11) Bentall and Kaney (1989); (12)
Heilbrun (1980) and Bentall and Slade (1985); (13) Harvey (1985). The causes
of the perceptual, cognitive, and metacognitive abnormalities remain
unspecified; it is likely that they will prove to be multiply determined by a range
of biological (disease) and historical (social-psychological) factors. Similarities of
symptoms and correlations between them are explained by their sharing of
underlying perceptual, cognitive, or metacognitive processes so that dysfunction
of a particular process may result in vulnerability to more than one symptom.
   Figure 2.3. should not be regarded as definitive or complete; rather, the
intention is to illustrate the value of a cognitive table of symptoms as a general
organizing principle. Some symptoms (for example, the negative symptoms) are
missing from the figure as shown. Moreover, a clearer understanding of the
relationships between the mental processes indicated would be needed for the
more accurate construction of the figure.

| | | Symptom | | | |
		Hallucinations	Delusions	Thought disorder	Depression
Perception	Perceptual Acuity	Slow loss of acuity related to vulnerability (1)	Deafness related to vulnerability (2)	Not implicated	Not implicated
	Perceptual Judgement	Rapid search for meaning (1)	Rapid search for meaning (4)	Not implicated	Not implicated
Cognition	Detection of Covariation	Not implicated	Over-detection of covariation (5)	Not implicated	Realistic under-detection of covariation (6)
	Attributions	Not implicated	*External*, global and stable for negative events (7)	Not implicated	*Internal*, global and stable for negative events (8)
Metacognition	Confidence in Judgements	Over-confident (9)	Over-confident (10)	Not known to be implicated	Under-confident (11)
	Reality Discrimination	Impaired (12)	Not implicated	Impaired (13)	Not implicated

Many of these problems can be avoided by taking the symptoms at face value. Symptoms are, after all, nothing more than classes of behaviour resulting from the interaction between cognitive processes and the environment. The first level of explanation of a symptom should therefore make reference to the cognitive organization of the patient and to environmental events that tend to make the symptom worse or better. Abnormalities of cognitive organization (the final common pathways of symptoms) may, in turn, be a consequence of a wide range of biological (genetic, biochemical, neurological) and historical (environmental) factors, but this second level of explanation will necessarily come later (biochemical abnormalities alone, for example, cannot *explain* mental disorder unless it can also be shown how they affect cognitive organization). By this strategy it should be possible to identify which kinds of cognitive abnormalities are implicated in which symptoms, and to thereby construct a kind of 'cognitive table' of psychopathological states analogous to the periodic table in chemistry (see Figure 2.3). The periodic table in chemistry locates each element according to its underlying atomic structure and thus explains the relationships between elements; a cognitive table would show how impairments in particular cognitive systems might lead to each symptom and would explain the relationships between symptoms. It is not surprising, for example, that persecutory delusions correlate with hallucinations to some degree (see Chapter 6 by Claridge in this volume) as a vulnerability to both results from a particular style of information processing (the over-confident attribution of meaning to ambiguous stimuli). Nor is it surprising that paranoid symptoms appear also to be related to depression as both depressed and paranoid thinking follows from making excessively global and stable attributions for unpleasant events. On this account, therefore, the question 'Is paranoia a form of schizophrenia or alternatively an affective disorder?' becomes meaningless.

This analysis suggests a completely new research programme for psychopathologists, a programme that more closely ties the study of madness to the cognitive and neurosciences and moves it away from the medical paradigm that present-day investigators have inherited from nineteenth-century psychiatrists. Inevitably some investigators will find this programme unattractive. It is only to be hoped that after a further hundred years students of psychopathology will no longer ask: Why has so little progress been made in the understanding of schizophrenia?

REFERENCES

Abramson, L.Y., Seligman, M.E.P., and Teasdale, J.D. (1978) 'Learned helplessness in humans: critique and reformulation', *Journal of Abnormal Psychology* 78: 40–74.

Alenen, Y.O., Rakkolainen, V., Laakso, J., Rasimus, R., and Kaljonen, A. (1986) *Towards a Need-specific Treatment of Schizophrenic Psychosis*, New York: Springer-Verlag.

Al-Issa, I. (1978) 'Social and cultural aspects of hallucinations', *Psychological Bulletin* 84: 570–87.

Alloy, C.B. and Abramson, L.Y. (1979) 'Judgement of contingency in depressed and non-depressed students: sadder but wiser', *Journal of Experimental Psychology: General* 108: 441–85.

Alpert, M. (1985) 'The signs and symptoms of schizophrenia', *Comprehensive Psychiatry* 26: 103–12.

American Psychiatric Association (1980) *Diagnostic and Statistical Manual of Mental Disorders, 3rd edn*, Washington, DC: American Psychiatric Association.

Andreasen, N.C. (1979) 'Thought, language and communication disorders: II. Diagnostic significance' *Archives of General Psychiatry* 36: 1325–30.

— (1982) 'Negative symptoms in schizophrenia: definition and reliability *Archives of General Psychiatry* 39: 784–8.

— (1985) 'Positive versus negative schizophrenia: a critical evaluation', *Schizophrenia Bulletin* 11: 380–9.

Arieti, S. (1974) *The Interpretation of Schizophrenia*, London: Crosby Lockwood Staples.

Asaad, G. and Shapiro, M.D. (1986) 'Hallucinations: theoretical and clinical overview', *American Journal of Psychiatry* 143: 1088–97.

Bagshaw, V.E. and McPherson, F.M. (1978) 'The applicability of the Foulds and Bedford hierarchy model to mania and hypomania', *British Journal of Psychiatry* 132: 293–5.

Bannister, D. (1968) 'The logical requirements of research into schizophrenia', *British Journal of Psychiatry* 114: 181–8.

— (1986) 'The psychotic disguise', in W. Dryden (ed.) *Therapist's Dilemmas*, Milton Keynes: Open University Press.

Bateson, G., Jackson, D.D., Haley, J., and Weakland, J. (1956) 'Towards a theory of schizophrenia', *Behavioural Science* 1: 251–64.

Beck, A.T. (1967) *Depression: Clinical, Experimental and Theoretical Aspects*, New York: Harper & Row.

— Ward, C.H., Mendelson, M., Mock, J.E., and Erbaugh, J.K. (1962) 'Reliability of psychiatric diagnosis: II. A study of consistency of clinical judgements and ratings', *American Journal of Psychiatry* 119: 351–7.

Beckman, H. and Haas, S. (1980) 'High dose diazepam in schizophrenia', *Psychopharmocology* 71: 79–82.

Bentall, R.P. (1986) 'The scientific validity of the schizophrenia diagnosis: a critical evaluation, in N. Eisenberg and D. Glasgow (eds) *Current Issues in Clinical Psychology, Vol. 5*, Aldershot: Gower.

The illusion of reality: a review and integration of
ogical research on hallucinations', *Psychological Bulletin* 107:

., Kaney, S., and Dewey, M.E. (1991) 'Persecutory delusions
al judgement: an attribution theory analysis', *British Journal of
Clinical Psychology* 30: 13–23.

Bentall, R.P., and Slade, P.D. (1985) 'Reality testing and auditory
hallucinations; a signal detection analysis', *British Journal of Clinical
Psychology* 24: 159–69.

— (1986) 'Verbal hallucinations, unintendedness and the schizophrenia
diagnosis', *The Behavioural and Brain Sciences* 9: 519–20.

Bentall, R.P., Jackson, H.F., and Pilgrim, D. (1988) 'Abandoning the
concept of "schizophrenia": some implications of validity arguments
for psychological research into psychotic phenomena', *British Journal
of Clinical Psychology* 27: 303–24.

Berenbaum, H., Oltmanns, T.F., and Gottesman, I. (1985) 'Formal
thought disorder in schizophrenics and their twins', *Journal of
Abnormal Psychology* 94: 3–16.

Beveridge, A.W. and Brown, K. (1985) 'A critique of Hoffman's analysis
of schizophrenic speech', *Brain and Language* 24: 174–81.

Blashfield, R.K. (1973) 'An evaluation of the DSM-II classification of
schizophrenia as a nomenclature', *Journal of Abnormal Psychology* 82: 382–9.

— (1984) *The Classification of Psychopathology: Neo-Kraepelinian and
Quantitative Approaches*, New York: Plenum.

Bleuler, E. (1911) *Dementia Praecox or the Group of Schizophrenias*, New York:
International Universities Press (English edn, 1955).

Bleuler, M. (1978) 'The long-term course of schizophrenic psychoses', in
L.C. Wynne, R.L. Cromwell, and S. Matthysse (eds) *The Nature of
Schizophrenia*, New York: Wiley.

Bourguignon, E. (1970) 'Hallucinations and trance: an anthropologist's
perspective', in W. Keup (ed.) *Origin and Mechanisms of Hallucination*,
New York: Wiley.

Brennan, J.H. and Hemsley, D.R. (1984) 'Illusory correlations in
paranoid and non-paranoid schizophrenia', *British Journal of Clinical
Psychology* 23: 225–6.

Brett, E.A. and Starker, S. (1977) 'Auditory imagery and hallucinations',
Journal of Nervous and Mental Disease 164: 394–400.

Brockington, I.F. and Wainwright, R.S. (1980) 'Depressed patients with
schizophrenic or paranoid symptoms', *Psychological Medicine* 10:
665–75.

Brockington, I.F., Kendell, R.E., and Leff, J.P. (1978) 'Definitions of
schizophrenia: concordance and prediction of outcome', *Psychological
Medicine* 8: 399–412.

Brown, G.W. and Birley, J.L.T. (1968) 'Crises and life changes and the
onset of schizophrenia', *Journal of Health and Social Behaviour* 9: 203–14.

Carpenter, W.T., McGlashan, T.H., and Strauss, J.S. (1977) 'The
treatment of acute schizophrenia without drugs: an investigation of
some current assumptions', *American Journal of Psychiatry* 134: 14–20.

Catts, S.V., Armstrong, M.S., Norcross, K., and McConaghy, N. (1980) 'Auditory hallucinations and the verbal transformation effect', *Psychological Medicine* 10: 139–44.

Chadwick, P., and Lowe, C.F., (1990) 'The measurement and modification of delusional beliefs', *Journal of Consulting and Clinical Psychology* 58: 225–32.

Child, D. (1970) *The Essentials of Factor Analysis*, London: Holt, Rinehart & Winston.

Ciompi, L. (1980) 'The natural history of schizophrenia in the long term', *British Journal of Psychiatry* 136: 413–20.

— (1984) 'Is there really a schizophrenia?: the long-term course of psychotic phenomena', *British Journal of Psychiatry* 145: 636–40.

Claridge, G. (1987) '"The schizophrenias as nervous types" revisited', *British Journal of Psychiatry* 151: 735–43.

Connor, S. and Kingman, S. (1988) *The Search for the Virus: The Scientific Discovery of AIDS and the Quest for a Cure*, Harmondsworth: Penguin.

Cooklin, R., Sturgeon, D., and Leff, J.P. (1983) 'The relationship between auditory hallucinations and spontaneous fluctuations of skin conductance in schizophrenia', *British Journal of Psychiatry* 142: 47–52.

Crow, T.J. (1980) 'Molecular pathology of schizophrenia: more than one disease process?', *British Medical Journal* 280: 66–8.

— (1984) 'A re-evaluation of the viral hypothesis: is psychosis the result of retroviral integration at a site close to the cerebral dominance gene?', *British Journal of Psychiatry* 145: 243–53.

— MacMillan, J.F., Johnson, A.L., and Johnstone, E.C. (1986) 'The Northwick Park study of first episodes of schizophrenia: II. A controlled trial of prophylactic neuroleptic treatment', *British Journal of Psychiatry* 148: 120–7.

Delva, N.J. and Letemendia, F.J.J. (1982) 'Lithium treatment in schizophrenia and schizo-affective disorders', *British Journal of Psychiatry* 141: 387–400.

Durbin, M. and Marshall, R.L. (1977) 'Speech in mania: syntactic aspects', *Brain and Language* 4: 208–18.

Eccleston, D. (1986) 'Organic aspects of schizophrenia: overview', in A. Kerr and P. Snaith (eds) *Contemporary Issues in Schizophrenia*, London: Royal College of Psychiatrists.

Everitt, B.S. (1980) *Cluster Analysis, 2nd edn*, Aldershot: Gower.

— Gourlay, A.J., and Kendell, R.E. (1971) 'An attempt at validation of traditional psychiatric syndromes by cluster analysis', *British Journal of Psychiatry* 119: 399–412.

Eysenck, H.J., Wakefield, J.A., and Friedman, A.F. (1983) 'Diagnosis and clinical assessment: the DSM-III', *Annual Review of Psychology* 34: 167–93.

Eysenck, M. (1976) 'Arousal, learning and memory', *Psychological Bulletin* 83: 389–404.

Faris, R.E.L. and Dunham, H.W. (1939) *Mental Disorders in Urban Areas: an Ecological Study of Schizophrenia and Other Psychoses*, Chicago: Chicago University Press.

Flavell, J.H. (1979) 'Metacognition and cognitive monitoring', *American Psychologist* 34: 906–11.

Foulds, G.A. and Bedford, A. (1975) 'Hierarchy and classes of personal illness', *Psychological Medicine* 5: 181–92.

Frith, C.D. (1979) 'Consciousness, information processing and schizophrenia', *British Journal of Psychiatry* 134: 225–35.

Gibbons, R.D., Lewine, F.J., Davis, J.M., Schooler, N.R., and Cole, J.O. (1985) 'An empirical test of a Kraepelinian versus a Bleulerian view of negative symptoms', *Schizophrenia Bulletin* 11: 390–6.

Gottesman, I. and Shields, J. (1982) *Schizophrenia: The Epigenetic Puzzle*, Cambridge: Cambridge University Press.

Green, A.R. and Costain, D.W. (1981) *Pharmacology and Biochemistry of Psychiatric Disorders*, London: Wiley.

Green, M. and Walker, E. (1985) 'Neuropsychological performance and positive and negative symptoms in schizophrenia', *Journal of Abnormal Psychology* 94: 460–9.

Hamilton, M. (ed.) (1984) *Fish's Schizophrenia*, London: Wright.

Hammeke, T.A., McQuillen, M.P., and Cohen, B.A. (1983) 'Musical hallucinations associated with acquired deafness', *Journal of Neurology, Neurosurgery and Psychiatry* 46: 570–2.

Harrow, M. and Miller, J.G. (1980) 'Schizophrenic thought disorders and impaired perspective', *Journal of Abnormal Psychology* 89: 717–27.

Harrow, M. and Prosen, M. (1978) 'Intermingling and disordered logic as influences on schizophrenic thought', *Archives of General Psychiatry* 35: 1213–18.

—— (1979) 'Schizophrenic thought disorders: bizarre associations and intermingling', *American Journal of Psychiatry* 136: 293–6.

Harrow, M., Grossman, L.S., Silverstein, M.L., Meltzer, H.Y., and Kettering, R.I. (1986) 'A longitudinal study of thought disorder in manic patients', *Archives of General Psychiatry* 43: 781–5.

Hartman, L.M. and Cashman, F.E. (1983) 'Cognitive-behavioural and psychopharmacological treatment of delusional symptoms: a preliminary report', *Behavioural Psychotherapy* 11: 50–61.

Harvey, P.D. (1983) 'Speech competence in manic and schizophrenic psychoses: the association between clinically rated thought disorder and cohesion and reference', *Journal of Abnormal Psychology* 92: 368–77.

—— (1985) 'Reality monitoring in mania and schizophrenia: the association of thought disorder and performance', *Journal of Nervous and Mental Disease* 173 (2): 67–73.

—— and Neale, J.M. (1983) 'The specificity of thought disorder to schizophrenia: research methods in their historical perspective', in B. Maher (ed) *Progress in Experimental Personality Research, Vol.12*. New York: Academic Press

Harvey, P.D., Earle-Boyer, E.A., and Weilgus, M.S. (1984) 'The consistency of thought disorder in mania and schizophrenia: an assessment of acute psychotics', *Journal of Nervous and Mental Disease* 172: 458–63.

Hawke, A.B., Strauss, J.S., and Carpenter, W.T. (1975) 'Diagnostic criteria and five-year outcome in schizophrenia', *Archives of General Psychiatry* 32: 343–7.

Hayman, M.A. and Abrams, R. (1977) 'Capgras syndrome and cerebral dysfunction', *British Journal of Psychiatry* 130: 68–71.

Heilbrun, A.R. (1980) 'Impaired recognition of self-expressed thought in patients with auditory hallucinations', *Journal of Abnormal Psychology* 89: 728–36.

— and Blum, N. (1984) 'Cognitive vulnerability to auditory hallucinations: impaired perception of meaning', *British Journal of Psychiatry* 144: 508–12.

Hemsley, D.R. and Garety, P.A. (1986) 'The formation and maintenance of delusions: a Bayesian analysis', *British Journal of Psychiatry* 149: 51–6.

Hewstone, M. (1985) 'Attribution theory and common-sense explanations: an overview', in M. Hewstone (ed.) *Attribution Theory: Social and Functional Extensions*, Oxford: Blackwell.

Hirsch, S. (1982) 'Depression revealed in schizophrenia', *British Journal of Psychiatry* 142: 624–5.

Hoffman, R.E. (1986) 'Verbal hallucinations and language production in schizophrenia', *The Behavioural and Brain Sciences* 9: 503–48.

— Kirstein, L., Stopek, S., and Cicchetti, D.V. (1982) 'Apprehending schizophrenic discourse: a structural analysis of the listener's task', *Brain and Language* 15: 207–33.

Hole, R.W., Rush, A.J., and Beck, A.T. (1979) 'A cognitive investigation of schizophrenic delusions', *Psychiatry* 42: 312–19.

Huber, G., Gross, G., Schuttler, R., and Linz, M. (1980) 'Longitudinal studies of schizophrenic patients', *Schizophrenia Bulletin* 6: 592–605.

Huq, S.F., Garety, P., and Hemsley, D.R. (1988) 'Probabilistic judgements in deluded and non-deluded subjects', *Quarterly Journal of Experimental Psychology* 40A: 801–12.

Inouye, T. and Shimizu, A. (1970) 'The electromyographic study of auditory hallucination', *Folia Psychiatrica et Japonica* 29: 123–43.

Johnson, D.A.W. (1986) 'Depressive symptoms in schizophrenia: some observations on the frequency, morbidity and possible causes', in A. Kerr and P. Snaith (eds) *Contemporary Issues in Schizophrenia*, London: Royal College of Psychiatrists.

Johnson, M.K. and Raye, C.L. (1981) 'Reality monitoring', *Psychological Review* 88: 67–85.

Johnson, R.L. and Miller, M.D. (1965) 'Auditory hallucinations and intellectual deficit', *Journal of Psychiatric Research* 3: 37–41.

Johnson, W.G., Ross, J.M., and Mastria, M.A. (1977) 'Delusional behaviour: an attributional analysis of development and modification', Journal of Abnormal Psychology 86: 421–6.

Johnstone, E.C., Crow, T.J., Frith, C.D., Husband, J., and Kreel, L. (1976) 'Cerebral ventricular size and cognitive impairment in chronic schizophrenia', *Lancet* ii: 924–6.

Johnstone, E.C., Owens, D.G.C., Gold, A., Crow, T., and MacMillan, J.F. (1981) 'Institutionalization and the defects of schizophrenia', *British Journal of Psychiatry* 139: 195–203.

RICHARD P. BENTALL

Kaney, S. and Bentall, R.P. (1989) 'Persecutory delusions and attributional style', *British Journal of Medical Psychology* 62: 191–8.

Karon, B.P. and VandenBos, G.R. (1981) *Psychotherapy and Schizophrenia: The Treatment of Choice*, New York: Jason Aronson.

Kasanin, J. (1933) 'The acute schizoaffective psychoses', *American Journal of Psychiatry* 13: 97–126.

Kay, D.W.K., Cooper, A.S., Garside, R.F., and Roth, M. (1976) 'The differentiation of paranoid from affective psychoses by patients' premorbid characteristics', *British Journal of Psychiatry* 129: 207–15.

Kendell, R.E. (1975) *The Role of Diagnosis in Psychiatry*, Oxford: Blackwell.

— and Brockington, I.F. (1980) 'The identification of disease entities and the relationship between schizophrenic and affective psychoses', *British Journal of Psychiatry* 137: 324–31.

Kendell, R.E. and Gourlay, J.A. (1970) 'The clinical distinction between the affective psychoses and schizophrenia', *British Journal of Psychiatry* 117: 261–6.

Koehler, K. (1979) 'First rank symptoms of schizophrenia: questions concerning clinical boundaries', *British Journal of Psychiatry* 134: 236–48.

Kornetsky, C. (1976) 'Hyporesponsivity of chronic schizophrenic patients to dextroamphetamine', *Archives of General Psychiatry* 33: 1425–8.

Kuriansky, J.B., Deming, W.E., and Gurland, B.J. (1974) 'On trends in the diagnosis of schizophrenia', *American Journal of Psychiatry* 131: 402–8.

Laing, R.D. (1967) *The Politics of Experience*, Harmondsworth: Penguin.

LaRusso, L. (1978) 'Sensitivity of paranoid patients to non-verbal cues', *Journal of Abnormal Psychology* 87: 463–71.

Lewine, R.R.J. (ed.) (1985) 'Negative symptoms in schizophrenia', *Schizophrenia Bulletin* 11: 361–486.

Lingjaerde, O. (1982) 'Effects of the benzodiazapine estazdam in patients with auditory hallucinations: a multicentre double-blind cross-over study', *Acta Psychiatrica Scandinavica* 63: 339–54.

Lonowski, D.J., Sterling, F.E., and Kennedy, J.C. (1978) 'Gradual reduction of neuroleptic drugs among chronic schizophrenics', *Acta Psychiatrica Scandinavica* 52: 99–102.

Luchins, D.J., Lewine, R., and Meltzer, H. (1984) 'Lateral ventricular size, psychopathology and medication responses in the psychoses', *Biological Psychiatry* 19: 29–44.

McCormick, D. and Broekma, V. (1978) 'Size estimation, perceptual recognition and cardiac rate response in acute paranoid and non-paranoid schizophrenia', *Journal of Abnormal Psychology* 87: 385–98.

McGuigan, F.J. (1966) 'Covert oral behaviour and auditory hallucinations', *Psychophysiology* 3: 73–80.

— (1978) *Cognitive Psychophysiology: Principles of Covert Behaviour*, Englewood Cliffs, NJ: Prentice Hall.

Mackay, A.V.P. (1980) 'Positive and negative schizophrenic symptoms and the role of dopamine', *British Journal of Psychiatry* 137: 379–84.

McPherson, F.M., Antram, M.C., Bagshaw, V.E., and Carmichael, S.K. (1977) 'A test of the hierarchical model of personal illness', *British Journal of Psychiatry* 131: 56–8.

Maher, B.A. (1974) 'Delusional thinking and perceptual disorder', *Journal of Individual Psychology* 30: 98–113.
— and Ross, J.S. (1984) 'Delusions', in H.E. Adams and P. Suther (eds) *Comprehensive Handbook of Psychopathology*, New York: Plenum.
Manos, M., Taratsidis, I., Pappas, K., and Routsoni, C. (1977) 'Maintenance anti-psychotic pharmacotherapy, relapse and length of stay out of the hospital in chronic schizophrenics in Greece', *Journal of Nervous and Mental Disease* 165: 361–3.
Margo, A., Hemsley, D.R., and Slade, P.D. (1981) 'The effects of varying auditory input on schizophrenic hallucinations', *British Journal of Psychiatry* 139: 122–7.
Mayer, M., Alpert, M., Stastny, P., Perlick, D., and Empfield, M. (1985) 'Multiple contributions to clinical presentation of flat affect in schizophrenia', *Schizophrenia Bulletin* 11: 420–6.
Miller, M.D., Johnson, R.I.., and Richmond, L.H. (1965) 'Auditory hallucinations and descriptive language skills', *Journal of Psychiatric Research* 3: 43–56.
Mintz, S. and Alpert, M. (1972) 'Imagery vividness, reality testing and schizophrenic hallucinations', *Journal of Abnormal Psychology* 79: 310–16.
Nair, N.P. (1977) 'Drug therapy of schizophrenia in the community', *Journal of Orthomolecular Psychiatry* 6: 348–53.
Naylor, G.J. and Scott, C.R. (1980) 'Depot injections for affective disorders', *British Journal of Psychiatry* 136: 105.
Neisser, U. (1967) *Cognitive Psychology*, New York: Appleton-Century-Crofts.
Nisbett, R.E. and Ross, L. (1980) *Human Inference: Strategies and Shortcomings of Social Judgement*, Englewood Cliffs, NJ: Prentice-Hall.
Ollerenshaw, D.P. (1973) 'The classification of the functional psychoses', *British Journal of Psychiatry* 122: 517–30.
Paul, G .L. and Lentz, R. (1977) *Psychosocial Treatment of Chronic Mental Patients*, Cambridge, Mass.: Harvard University Press.
Persons, J.B. (1986) 'The advantages of studying psychological phenomena rather than psychiatric diagnoses', *American Psychologist* 41: 1252–60.
Pincus, J.H. and Tucker, G.J. (1978) *Behavioural Neurology*, New York: Oxford University Press.
Pohue-Geile, M.F. and Harrow, M. (1984) 'Negative and positive symptoms in schizophrenia and depression: a followup study', *Schizophrenia Bulletin* 10: 371–81.
Posey, T.B. (1986) 'Verbal hallucinations also occur in humans', *The Behavioural and Brain Sciences* 9: 530.
Reese, W.D. (1971) 'The hallucinations of widowhood', *British Medical Journal* 210: 37–41.
Rochester, S. and Martin, J.R. (1979) *Crazy Talk: A Study of the Discourse of Schizophrenic Speakers*, New York: Plenum.
Ryle, G. (1949) *The Concept of Mind*, Harmondsworth: Penguin.
Sandifer, M.G., Pettus, C., and Quade, D. (1964) 'A study of psychiatric diagnosis', *Journal of Nervous and Mental Disease* 139: 350–6.

Schneider, K. (1959) *Clinical Psychopathology*, New York: Grune & Stratton.

Schneider, S.J. and Wilson, C.R. (1983) 'Perceptual discrimination and reaction time in hallucinatory schizophrenics', *Psychiatry Research* 9: 243–53.

Schwartz, S. (1975) 'Individual differences in cognition: some relationships between personality and memory', *Journal of Research in Personality* 9: 217–25.

Shoham-Salomon, V. (1985) 'Are schizophrenics' behaviours schizophrenic?: what medically versus psychologically orientated therapists attribute to schizophrenic persons', *Journal of Abnormal Psychology* 94: 443–53.

Siegel, R.K. (1984) 'Hostage hallucinations: visual imagery induced by isolation and life-threatening stress', *Journal of Nervous and Mental Disease* 172: 264–72.

Singer, M.T. and Wynne, L.C. (1965) 'Thought disorder and family relations of schizophrenics: IV. Results and implications', *Archives of General Psychiatry* 12: 201–12.

Singh, M.M. and Kay, S.R. (1976) 'Wheat gluten as a pathogenic factor in schizophrenia', *Science* 191: 401–2.

Slade, P.D. (1972) 'The effects of systematic desensitization on auditory hallucinations', *Behaviour Research and Therapy* 10: 85–91.

— (1973) 'The psychological investigation and treatment of auditory hallucinations: a second case report', *British Journal of Medical Psychology* 46: 293–6.

— (1974) 'The external control of auditory hallucinations: an information theory analysis', *British Journal of Social and Clinical Psychology* 15: 415–23.

— (1976a) 'Towards a theory of auditory hallucinations: an outline of a hypothetical four-factor model', *British Journal of Social and Clinical Psychology* 15: 415–23.

— (1976b) 'An investigation of psychological factors involved in the predisposition to auditory hallucinations', *Psychological Medicine* 6: 123–32.

— and Bentall, R.P. (1988) *Sensory Deception: A Scientific Analysis of Hallucination*, London: Croom Helm.

Slade, P.D. and Cooper, R. (1979) 'Some conceptual difficulties with the term "schizophrenia": an alternative model', *British Journal of Social and Clinical Psychology* 18: 309–17.

Sommers, A.A. (1985) 'Negative symptoms: conceptual and methodological problems', *Schizophrenia Bulletin* 11: 364–79.

Spitzer, R.L. and Fliess, J.L. (1974) 'A reanalysis of the reliability of psychiatric diagnosis', *British Journal of Psychiatry* 123: 341–7.

Spitzer, R.L., Endicott, J., and Robins, E. (1978) *Research Diagnostic Criteria for a Selected Group of Functional Disorders*, New York: Biometrics Research.

Stanton, A.H., Gunderson. J.G, Knapp, P.H., Frank, A.F., Vannicelli, M.C., Schnitzer, R., and Rosenthal, R. (1984) 'Effects of psychotherapy in schizophrenia: I. Design and implementation of a controlled study', *Schizophrenia Bulletin* 10: 520–65.

Strauss, J.S. and Carpenter, W.T. (1974a) 'The prediction of outcome in schizophrenia: II. Relationships between predictor and outcome variables', *Archives of General Psychiatry* 31: 37–42.

— (1974b) 'Characteristic symptoms and outcome in schizophrenia', *Archives of General Psychiatry* 30: 429–34.

— (1977) 'Prediction of outcome in schizophrenia III: Five year outcome and its predictors', *Archives of General Psychiatry* 34: 159–63.

Sturt, E. (1981) 'Hierarchical patterns in the distribution of psychiatric symptoms', *Psychological Medicine* 11: 783–94.

Toone, B.K., Cooke, E., and Lader, M.H. (1981) 'Electrodermal activity in the affective disorders and schizophrenia', *Psychological Medicine* 11: 497–508.

Torrey, E.F. (1987) 'Prevalence studies in schizophrenia', *British Journal of Psychiatry* 150: 598–608.

Trouton, D.S. and Maxwell, A.E. (1956) 'The relation between neurosis and psychosis: an analysis of symptoms and past history of 819 psychotics and neurotics', *Journal of Mental Science* 102: 1–21.

Warner, R. (1985) *Recovery from Schizophrenia: Psychiatry and Political Economy*, London: Routledge & Kegan Paul.

Watson, C.G., Kacula, T., Anguluski, G., and Bruun, G. (1982) 'Season of birth and schizophrenia: a response to the Lewis and Griffin critique', *Journal of Abnormal Psychology* 91: 120–5.

Watts, F.N., Powell, E.G., and Austin, S.V. (1973) 'The modification of abnormal beliefs', *British Journal of Medical Psychology* 46: 359–63.

Wilding, J.M. (1982) *Perception: From Sense to Object*, London: Hutchinson.

Williams, E.B. (1964) 'Deductive reasoning in schizophrenia', *Journal of Abnormal and Social Psychology* 69: 47–61.

Wing, J.K. (1978) *Reasoning about Madness*, Oxford: Oxford University Press.

— and Brown, G.W. (1970) *Institutionalism and Schizophrenia*, London: Cambridge University Press.

Wing, J.K., Cooper, J.E., and Sartorius, N. (1974) *The Measurement and Classification of Psychiatric Syndromes*, Cambridge: Cambridge University Press.

Winters, K.C. and Neale, J.M. (1983) 'Delusions and delusional thinking: a review of the literature', *Clinical Psychology Review* 3: 227–53.

World Health Organization (1975) *Schizophrenia: A Multinational Study*, Geneva: WHO.

Wynne, L.C., Singer, M.T., and Toohey, M.L. (1976) 'Communications of adoptive parents of schizophrenics', in J. Jorstad and E. Ugelstad (eds) *Schizophrenia 75: Psychotherapy, Family Studies, Research*, Oslo: Universtetsforlaget.

Young, H.F., Bentall, R.P., Slade, P.D., and Dewey, M.E. (1987) 'The role of brief instructions and suggestibility in the elicitation of auditory and visual hallucinations in normal and psychiatric subjects', *Journal of Nervous and Mental Disease* 175: 41–8.

Zigler, E. and Glick, M. (1988) 'Is paranoid schizophrenia really camouflaged depression?', *American Psychologist* 43: 284–90.

Zigler, E. and Phillips, L. (1961) 'Psychiatric diagnosis and symptomatology', *Journal of Abnormal and Social Psychology* 63: 69–75.

Zimbardo, P., Andersen, S., and Kabat, L. (1981) 'Induced hearing deficit generates experimental paranoia', *Science* 212: 1529–31.

Chapter Three

SCHIZOPHRENIA AS A LIFE PROCESS

PETER BARHAM AND ROBERT HAYWARD

INTRODUCTION

What has traditionally been called the course of schizophrenia, asserts the Swiss psychiatrist Luc Ciompi, does not exist, and the development of a person who has once become psychotic must be viewed more as an open life-process, dependent upon a wide variety of biographical and social influences of all kinds, than as a disease process (Ciompi 1980a). In similar terms, Rue Cromwell has argued that the schizophrenic's 'destiny is determined much the same as the destinies of all people are determined' and that schizophrenia is not therefore an 'all-encompassing illness which sets the patient apart from his fellow man' (Cromwell 1978: 646; see also Zubin et al. 1983).

From the formulations of psychiatrists in the late nineteenth and early twentieth centuries we have inherited a highly determinate view of the unfolding of schizophrenic lives (see Barham 1984). In this chapter we shall describe some of the evidence which requires that we part company with these conceptions and look more closely at what is involved in attempting to understand the vicissitudes of people who have had a schizophrenic illness.

VARIATIONS IN COURSE

First there is the evidence that the clinical course of schizophrenia is much more varied than had been supposed. The most revealing studies in this respect are those of Luc Ciompi and Christian Muller (1976) and of Manfred Bleuler (1972).

In an enquiry undertaken in Lausanne, the Swiss psychiatrists Ciompi and Muller provided a historical retrospect on the destinies of 228 schizophrenics born between 1873 and 1897. The lives of the patients were charted over a minimum period of 37 years from first admission to hospital to re-examination, in many instances for much longer. As Ciompi remarks, these are probably the longest follow-ups of such a large group of schizophrenics in the world literature. It was shown that the various forms of schizophrenia run a much more polymorphic course of development than had previously been assumed and that the outcome is much better. Ciompi and Muller, and also Bleuler in an independent study, were able to identify eight developmental types. As Ciompi comments:

> These observations lead us to the conclusion that the developmental course of schizophrenia is not compatible with the conception of a progressive disease process but, rather, that such courses, upon closer inspection, show themselves as being almost as protean as life itself.
>
> (Ciompi 1980a: 240)

Almost half of the patients in the Ciompi and Muller study achieved a favourable outcome (27 per cent complete remissions and 22 per cent 'minor residuals'), 24 per cent achieved an intermediate outcome, and 22 per cent a severe outcome. (The remaining 9 per cent fell into an unstable or uncertain category.) Only 6 per cent of the subjects were judged to be suffering from the so-called 'catastrophic schizophrenia', an acute form of schizophrenia leading directly to a severe and unremitting chronic psychosis. Furthermore, a comparison of the clinical condition at follow-up with that at first admission revealed that 'mental health was completely or partially improved in about two-thirds of the cases' (Ciompi 1980b: 416). Over the period of study, about one-quarter of the group spent more than 20 years in hospital, but as many as 47 per cent spent less than one year. At the time of follow-up the mean age of the subjects was 74, yet more than half were still working, about two-thirds of these in part-time and the remaining third in full-time occupations.

The individual who has perhaps made the most notable and determined effort to tackle the mistakes and biases in the formulation of schizophrenia as a unitary disease process is the

SCHIZOPHRENIA AS A LIFE PROCESS

Swiss psychiatrist Manfred Bleuler. The son of Eugen Bleuler who introduced the term schizophrenia as an alternative to Kraepelin's concept of dementia praecox, Manfred Bleuler was brought up in the renowned Burgholzli Hospital in Zurich where his father was the director and where Jung, among others, served his apprenticeship. Manfred Bleuler himself subsequently became director of the Burgholzli, and it was here that he conducted his most important clinical work. (For a discussion of Bleuler in the context of the history of schizophrenia, see Barham 1984.)

In his major study *The Schizophrenic Disorders* Manfred Bleuler set out to depict the 'life vicissitudes of 208 schizophrenics and their families' as he had 'personally experienced these, together with them, over a period of more than 20 years'. Previous studies had described the long-term courses only of hospitalized patients and in consequence 'nothing was really known about the fates of the great number of patients with whom, after their release, the doctor lost contact'. The account which Bleuler gives of the variations in the course of schizophrenia and of outcome is in all important respects complementary to that of Ciompi and Muller. Bleuler concludes that about 25 per cent of schizophrenics recover entirely and remain recovered for good; about 65 per cent alternate for decades between phases of improvement or recovery and acute psychotic lapses; and about 10 per cent remain severely psychotic and in need of hospital care. On average after 5 years' duration the psychosis does not progress any further but tends rather to improve.

A recurring emphasis in Bleuler's writing is on the unpredictability of the individual life:

> The closer we live together with patients, even the most chronic ones, the more astonished we are at fluctuations in their condition. The great majority of the alterations in the course of many years after the onset of psychosis are clearly in the direction of improvement. The improvements are manifold in nature. Some of the patients who have hardly ever uttered coherent sentences start to speak or behave as if they were healthy on certain occasions, for instance, when on leave, at hospital festivities, or on the occasion of a catastrophe such as exploding bombs in wartime.
>
> (Bleuler 1978: 633)

The following is an example of the kind of improvement which Bleuler identifies. Edouard S. was born in 1912 and hospitalized as a schizophrenic at the age of 30. From 1943 to 1963 he lived at home but in all this time:

> was able to perform only the simplest tasks, and continued to show peculiar behaviour stereotypes. For instance, every day he scrubbed three steps of the staircase. He voiced numerous delusional associations. If, for instance, an object was broken he declared stereotypically that it could only be repaired if this or that person would live in a specified location or would die.
>
> (Bleuler 1972: 226)

However,

> Beginning in 1963, that is, 21 years after onset of illness, a period of improvement set in. It seemed related to the death of his mother, although he had enjoyed a good relationship to her. The proband began to take an interest in many things; he began to read the newspaper again, which he had not done for many years, and especially, he speaks again with his relatives and has become their accepted and beloved family member again. His family no longer regards him as mentally ill, but simply as somewhat odd. After many years he again attends church with his family. To be sure, his case cannot be considered a complete recovery. He still voices delusional associations, as described, and leads a retired life limited to the confines of his family. This marked state of improvement has held for the past two years, to the conclusion of the observation period.
>
> (ibid.)

In Bleuler's view, for all that is known about the factors which influence prognosis,

> the individual prognosis is never certain; it always remains a guess...Frequently course and outcome do not correspond to the prognostic rules. Unexpected ameliorations do occur. We should never think and maintain that there is absolutely no hope of improvement.
>
> (Bleuler 1982: 5).

64

CONTRASTING OUTCOMES: FIRST AND THIRD WORLDS

The work of Bleuler and Ciompi provides strong grounds for thinking that we must try to locate the course of schizophrenic lives within the framework not of a natural history but of a social history. Bleuler and Ciompi were of course concerned with the variations and fluctuations of schizophrenic lives within a single society, and it is therefore of great importance to be able to explore the same issues on a wider dimension by comparison between societies.

Table 3.1 Percentage of schizophrenic patients in different overall outcome groups in the WHO international outcome study

Centres	Best - outcome group	Two best - outcome groups combined	Two worst - outcome groups combined	Worst - outcome group
	%	%	%	%
Aarhus	6	35	48	31
Agra	48	66	21	15
Cali	21	53	28	15
Ibadan	57	86	7	5
London	24	36	41	31
Moscow	9	48	20	11
Prague	14	34	39	30
Taipei	15	38	35	15
Washington	23	39	45	19
Developed nations	15	39	37	28
Developing nations	35	59	23	13

Reproduced from Warner 1985.

International comparisons have in the past often been vitiated by differences in criteria of selection and diagnosis. A study which succeeded in overcoming these weaknesses is the World Health Organization follow-up study of schizophrenia in which psychotic patients from nine countries in the industrial and non-industrial worlds were diagnosed and followed up by standardized methods (WHO 1979). In each of the nine participating centres, groups of acute and chronic schizophrenics were followed up 2 years after entry into the study. As can be seen from Table 3.1 the schizophrenic patients from the Third World fared much better than their counterparts from the west. Only 13 per cent of Third World patients were in the worst-outcome group by comparison with 28 per cent from the west. The best-outcome group, in contrast, contains only 15 per cent of patients from the west by comparison with 35 per cent of the Third World group.

Preliminary results have recently been published from the 5-year follow-up of the WHO study (Sartorius et al. 1987), and here again the same trend emerges. Two criticisms had been made about the results of the 2-year follow-up. One is that the differences observed could be accounted for by a sampling bias in which, for example, good-prognosis patients from Third World countries were over represented. To answer this question WHO launched a second study entitled Determinants of Outcome of Severe Mental Disorder, which involved participating centres in ten countries and more stringent criteria of selection. The results of this study have yet to be published in detail but preliminary reports of the investigators suggest that the course and outcome differences found in the main study would appear to have been replicated (ibid.).

Table 3.2 Pattern of course (by percentage of cases) in schizophrenia: 5-year follow-up

	1	2	3	4	5
Developed countries (297 cases)	8	17	9	41	24
Developing countries (235 cases)	27	12	23	23	14

Key: 1: Only one episode with full remission; 2: Only one episode with incomplete remission; 3: Several episodes with full remissions; 4: Several episodes with incomplete remission; 5: Continuous illness.

The second suggestion was that the differences found in the 2-year follow-up might disappear by the 5-year follow-up. As can be seen from Table 3.2, however, this was not the case, and the contrasting patterns of course are once again very striking. Some 27 per cent of patients in Third World countries had only one single psychotic episode followed by full remission, compared with 8 per cent of Western patients. Furthermore, 50 per cent of Third World patients had full remissions between episodes as compared with 17 per cent of patients from the West. The same trend is repeated if we look at measures of social functioning (occupational adjustment, sexual adjustment, interpersonal relations, and so on). Thus, we see from Table 3.3 that only 33 per cent of Third World patients experienced moderate or severe difficulties in social functioning by comparison with 65 per cent of patients from the west.

Table 3.3 Impairment in social functions (by percentage of cases) in schizophrenia: 5-year follow-up

	Number of cases	None or mild	Moderate or severe
Developed countries	297	43	56
Developing countries	235	65	33

Reproduced from Sartorius et al. 1987.

As Richard Warner has commented on the 2-year follow-up of the WHO study:

> The general conclusion is unavoidable. Schizophrenia in the Third World has a course and prognosis quite unlike the condition as we recognise it in the West. The progressive deterioration which Kraepelin considered central to his definition of the disease is a rare event in non-industrial societies, except perhaps under the dehumanizing restrictions of a traditional asylum. The majority of Third World schizophrenics achieve a favourable outcome. The more urbanized and industrialized the setting, the more malignant becomes the illness.
>
> (Warner 1985: 156)

CHRONIC SCHIZOPHRENIA IN A PSYCHO-SOCIAL AND ECONOMIC CONTEXTS

In a provocative article under the title 'Is chronic schizophrenia an artefact?', Ciompi (1980b; see also Ciompi 1981) has examined the arguments and counter-arguments for the hypothesis that chronic schizophrenia could to a large extent be a psycho-social 'artefact' in the sense of a situationally determined consequence of acute illness. By chronic schizophrenia Ciompi means the chronic syndrome characterized largely by 'negative' symptomatology (as distinct from the 'positive' or 'productive' symptomatology of the acute syndrome), such as passivity, hopelessness, purposelessness, affective withdrawal, lowered self-esteem, mannerisms, and stereotypic behaviours. Ciompi shows under a number of headings how different traditions of evidence converge to suggest such a hypothesis.

Institutionalism and understimulation

There is evidence that the 'negative' symptomatology of schizophrenia is associated to a large extent with social understimulation in 'impoverished' environments such as large psychiatric institutions, inadequately staffed day centres, and so on (see, in particular, Wing and Brown 1970). J.K. Wing and his colleagues have also shown (for example, Wing 1978) that social overstimulation, through for example overzealous therapeutic endeavours, may lead to 'productive' psychotic relapses, but in protected therapeutic settings with 'minimal supervision according to needs', argues Ciompi, the so-called 'defect-syndromes' of schizophrenia 'often improve to an astonishing degree even after decades of hospitalization'.

The non-specificity of 'chronic schizophrenia'

Ciompi argues that many of the symptoms attributed to chronic schizophrenia are not specific to schizophrenics but are instead much more generally characteristic of the inmates (regardless of diagnosis) of large psychiatric institutions and of prisons and concentration camps. (Compare Manfred Bleuler's remark in the contrast he draws between his own conception of chronic schizophrenia and that of the Swiss psychiatrist Gert Huber. Huber, he writes, 'is inclined to compare the impoverished personality after a schizophrenic psychosis with the condition after psychosurgery or localized cerebral diseases. I should prefer to compare it with the impoverished personality after long-standing frustration in a concentration camp or after an uneventful unsatisfactory life during which the person's talents and abilities had no occasion to develop.' (Bleuler 1978: 633-4))

Heredity and course

Ciompi points to the evidence discussed above of the *polymorphicity of the long-term course of schizophrenia*, and to the finding (Bleuler 1972; Ciompi and Muller 1976; Huber et al. 1979) that the long-term course of schizophrenia, in contrast to the primary disorder, would appear to be independent of hereditary factors.

Social factors and long-term course

Data from a prospective longitudinal study of prognostic factors pertaining to the rehabilitation of chronic schizophrenics (Ciompi et al. 1979) indicated that of all the variables studied the future expectations of patients and families, along with length of preceding hospitalization and social isolation, was the most predictive of a good outcome. Psychopathology and diagnosis, by contrast, had little or no bearing on outcome. Ciompi postulates the notion of a 'general principle of psycho-social inertia' to indicate the way in which a number of forces (including traditional psychiatric conceptions of chronic schizophrenia) combine to reproduce and maintain the social type of the 'chronic schizophrenic'. So, for example a vicious circle may arise in which a patient's negative expectations are confirmed and strengthened by repeated experiences of failure in, for example, attempting to find work or adequate housing. As a consequence, 'a regression into resigned passivity may, for the patient himself as well as for his family and environment, represent the most logical...solution' (Ciompi 1980a: 241).

Family influences

There is evidence that the dynamics within certain kinds of family situations may contribute to the perpetuation and maintenance of a once-defined sickness role in a family member and thus to the production of chronicity (see, for example, Scott 1975; for a discussion of 'expressed emotion' research see Chapter 10 by Tarrier in this volume).

Luc Ciompi's concern has therefore largely been to conceptualize schizophrenia as a life process within a micro-social context but Richard Warner (1985) has attempted to cast the whole problem of schizophrenia within the wider dimension of political economy. He has attempted to demonstrate that the fate of people with a schizophrenic disorder is to a large extent shaped and determined by the organization of the material conditions of life in a given society and in particular by the forces of production and reproduction. A psychiatrist who has also trained as an anthropologist, Warner is able to bring to this difficult subject the benefit of two disciplines.

Warner's concern is to set the evidence discussed above in the context of the economic conditions of the industrialized world and the Third World. This perspective also attempts to embrace related questions concerning the impact of the industrial revolution upon insanity and the influence on schizophrenia of labour dynamics, class status, and sex roles. Briefly stated, Warner's argument is that, viewed historically, changes in the outcome of schizophrenic illness reflect shifts in the perceived usefulness of the schizophrenic in the productive process. Thus, for example, the successful rehabilitation and social integration of the mentally ill is closely related to the demand for labour. Warner provides evidence for the following theses:

- 'Rehabilitation of the mentally and physically disabled is more successful in wartime and during periods of labour shortage.'
- 'Deinstitutionalization began, before the introduction of the antipsychotic drugs, in those North European countries that had low unemployment rates.'
- 'The number of mental hospital beds provided in the industrial nations in 1965 was related to the national unemployment rate.'
- 'The proportion of schizophrenics in hospital at follow-up increased during the Great Depression.'

(Warner 1985: 137)

In much the same terms as Bleuler and Ciompi, Warner remarks on the striking similarity of many features of chronic schizophrenia to the psychological effects of long-term unemployment. The common fate of the schizophrenic in Western societies is to be unemployed, seemingly of no value either to oneself or to others:

In the stigma of mental illness, the most debased status in our society, we see the utmost in painful estrangement of one human from another. And in the schizophrenic's own acceptance of this same dehumanized stereotype we witness the loss of his or her sense of fully belonging to humankind....The schizophrenic, then, is amongst the most alienated of industrial society, and it is in this condition that one may perceive the causes of the malignancy of the illness. Looking beyond this, the origins of the schizophrenic's alienation are to be found in the political and economic structure of society – in the division of labour and development of wage work. For it is these aspects of production which have rendered the schizophrenic – with his or her limited ability to withstand stress, limited productive capacity and limited drive – marginal to the industrial work force, marginal members of (what anthropologist Jules Henry terms) 'the driven society'.

(Warner 1985: 181)

SCHIZOPHRENIA AND THE PROBLEM OF THE PERSON

As we have seen there is strong evidence for the view that it is useful to examine the problem of outcome in schizophrenia, and hence the histories of schizophrenic lives, in the context of the personal and social consequences of a schizophrenic illness. In this section we shall provide some direct illustrations of these consequences.

We can focus on some of the difficulties in this area by asking: What is involved in accepting a diagnosis of major mental illness? What effect does it have on the agent's sense of himself or herself as a person? How does the agent negotiate re-entry to the 'ordinary person' frame after being defined as a mental patient suffering from schizophrenia? Discussing these questions Warner proposes counter-intuitively that

patients who accept that they are mentally ill will have the worst course to their illness, that those who reject the label from the outset might do better and that the patients who show the most improvement will be those who accept the label of mental illness but subsequently are able to shake it off (Warner 1985: 186; for evidence in support of these contentions, see Doherty 1975).

71

Issues about stigma and labelling are implicated here but these concepts are inadequate to identify the full range of issues that are involved and they can be misleading. Above all we need to frame the issue in terms of an agent contending with a set of problems rather than in terms of a patient entrapped in a sick role or borne along by a disease process. If we are to try to understand schizophrenia as a life process we need, in other words, to describe the lives of people who have suffered from schizophrenia in terms that are appropriate to the person in the sphere of the social world rather than in terms of the patient in the sphere of the clinic.

Some of the questions and dilemmas which arise for the hypothetical agent who is trying to negotiate re-entry from mental-patient status into a more ordinary form of social existence may include these:

I've been through an experience of breakdown, its definition, and treatment, and I'm scarred by it. I may feel better but I am still scarred by what I have been through; it has left its mark on me. I don't see myself as an incapacitated person, but I do see myself as having to cope with a vulnerability.

Define it as I may for myself, I recognize that it is the kind of vulnerability for which I may continue to need help. But how can I seek help without finding myself permanently defined as a mental patient? How can I acknowledge the reality of my vulnerability and still retain my sense of integrity and value as a person? What has this whole experience done to me? Who can I say that I now am? What can I make of myself become? How am I to describe myself, account for myself, to others?

Some of these questions and concerns are a matter of self-understanding, of a dialogue that the agent has with him- or herself. Others involve negotiation with other people. Clearly not every person in our society who has suffered from schizophrenia will put the kinds of questions or return the kinds of answers which we have sketched here. However, we may see these questions and answers as indicating the kinds of considerations which are brought into focus when we try to step outside the clinical framework and to conceive the person who has suffered from schizophrenia as an agent who is attempting to make sense of the hiatus in his or her life.

Sarah, for example, a young woman in her mid-twenties, who has had a serious schizophrenic breakdown, describes how her experience of illness has brought about a 'definite change' in her. She no longer has such a clear idea of who she is:

> If you're a schizophrenic or whatever, you have to fight more for your individuality. You lose your individuality, you completely lose it. You sort cf merge with other people and listen to their ideas, get their ideas into your head and you just lose yourself completely because you haven't got that barrier in your head which says 'I disagree with you, I'm going to say this.' You haven't got that in your head anymore.

Despite the change in her, Sarah refuses to permit her identity to be defined by her illness;

> My fight, my personal fight, would be to say: 'No, it's not going to affect the rest of my life', and that's why I struggle so much, because I don't want this illness. I don't particularly cherish it or want it or go on about it as if it were the bee's knees. I'd rather be normal. That's just me. Like a lot of people react in a different way. There's one I know who says, 'I'm going to be a professional nutter for the rest of my life', and he laughs about it and is able to joke about it and that's his way of *accepting* it. But I can't do that...I've never accepted it, I don't think I've ever accepted it.

One aspect of Sarah's struggle is to achieve equality with other people:

> It's important to me to feel equal to other people....I like *pretending* to people when I go into a pub, I like doing that, I like just starting a conversation with someone and letting it flow and not saying anything. I like doing that, but if they were to get to know me really well, I'd have to tell them and then I wouldn't be on a par with them.

Sarah says that there is something about the admission of illness that makes her feel: 'less of a person. You have to fight more....Like in my own family I've had to fight and say, "Look, my mind's as good as yours or as strong as yours".'

The diagnosis of schizophrenia has in itself contributed to her difficulties:

> You wake up every morning and you think 'Oh God, I'm a schizophrenic!' If the doctor hadn't told me I'd just have woken up and thought, 'Well I'm just going through some sort of illness and I'll probably get over it.' But once you get diagnosed you start thinking all sorts from different corners about the illness and it just gets worse and worse.

Sarah is one of a number of participants in a project in which we have been engaged over the past 2 years which has attempted to look at the personal and social consequences of a schizophrenic illness from the point of view of those who have been through the experience. (This is the Bradford Mental Health Project, based at the School of Applied Social Studies, University of Bradford, and supported by the Joseph Rowntree Memorial Trust. For a full account of the project see Barham and Hayward 1991 and Barham 1992.)

In this study we have been concerned with the question: How is the agent to rebuild and maintain his or her life in the face of disruption and its consequences? We shall suggest that there are two main and interconnected areas of difficulty, one which we shall describe as the problem of *incorporation,* the other as the problem of *structural isolation.* Incorporation we shall define as the set of social forces that make it difficult for people who have suffered from schizophrenia to extricate themselves from a condition of 'mental patienthood' in which the ways in which they come to think of themselves, and are regarded by others, are determined by their clinical condition. The classic type of the incorporated mental patient is the long-stay schizophrenic of the old asylums. Yet as history has shown there is nothing about discharge as such that guarantees success or acceptance in the effort to re-establish oneself as an ordinary agent whose life is not wholly defined by one's clinical condition.

Broadly, there are two aspects of incorporation. One concerns incorporation within the role of mental patient, within a service-dominated frame of existence in which there are only restricted opportunities to practise as an ordinary social agent. The other is incorporation within a set of images and assumptions about schizophrenia and the mentally ill that put the person 'off the map', outside the community of ordinary human beings. Structural isolation we shall define as the field of forces in our society which serve to marginalize the lives of ex-mental patients (as of other disadvantaged groups) in such spheres as housing, employment, and social relations.

We may thus attempt to understand the lives of people who have had a schizophrenic illness in terms of two kinds of *resistance*, resistance to incorporation, and resistance to structural isolation. In the discussion here we shall look mainly at the problem of incorporation. The problem of how to fashion a way of life that is not dominated by one's clinical condition and by mental-patient status will, clearly, not present itself as the same kind of problem for all ex-schizophrenics but it follows from our account of it that as a condition of recovery it should present itself as a problem of *some* kind. We should not think of the problem of incorporation as a unitary problem for which there can be a singular solution, but rather as a field of forces, thick with tension and ambiguity, which focus on the ex-mental patient. We shall now attempt to illustrate some of these points in more detail.

Barry is a man in his mid-thirties, a gentlemen's hairdresser by training, who has been hospitalized on a number of occasions for schizophrenia and now lives on his own in a flat rented from a local housing association. He sees himself as someone who has had a mental illness and is still vulnerable in certain respects but at the same time he is intent upon managing his life and his relations with psychiatric services on his own terms. Thus, for example, he describes how over the past 5 years he has resisted pressure on him to affiliate himself more closely to the official spaces for ex-mental patients in the community. He lived for a time in a house owned by an elderly woman called Alice who herself had a history of mental illness and by Barry's account was often in a bad way. A community psychiatric nurse used to visit once a week and tried to encourage Barry to attend a day centre and leave Alice by herself during the day. However, Barry felt that he had a responsibility for Alice and moreover he derived some pleasure from caring for her and so he refused to go. Since then Barry's circumstances have changed. Alice has been taken to a nursing home and Barry lives on his own. He is still under pressure to attend the day centre and still he refuses. He describes his experience:

Well I went for an hour. It was full of smoke, someone playing snooker, the radio on blasting, people talking. The social worker took me down and I found out it would cost 60p for my dinner which I didn't have, so that was that. They asked why did I bugger off and I said I couldn't stand the place.... There must have been six to eight people I knew, the rest of them I didn't know. Twelve or fifteen in the room, maybe more. They were doing keep fit when I came away.... That frightened me off! What a thing to do, keep fit in all this smoke.

According to Barry the staff at the centre also wanted him to attend occupational therapy to which he said, 'No, I'm doing my own therapy cutting hair.' As he describes the therapy it is apparent it didn't appeal to him because the only activity on offer was 'cutting paper and colouring boxes' and he 'just didn't see where it was going to lead'.

On Barry's own account it is his skill as a hairdresser which has helped him maintain some sense of point and worth in his life over the years since he has been ill. Since his illness he has only been able to practise his trade on an informal basis but he has been able to practise nevertheless – for example, he describes how the previous week his community psychiatric nurse came to have his hair cut. He complains also that whilst in hospital he did a lot of haircutting for which he did not get paid. So what he would like now is paid employment cutting hair. He has considered other options but feels they are less feasible:

I had a go at cooking when I was in hospital, when I was on self-care 7 or 8 years back. I was cooking meals, I cooked for about seven or eight people, three meals a day. So I thought I could work in a café. They said they'd try and find me something but it just fizzled out and so I thought, well I'm back to hairdressing again.

For all the difficulties, Barry is intent on maintaining his identity as a hairdresser and refuses to be drawn into activities that seem to him not to lead anywhere, that hold no meaning for him within the narrative of his life. It is in part this sense of the integrity of his life project that gives him the motivation and the capacity to resist incorporation into a service-dominated form of life and instead to regard services as a resource or support on which he can draw on his own terms. Thus, for example, he values the social contacts he made at the hospital and sometimes still attends a support group for ex-patients:

> If I go anywhere else like a pub I don't know what is going on. If I go to hospital I can relate to people. They tell me what they are going through and I tell them what I am going through....Sometimes it works, sometimes it doesn't....That's how you meet people.

Barry seems able to draw on 'mental patient' space for his informal contacts, to move in and out of it on his own terms, without feeling defined or contained by it. Yet for other people social relationships with ex-mental patients may sometimes put in question their membership of a wider community. Here we have one of the points of tension and ambiguity with which people who have had a schizophrenic illness have to contend. People who associate with other ex-mental patients may risk incorporation into a mental-patient subculture and into marginalized self-definitions; the price of the integrity of going it alone, on the other hand, may be the loss of real relations of value and the risk of painful social isolation.

In a group discussion Vaughan puts the strong case for severing connections with other people who have had a mental illness:

> It's all right when you come out of hospital, you need that sort of security. But when you have been out for about a year you should start building your own life and looking for new horizons and mixing with other people who have never had it – even if you have to put a bold front on it, a false image if you like, but you have definitely got to try.

Sarah strongly disagrees:

> I don't feel in the people I meet, I am involved in a lot of groups with people who have had a mental illness, I don't see them as being any *different*. I'm learning from them in how to cope with the illness itself, and learning from their experiences and I think talking to them is rather rewarding and I don't see them as being different or totally abnormal....I don't agree with this feeling that you've got to get back and go out with 'normal people'.

Sarah does not want to trade in 'false images':

> With normal people you have got to put on a front, you have
> got to act normal and you can't relax and just be yourself.
> You have got to act like they expect you to act. That's what
> makes it a lot harder. Why should you have to act like that?

The idea that there is an integrity to relationships between ex-
mental patients is also brought out by Simon:

> I realize I am very limited in the number of people I know
> and it will probably stay that way because although I have
> made friends...it is with people who are either psychiatric or
> ex-psychiatric or whatever you want to call it. I have known
> some great people with great stories to tell and it almost
> seems like going through this psychiatric problem makes
> people more human and more down to earth and ordinary
> people seem a bit stuck up and stand-offish – you generally
> find that people who are ex-psychiatric have been through
> the mill and are a bit more open, a lot more honest and a
> lot more accessible.

A different, and more ambiguous, cast on this problem is given by
Ben. Ben, who is in his mid-thirties and lives on his own in a
council flat on a large housing estate, describes the kind of
prejudice in the mental-patient subculture in which the low self-
expectations of ex-schizophrenics may come to be reproduced
and reinforced in a way that is at once protective and harsh:

> It's a funny subculture. How can I put it? There is a certain
> amount of mockery in it as if they are saying to you: 'Come
> on, take your tablets' kind of thing. There is a strange sort of
> subculture there where they may say to you, 'You haven't got
> a job have you? How did you get a job? You're a mental
> patient!' – because I'm known as a mental patient, that's all
> they know me as....There is that kind of prejudice there and
> I do it myself. I say, 'You're not really going to make a
> record' when someone's talking about making a record,
> because I know he's had mental illness, whereas I wouldn't
> really react in that way if I hadn't known.

Ben describes himself as someone who likes to 'take part in
things' and so, for example, he is active in the local Labour Party

and in the World Development Movement. However, for an unemployed person to forge a firm identity that can transcend mental-patient status is not easy. All too often:

> People can just treat you as a patient. It's like a role in a way. Because especially in the hospital there is not a lot to do and your role as a patient is to get better...and if you are unemployed for a long time you haven't got a role and a lot of my difficulties come from the rolelessness....When somebody asks me what I do or what are you there is no definite answer – I'm just unemployed or I could say I'm an ex-mental patient.

Ben's sense of what he is depends to a considerable degree on the willingness of the other person to regard him as someone other than a mental patient:

> But you don't feel yourself still to be a mental patient do you? (P.B.)
> No, but sometimes.
> It depends on how you are feeling in yourself?
> Yes, I don't feel like that today, particularly as I am talking to you, but sometimes I feel like that.
> But at the moment we're talking about something that happened in the past.
> That's right. You are not looking at me because I've got problems.

Until a year ago Ben thought that he had worked himself out of the 'psychiatric system':

> I thought I had got rid of it. I had been out of hospital four years and I was going along fine and there were no problems but this year it really upset me going back into hospital and I do now see myself as a person who has had a mental problem and could quite well have it again.

His readmission to hospital posed problems for his social relationships:

> It was upsetting with the friends I had made on the estate independent of the hospital. Some of them knew I had been in hospital in the past, a lot of them didn't. But for me to go

79

into hospital and for them to visit me was upsetting. I felt, if you like, I had grown in self-confidence and it was a reduction, a step back, and whereas I like people to feel 'Oh he's all right' I have to *convince* them because of that and I have to re-establish that.

From Ben we get a keen sense of how difficult it is for the ex-mental patient to establish a firm foothold in social life as an ordinary person. Relationships between people repose on a considerable degree of trust and Ben describes how after his last breakdown he had to rebuild trust in his relationships, 'a trust that you have to build up with any kind of human being'. Such trust is difficult to achieve for people who have had a mental illness, and in particular a schizophrenic illness, because of the suspicion ('Is it safe to leave him alone with the children?', as Ben puts it) with which they are regarded. Sarah makes the same point in a different way when she says that people who have had a schizophrenic illness have to 'try twice as hard to be accepted. Like if you go for an interview or go for a job you have to try twice as hard because you have to prove to them that there is nothing wrong with you.'

Re-entry into social life holds out the potential of a return to ordinary-agent status but it may also carry with it the loss of valuable support from the psychiatric system:

> When I am in the flat I can lead a life on my own but I won't wash up and clean up and things like that, and when you are unemployed you have got no external disciplines to make you do anything and no one comes across your door – certainly no one from the hospital has been across my door since I came out.
> Would you want them to? (P.B.)
> I am not sure. I don't seem to have an opinion. I don't particularly want them to but I think perhaps they could have visited me to see if I was coping.

It is then a question of how to secure support without seeming to invite reincorporation into a view of oneself as ill or incompetent:

> Isn't there a problem of interference or invasion of people's privacy? For community psychiatric nurses to start banging on the doors of people...(P.B.)

80

That's only because you have got this stigma about being helped because you are ill – nurses coming in and doing it for you when you should be doing it for yourself. I know from my own self that I need people to come and give me a push, and if you are not married and you are not working there is nobody to force you to do anything and I think sometimes we need a bit of a push because self-discipline is one of the hardest things to achieve so you can get problems from being lonely. Women seem to cope with it better – keeping flats nice and tidy – maybe it's the way we were brought up as men.

Ben now feels that he has reached a stage in many of his relationships where knowledge of his history and of his enduring vulnerability need not put everything in jeopardy:

As people get to know me they make contact and come to expect things from me and I expect things from them.... They know the kinds of things I can do. Usually, and certainly in the kindest possible way, people know I have had an illness and say 'don't let yourself get too pressured' and although they are reacting to me in my illness I certainly don't think they are doing it in any kind of malevolent way, they are doing it in a 'we know if you do too much, or get too pressured, then you are going to have a problem' kind of way, and they are very kind about that, people who know.

In Ben's case people are able to 'react to him in his illness', as he nicely puts it, and still treat and respect him as an ordinary and capable human being. That he should be able to say this is a measure of his own achievement and we should not underestimate the formidable cultural obstacles to this form of integration. For most people who have had a schizophrenic illness, to be 'reacted to in their illness' is to find themselves swiftly reincorporated into an entirely alien set of categories. As Sarah puts it,

you can't mention it to people when you go out with them – you can't say 'I suffer from a mental illness', you can mention 'I have had cancer' or you can mention other things, but this is something that's very difficult to talk about as a problem.

It is a commonplace that under different circumstances we all have a need to talk about our lives and that in doing so in relation to others we lend our lives coherence and acquire a sense of recognizing each other through a shared history. It is, then, not difficult to see that the pressure to hide a significant part of one's history may engender an internal sense of dissonance and also create formidable problems of self-disclosure for people whose capacity for making relationships is in any case already precarious. Henry, for example, says that people tend to treat him with aggression if they know he has been diagnosed schizophrenic:

> What about people who don't know? Milkmen or whatever, do they treat you normally? (R.H.)
> Yes, that's why you've got to keep it a secret because people treat you better if they don't know you are schizophrenic. I am afraid of people finding out that I am schizophrenic.... There is something I regret. I went not long since to the Job Centre and I had to tell them I was schizophrenic....I was sat in front of the lady, I didn't want to tell them, but the hospital made me tell them. They had got a report from the doctor saying I was schizophrenic. But people are nervy – there was this lady sat in front of me as if she didn't know what to expect. People are nervy because they know you're schizophrenic, as though they feel 'what's he going to do next?'. It's all out of perspective.

CONCLUSIONS

On Manfred Bleuler's view of it, to react to a schizophrenic person in his or her illness is to recognize in the person 'a fellow sufferer or comrade in arms' rather than someone whom 'a pathological heritage or a degenerate brain has rendered inaccessible, inhuman, different or strange' (Bleuler 1972: 502). An important part of Bleuler's concern has been to forge a concept of schizophrenic illness not as a discrete and encapsulated aberration but as 'staged in the same general spheres of life where the neuroses are formed, and in which the human personality is shaped in a constant interplay between hereditary developmental tendencies and environmental experience'. In Bleuler's account, therefore, schizophrenics can be seen to 'founder under the same difficulties with which all of us struggle all our lives' (ibid.: 457, 502). (For a biological grounding of this perspective see Chapter 6 by Claridge in this volume. Compare also the view of the British psychoanalyst D.W. Winnicott: 'While we recognize the hereditary factor in schizophrenia and while we are willing to see the contributions made in individual cases by physical disorders, we look with suspicion on any theory of schizophrenia that divorces the subject from the problems of ordinary living and the universals of individual development in a given environment.' (Winnicott 1971: 66))

Historically, however, people with a schizophrenic illness have been reacted to in rather less encouraging ways. We have seen from our discussion of the course of schizophrenia that how a schizophrenic condition turns out in a given life and how it is reacted to are closely interconnected matters. Warner argues that much of what is regarded as characteristic of chronic schizophrenia may be 'attributed to the purposeless lifestyle and second-class citizenship of the schizophrenic' (Warner 1985: 299). In the examples discussed briefly above we have identified some of the obstacles and dilemmas with which people in our society who have had a schizophrenic illness have to contend in order to achieve some measure of self-recognition and recognition by others as persons. (Clearly, a full account would need to address a number of other aspects which we have not had space to address here.)

To conceive schizophrenia as an open-ended life process in this way, and to explore the contexts of option and constraint in which lives unfold, provides grounds for therapeutic optimism. The evidence from projects like the WHO comparative study shows us that schizophrenics, for all their vulnerabilities, are in the full sense responsive social beings like the rest of us. Evidence of this kind can be used against the pessimism of people like the Dean of the Institute of Psychiatry who, in making a claim for increased expenditure on biological research into the causes of schizophrenia rather than on services, asserted that 'even if we had the best social policy' we would not be able to 'substantially alter the situation' for patients with the condition (Herbst 1987: 90).

At the same time a close reading of Warner should caution us against underestimating the difficulties that stand in the way of remedying the characteristic fate of schizophrenic lives in our society. In Warner's account the course and perhaps also the occurrence of schizophrenia is governed by political and economic forces, and one way to read his argument is to view the degradation and exclusion of the schizophrenic as the price that is to be exacted for the privilege of living in our type of society. 'We have far to go before the schizophrenic is welcome in Western society', he argues; and whilst we now possess the knowledge to render schizophrenia benign, 'we may, in essence, have to restructure Western society' in order to do so (Warner 1985: 307).

REFERENCES

Barham, P. (1984) *Schizophrenia and Human Value*, Oxford: Basil Blackwell.
— (1992) *Closing the Asylum.* London: Penguin (in press).
Barham, P. and Hayward, R. (1991) *From the Mental Patient to the Person*, London: Routledge.
Bleuler, M. (1972) *Die Schizophrenen Geistesstörungen im Lichte Langjahriger Kranken und Familiengeschichten*, Stuttgart: Georg Thieme (translated as: *The Schizophrenic Disorders: Long-term Patient and Family Studies*, New Haven: Yale University Press, 1978).
— (1978) 'The long-term course of schizophrenic psychoses', in L.C. Wynne, R.L. Cromwell, and S. Matthysse (eds) *The Nature of Schizophrenia*, New York: Wiley.
— (1982) 'Prognosis of schizophrenic psychoses: a summary of life-long personal research compared with the research of other psychiatrists, lesson 31' in F.F. Flack, (ed.) *Directions in Psychiatry*, New York: Hatherleigh.
— (1980a) 'The natural history of schizophrenia in the long term', *British Journal Psychiatry* 136: 413–20.
Ciompi, L. (1980b) 'Ist die chronische Schizophrenie ein Artefakt?: Argumente und Gegenargumente', *Fortschritte der Neurologie und Psychiatrie* 48: 237–48.
— (1981) 'The social outcome of schizophrenia', in J.K. Wing, P. Kielholtz, and W.M. Zinn (eds) *Rehabilitation of Patients with Schizophrenia and Depression*, Bern: Hans Huber.
— and Muller, C. (1976) *Lebensweg und Alter der Schizophrenen*, Berlin: Springer.
Ciompi, L., Dauwalder, H.-P., and Ague, C. (1979) 'Ein Forschungsprogramm uber die Rehabilitation psychisch Kranker. II. Querschnittuntersuchung einer Population von chronischen Spitalpatienten', *Nervenarzt* 49: 332–8.
Cromwell, R.L (1978) 'Integration and editorial comment', in L.C. Wynne, R.L. Cromwell, and S. Matthysse (eds) *The Nature of Schizophrenia*, Wiley: New York.

Doherty, E.G. (1975) 'Labelling effects in psychiatric hospitalization: a study of diverging patterns of inpatient self-labeling processes', *Archives of General Psychiatry* 32: 562–8.

Herbst, K.G. (ed.) (1987) *Schizophrenia*, London: Mental Health Foundation.

Huber, G., Gross, G., and Schuttler, R. (1979) *Schizophrenie: Eine Verlaufs- und Sozialpsychiatrische Langzeitstudie*, Berlin: Springer.

Sartorius, N., Jablensky, A., Ernberg, G., Leff, J., Korten, A., and Gulbinat, W. (1987) 'Course of schizophrenia in different countries: some results of a WHO international comparative 5-year follow-up study', in H. Hafner, W.G. Gattaz, and W. Janzarik (eds) *Search for the Causes of Schizophrenia*, Berlin: Springer.

Scott, R.D., (1975) 'Family patterns and outcome in schizophrenia', in A. Forrest and J. Affleck, (eds) *New Perspectives in Schizophrenia*, Edinburgh: Churchill Livingstone.

Warner, R. (1985) *Recovery from Schizophrenia: Psychiatry and Political Economy*, London: Routledge.

Wing, J.K. (1978) 'Social influence on the course of schizophrenia', in L.C. Wynne, R.L. Cromwell, and S. Matthysse (eds) *The Nature of Schizophrenia*, New York: Wiley

— and Brown, G.W. (1970) *Institutionalism and Schizophrenia*, Cambridge: Cambridge University Press.

Winnicott, D.W. (1971) *Playing and Reality*, London: Tavistock.

World Health Organization (1979) *Schizophrenia: An International Follow-up Study*, Chichester: Wiley.

Zubin, J., Magaziner, J., and Steinhauer, S. (1983) The metamorphosis of schizophrenia: from chronicity to vulnerability; *Psychological medicine* 13: 551–71

Part Two

THE ROLE OF BIOLOGY IN SCHIZOPHRENIC BEHAVIOUR

Chapter Four

THE GENETICS OF SCHIZOPHRENIA

Axiom or hypothesis?
RICHARD MARSHALL

THE GENETIC STANCE IN HISTORICAL CONTEXT

A review of evidence concerning the genetic basis of the disorder called 'schizophrenia' would be more than incomplete without some attempt to place it within a historical perspective. My purpose is not to provide an account of past work on which more recent approaches have been built, but to illustrate that the fundamental issues have changed little over the past century. Of course, theorizing about the *mode* of genetic inheritance has altered with developments in the field of genetics generally, but the underlying attempts to establish schizophrenia as genetically determined have been pursued with greater or lesser conviction since disordered conduct was first construed as some form of illness. It is my contention that this medicalization process required as a cornerstone the resort to biological explanation, and that this, in turn, could only gain scientific respectability if the source of the disorder could be located in genetic transmission. Evidence for this assertion will be provided later in the chapter.

It is apparent, then, that this chapter will not be restricted to a critical examination of recent studies concerning the genetics of conduct described as schizophrenia. Developments in the field of sociology of knowledge now allow us to see that knowledge is in itself subject to influence from a variety of sources, including the beliefs and values of scientists, and the very *Zeitgeist* of the society in which research is formulated and interpreted. Such considerations imply that some form of meta-analysis is essential if we are to move beyond the apparently factual to the form of understanding which we call knowledge.

89

Sociologists of knowledge have recently tended to confine their attentions to the harder sciences, presumably because if it can be shown such knowledge bases are markedly influenced by social factors, then it is even more likely that the softer sciences will be subject to at least an equal degree of distortion. A detailed example of this approach is provided in Gould's *Mismeasure of Man* (1981), which reveals how scientific claims about the nature of intelligence owe much to the beliefs and attitudes of dominant groups in wider society. Gould points out that some topics are invested with enormous social importance but blessed with very little reliable information. Thus, when the ratio of data to social impact is low a history of scientific attitudes may be little more than an oblique record of social change.

It would be possible to argue that the disorder under consideration in the present volume fits closely with Gould's prescription for likely social influence upon scientific thinking. The very title of the present volume indicates that 'schizophrenia' is hardly a scientifically validated entity but that what we term schizophrenia is a construction, that to some degree it is a social construction, and as such that it is likely to reflect the ethos and attitudes of a wider society. Consider, for example, the description of a schizophrenic in a well-respected textbook of psychiatry:

> He can make no decisions, and if he is not supported by indulgent relatives he drifts into poverty and lives in the lowest stratum of society as an unemployable idler, tramp, petty criminal, or prostitute etc. Many ineffectual, talentless, and sterile dilettantes are simple schizophrenics, as also are some of the hangers on of harmless sects and philosophies, or aiders and abetters of criminal gangs.
>
> (Mayer-Gross et al. 1970: 242-3)

Such accounts appear to be more prescriptions of social values than scientific descriptions of disordered conduct. It is hardly unexpected that agreement between experienced assessors of schizophrenia is far from perfect (see Chapter 2 by Bentall in this volume).

One of the chief investigators in the field of schizophrenic genetics, whose work will be considered in more detail later, had views about the nature of schizophrenia which seem a long way from the description of a disinterested scientist. Kallmann's understanding of schizophrenia was of a disease group 'which continues to crowd mental hospitals all over the world, and affords an unceasing source of maladjusted cranks, asocial eccentrics, and the lowest type of criminal offenders' (Kallmann 1938: xiii). Such sentiments, and Kallmann's strongly held eugenic beliefs, are examples of the less objective and disinterested attitudes which emerge from time to time in the history of schizophrenia genetics.

It is interesting to note how the *belief* in the biological approach has resulted in very little attention being paid to the possibility that what we term schizophrenia exists on a continuum with what we might call normal behaviour. It was pointed out by Strauss (1969) that hallucinations and delusions, the hallmarks of schizophrenia, are usually considered to be discrete and discontinuous – a person either has them or does not: 'The notion of the discreteness of these symptoms encourages the conception of psychosis and schizophrenia as states that are also discrete and the further conception that patients with these diagnoses are somehow qualitatively different from other people.' (ibid.: 581) Strauss went on to demonstrate that, in fact, hallucinations and delusions are not discrete phenomena but on continua of experiences, thereby suggesting that schizophrenia and the symptoms that characterize it are understandable exaggerations of normal function (see also Claridge's discussion of schizotypal traits in Chapter 6 of this volume).

The notion that schizophrenia is a discrete entity and the belief that it is a disorder of largely genetic origins are mutually reinforcing and, in turn, both assist in the transformation of an abstract, hypothetical concept into a 'thing'. Throughout the past century this circular and self-fulfilling mode of reasoning has been characteristic of much of the theorizing about the conduct we term schizophrenia, so that the emphasis on genetics has contributed to the reification process, and still continues to do so. As I hope will become clear, the *evidence* for a genetic account is far from as conclusive as the majority of current texts would lead us to believe. There may well be important underlying reasons for the existence of this discrepancy between what has been demonstrated and what is said has been demonstrated.

The writings of Szasz, unpopular as they are in psychiatry, may provide some understanding of this discrepancy. Szasz (1976) attempts to portray the development of psychiatry from a socio-historical perspective. In this analysis of the history of the discipline he outlines the way in which modern psychiatry began with the study of paresis, and efforts to cure it. Psychiatry soon turned into the study of psychopathology and the efforts to control it: 'It has now become, the world over, the study of misbehaviour, and the efforts to manage it. And schizophrenia is the sacred symbol.' (ibid.: 313) By this Szasz means that schizophrenia is the core concept of modern institutional psychiatry, and that it therefore cannot be understood and unravelled except by a careful historical and epistemological re-examination of the origin and development of the psychiatric profession. Of importance in this development has been the authoritative literalization of the psychiatric nomenclature, so that the norms of psychiatric diseases become the unquestioned and unquestionable proofs of the existence of such diseases.

The circularity of the genetic-disease model played an important role in this achievement, long before any research into the genetic aetiology of schizophrenia. It was a role which fitted neatly with the prevailing ethos of the dominant thinking in nine-teenth-century Western societies. McDonald (1984), for instance, points out that the most predominant myth of the Victorian period was of the inheritance of delicate, weak, or raw nerves, followed closely by the myth of the 'degenerate'. Degeneracy was considered to be passed from one tainted generation to the next, with each generation becoming progressively worse: the alcoholic father was likely to have a prostitute daughter, or a criminal, even idiot, son.

In a recent analysis Dowbiggin (1985) traces the development of ideas about hereditary degeneracy in nineteenth-century French psychiatry, and illustrates how the theory of morbid heredity served as an intellectual weapon in psychiatry's claim of medico-scientific respectability. Thus, the theory of morbid heredity can now be understood as an intellectual response to a period of socio-political pressure, and crises within the medical profession. According to Dowbiggin the hereditarian theory proved to be beneficial as a culturally consonant idea, one of great political, social, and religious currency.

This process bears more than a passing resemblance to that recognized by Bernal, writing from the perspective of the harder sciences:

> Often enough the ideas which statesmen and divines think
> they have taken from the latest phase of scientific thought
> are just the ideas of their class and time reflected in the
> minds of scientists subjected to the same social influences.
>
> (Bernal 1965: xiii)

In Victorian psychiatry and in the monolithic theory of hereditary
degeneration upon which psychiatry had based its social and
scientific vision, we find an excellent illustration of Bernal's
account of the interaction between science and society. Of course
there was a certain kind of 'evidence' for the notion of
inheritance. Observations did reveal that certain conducts tended
to run in families over several generations. If it is accepted,
however, that criminality, alcohol dependence, prostitution, and
madness reflect, at least to some degree, the structures of the
societies in which they are located, then their occurrence in
families may be considered to indicate as much about social
structure and economic conditions as some form of hypothesized
inherited disposition.

As Jackson (1960) argues, there is no doubt that the culture of
the time (including, as it did, fixed ideas about good and evil and
hierarchical social classes without much mobility) rendered such
ideas acceptable. Hereditarian beliefs allow the possible
deleterious impact of social forces upon individuals to be
neglected and locate the source of social dysfunction firmly
within the individual. The genetical level of explanation provides
a ready apersonal, ahistorical, asocial focus. It bears the hallmark
of scientific respectability, avoids immediate personal blame for
social failure, but furthers the notion that the organization of
society is not the appropriate place at which to begin any attempt
to understand those who are outside 'normality'.

In recent years the social constructionist movement in modern
psychology (Gergen 1985) has viewed discourse about the world,
not as a reflection or map of the world, but as an artefact of
communal interchange. Albee (1982), for example, describes how
the whole 'scientific' process can be seen in reverse: instead of
facts being useful as the building blocks of theories, rather it is
more accurate to say that people, and especially social scientists,
select theories that are consistent with their personal values,
attitudes, and prejudices, and then go into the world, or into the

laboratory, to seek facts which validate those beliefs, neglecting or denying observations that contradict their personal prejudices. With reference to the appeal of genetic determinisim, Albee points to the powerful influence of Calvinism with its concepts of predestination and dualism, and especially the concept of 'unchangeable man' which is rooted in Calvin's doctrine. The ideological path was from Calvinism to social Darwinism, which emphasized the elimination of the unfit for the improvement of the species.

Now it may appear, at this point, that the writer has strayed from schizophrenia into areas which are at best tangential, and at worst irrelevant. Yet I believe that it is precisely the dearth of a social and historical context which allows and encourages the belief in a pure factual reality in science, and in the social and human sciences in particular. Consequently, this belief leads to a situation in which the most powerful voices are heard. Yet a meta-analysis may well reveal that the correctness of an argument is not necessarily a function of the power of its advocates. In the field under consideration, for instance, the current influence of the pharmaceutical companies cannot be underestimated. As I hope to show, the genetic evidence, as portrayed in knowledge bases, is a cornerstone of attempts to show a biological aetiology in schizophrenia. In turn the pharmaceutical industry's interest in mental disorders is based upon a molecular, individualistic model of disturbance, and in turn the industry, directly or otherwise, sponsors a biological approach. One example of this is a recent publication entitled *Transmission: Biological Psychiatry in Clinical Practice* (Crow and Deakin 1987), published by 'Education in Practice', and sponsored by Dunphar Laboratories Ltd. In the publication's editorial it is predicted that progress in psychiatry will depend upon biochemical developments based upon genetic underpinnings. The studies mentioned relate to depression, 'from both the genetic and clinical viewpoints'. The sponsoring firm advertises in this publication a drug which aims to combat 'worry, tiredness, aches and pains, agitation, low mood, etc.'.

It is difficult to underestimate the influence of pharmaceutical interests on the shaping of the knowledge base in psychiatry, and to a lesser extent clinical psychology. In a book advocating psychotherapy as a treatment of choice in schizophrenia, Karon and VandenBos (1981) provide evidence from both controlled trials and individual case-studies to support the psychotherapeutic approach. However, in a later interview, Karon describes how he had not fully taken into account the power of the pharmaceutical industry to direct psychiatric theory:

> I was too kind to medication in the book. I now think that drugs are causing as much mental illness as they cure. And because of the money manufacturers spend on research, psychotherapy is having less influence on mental policy, despite our findings.

> (*Guardian* 22 February 1984)

Such influences can add confusion in a field which is already riddled with value-judgements, professional interests, and distorted research results (as I hope to demonstrate later). However, perhaps the most fundamental and yet most difficult-to-perceive influence on what we consider to be the scientific process derives from far less tangible sources. Gould (1981) has shown in his account of the history of intelligence testing that psychology, as with other sciences, is a socially embedded activity which must be understood as a social phenomenon, at times serving as a mirror of social movements. Gould does not suggest that a factual reality does not exist, but that the roads to it are lined with preconceived attitudes which exert distorting influences. He quotes from Myrdal (1944):

> there must be still other countless errors of the same sort that no living man can yet detect, because of the fog within which our type of Western culture envelops us. Cultural influences have set up the assumptions about the mind, the body, and the universe with which we begin, pose the questions we ask; influence the facts we seek; determine the interpretations we give these facts; and direct our reaction to these interpretations and conclusions.

> (quoted by Gould 1981: 23)

I have mentioned how Albee (1982) attempts to penetrate this enveloping fog by arguing that underlying the evidence in the genetic-versus-environmentalist positions are contrasting philosophies about the nature of humankind. Genetic beliefs are traditionally associated with a cluster of other beliefs, as was shown by Pastore (1949a). In his study Pastore found that scientists in the US took up stances on the nature–nurture debate which related to their wider political beliefs: specifically he found that liberals and radicals were more likely to support an environmentalist position in contrast to conservatives, who favoured an understanding which emphasized genetic and organic factors.

These effects are most clearly seen in the controversy about the determinants of intelligence, and are most dramatically illustrated by the Burt affair. Sir Cyril Burt's work, very widely quoted, purported to show that intelligence was largely genetically determined, a notion which had been advanced in the nineteenth century by Galton. It seems likely that Burt was so committed to a genetic explanation that he actually went so far as to contrive data. Now, although Burt has been censored posthumously, the main point has been largely overlooked. By focusing on Burt's fraud and his personal disposition we have, by and large, missed the opportunity to consider several most pertinent processes. We could for instance examine the ways in which Burt's data became established as essential evidence in the geneticists' stance. It is surely not a sufficient explanation to locate the source of distortion in one individual, when a scientific community grasped his findings with such zeal, especially in view of the fact that clues to Burt's deviousness were apparent for all to see.

Burt's 'findings' fitted neatly into expectations concerning the nature of intelligence, and lent further support to a *belief* which had its roots in the previous century. Fixed notions concerning heredity of ability were in tune with the rather rigid hierarchies of the period, and Galton's work had seemed to provide evidence which confirmed that intellectual ability ran in families. The obvious neglected influence was the potential impact of environment upon ability. Burt was manipulating data to make it fit what he *knew* from his own social and academic learning to be the case.

In many ways there are parallels between the work of Franz Kallmann, one of the founding fathers of schizophrenia genetics, and that of Burt. Both were using identical twins to prove what they already knew – the importance of genetics in behaviour. In each case scientific evidence which demonstrated such links would have vital consequences for many people. Both researchers were committed eugenicists who firmly believed that the 'quality' of the race could be improved by the elimination of those who were least equipped to compete in a society which required well-functioning people. Kallmann and Burt were strongly influenced by their cultural and scientific *Zeitgeist*. The former reflected many of the German values of the 1920s and 1930s (the need for a purposeful, hard-working, conforming society) and advocated the role of eugenics in moving society towards perfection based upon hereditarian principles. Kallmann's eugenics were based upon the family as the 'indisputable biological, social and educational unit'; therefore 'work in human genetics favours the promotion of an intelligently planned and well-integrated family organisation' (Kallmann 1953: 276). Burt did not feel that races varied much in inherited intelligence, but that social-class differences reflected differential innate intellectual ability. The poor were poor simply because they were of limited intellect. (Gould has pointed out that, whereas race has been the US's primary social problem, class has been Britain's corresponding concern.)

Very many years before Burt carried out research into the genetic basis of intelligence he had argued that intellect is largely a result of innate factors (1909). For the next 60 years he showed little sign of change in this philosophy. Similarly, Kallmann, long before presenting the results of his twin research, was strongly committed to the genetic theory of schizophrenia.

In fact, the earliest research which obtained schizophrenia concordance rates for monozygotic (MZ) and dyzygotic (DZ) twins came out of an institute at which Kallmann spent some time during his early research days. Luxenburger's (1928) paper seemed to set the seal on the genetic theory of schizophrenia and was published around the time that Kallmann was beginning his research in that institute.

EVIDENCE FOR THE GENETIC AETIOLOGY OF SCHIZOPHRENIA

Kallmann's Twin Studies

My discussion of Burt in no way implies that there has been any fraud in schizophrenia research. My aim was to show that any enquiry into the genetics-versus-environment debate requires a historical context in which evidence can be evaluated. We begin our investigation into the evidence in the field of schizophrenia genetics with some quite definitive statements by two of the contemporary authorities in the field.

Gottesman and Shields (1982) estimate that the variation in the liability of developing schizophrenia appears to be under a high degree of genetic control, approximately 70 per cent, whilst only 20 per cent of the variance is culturally transmitted. Such assertions have major implications for the ways in which the conduct we term schizophrenia is conceptualized and particularly for the ways in which individuals so labelled are to be treated. Gottesman and Shields (1982) are quite explicit about their interpretations:

> Our case for the role of genetic factors in the aetiology of schizophrenia is built on clinical–population genetics data, but it implies a biochemical and/or biophysical cause for the malfunctioning of the brain that leads to the development of schizophrenia.
>
> (ibid.: 235-6)

Thus, these authors make it quite clear that strong genetic evidence implies that schizophrenia is, indeed, a disease of the brain, in spite of several decades of unsuccessful attempts to demonstrate this. In the absence of such support one might expect that research evidence would be most carefully evaluated in attempts to resolve the genetics-versus-environment question. After all, the actual therapeutic approach resulting from whichever factor is considered dominant will have major consequences for those called schizophrenic. The biochemical/biological causation model leads to modes of treatment of a biophysical or chemical nature, whereas an environmental model leads to socio-psychological approaches. Damage may be incurred by patients if the inappropriate therapeutic approach is used.

Yet a careful examination of the genetic evidence suggests that the methodologies, statistics, and inferences employed often fall far short of what should be required in a matter of such social importance. Elsewhere I have considered the work of Kallmann (Marshall 1984, 1985, 1986). Kallmann's research (1938, 1946), although said by some to be of little importance today, still continues to dominate many reviews and textbook accounts of the genetics of schizophrenia.

Kallmann's earlier study (1938) examined the family histories of those designated as schizophrenic. Although this study included more than 1,000 subjects, it contains the basic flaw of any study which seeks to assess the relative contributions of heredity and environment by simply considering family histories. There is no doubt that characteristics of all kinds tend to run in families, but of course this same data could be used to support either a genetic or environmentalist stance. Yet Kallmann chose to interpret his findings as pointing to a strong hereditarian influence in schizophrenia, and his conclusions have, over half a century, been widely quoted and accepted. One critique of this study, written by Jackson (1960), is particularly thorough and detailed. Jackson finds little in Kallmann's work which would provide any certainty for the belief in the genetic causation of schizophrenia, and still less for Kallmann's deep commitment to eugenics and to techniques such as sterilization.

Yet today Kallmann's work is frequently referred to, directly or indirectly, in support of the genetic stance. The major compilation of family studies has been made by Zerbin-Rudin (1967a, 1967b), in German, and this was translated for English readers by Slater and Cowie (1971). In turn this material is reproduced by Gottesman and Shields (1982). It is not immediately obvious that the combined figures are dominated by Kallmann's massive sample.

The methodology of Kallmann's 1938 study depended upon the examination of hospital records of those admitted to a Berlin state mental hospital between 1893 and 1902. Next, he attempted to trace their relatives, many of whom were dead at the time of the study. Only 23 per cent of the probands were alive by this time. He did not attempt to be blind to the mental status of probands when assessing the mental status of relatives, and this basic methodological weakness is compounded by his overinclusive notion of schizophrenia. Detailed criticisms (Pastore 1949b; Jackson 1960; Laing 1976) lead to the conclusion that Kallmann's family studies are quite unsound.

Furthermore, Kallmann's own expectations and beliefs caution against accepting his research as objectively derived and untainted by his attitudes. It is quite clear that, from the outset, Kallmann saw his work as having significance in the wider perspective. His concerns centred around the scientific underpinning of eugenics, and the establishment of a psychiatry informed by biological principles. Eight years prior to the publication of Kallmann's twin study, the aim of which was to control for the separate effects of heredity and environment, he was already so convinced of the nature of the aetiology of schizophrenia that he insisted that

> cases which present a schizophrenic picture clinically but lack the hereditary predisposition, must be excluded from the disease group of 'genuine' schizophrenias and differentiated as 'schizoform' psychoses of exogenous origin...let us repeat that each case of genuine schizophrenia must actually be 'inherited'.
>
> (Kallmann 1938: 264)

Even at this point, then, for Kallmann no individual could legitimately be labelled schizophrenic unless there was some form of family history which would warrant it. Not only did he have firm ideas about the origins of schizophrenia, Kallmann also provides us with his reflections about the nature of those designated schizophrenic, or closely related to them:

> Even the faithful believer in the predominance of individual liberty, theoretically opposed to every eugenic measure on behalf of society as a whole, will admit that mankind would be much happier without these numerous adventurers, fanatics, and pseudo-saviours of the world who are found again and again to come from the schizophrenic genotype.
>
> (ibid.: xiii)

It is difficult to avoid the impression that Kallmann is straying from the realms of science in his idiosyncratic understanding of those who are supposedly inflicted with an *illness*. This is even more surprising in view of Kallmann's insistence on a scientific psychiatry. In fact, the impetus behind Kallmann's massive studies is quite explicit – the assumption that psychiatry should develop along biological lines:

> Despite various advances in recent years, psychiatric research is still battling on many fronts...for general recognition of genetic concepts and for practical realisation of biological principles. The key position of this battle seems

to be held by the disease group of schizophrenia, which continues to crowd mental hospitals all over the world and affords an unceasing source of maladjusted cranks, asocial eccentrics, and the lowest type of criminal offenders.

(ibid.: xii)

The practical realization of biological concepts is the ultimate goal of Kallmann's future psychiatry, and he promotes the development of eugenics as a way of reducing not only the population of schizophrenics, but others whom he appears to have considered undesirable:

In this way psychiatry would accomplish its part in making the biological quality of future generations an important matter for medical concern and activity, by decreasing not only the number of schizophrenic patients but also the number of heterozygotic trait-carriers, such as schizoid eccentrics, criminal adventurers, and other members of the lunatic fringe.

(ibid.: 3)

Kallmann seems unaware that he is confusing belief with evidence as he goes on to prescribe action for those whom he considers to be tainted with the schizophrenia gene: 'Compulsory sterilization could then be confined to absolutely incorrigible schizophrenics who do not need hospitalization and who may be expected to propagate, even out of wedlock, and against medical advice.' (ibid.: 267) The 'incorrigible' schizophrenics who do not need hospitalization were, in Kallmann's terms, the most dangerous because they were 'diseased trait-carriers' who manifested the disorder in what he considered to be antisocial behaviours rather than in florid symptoms of schizophrenia. Thus, as well as the 'schizophrenic homozygote' Kallmann emphasized that we should pay particular attention to the 'heterozygotic trait-carriers' of schizophrenia, for 'we cannot expect sufficient success from the prevention of reproduction in the symptom-carriers alone' (ibid: 267).

I have considered Kallmann's (1946) twin study in detail elsewhere (Marshall 1984, 1985, 1986). Working in New York State he set himself the task of tracking down the relatives of all those twins in the state who had been diagnosed as schizophrenic.

By 1946 he had collected data on 691 pairs, together with information on 3,394 relatives. The results of this study had a resounding impact upon our present-day conceptualization of schizophrenia. The crucial concordance figures reported by Kallmann were 86 per cent for identical (monozygotic or MZ twins and 15 per cent for fraternal (dyzgotic or DZ) twins. It is hardly surprising that such results, based as they were upon the largest sample of schizophrenic twins ever located even to the present day, should have such an effect upon thinking about mental disorder in general, and schizophrenia in particular. The figures seemed finally to answer the major questions concerning schizophrenic aetiology.

Yet the methodology of this influential work was very poorly reported, and many pertinent questions unanswered. In fact, Kallmann allocated only a few sentences in his report to a discussion of the means whereby he carried out his study, in spite of the well-known existence of major pitfalls in this type of investigation. There are serious omissions concerning the way in which zygosity (whether twins were identical or fraternal) was determined – one of the crucial factors in such an investigation. Those interested in the vital omissions had to content themselves with a 21-year wait, until colleagues of Kallmann published a defence of his methods, based largely upon Kallmann's correspondence with others (Shields et al. 1967). By this time Kallmann had died, and only at this point is it discovered that a series of factors had combined to increase concordance rates. We find that Kallmann had included suspected, untreated schizophrenics in his co-twin sample, thereby raising the uncorrected concordance from 59 to 69 per cent for MZ twins (9 to 10 per cent for DZ twins). It was already known from Kallmann's paper that a correction factor for age had increased the 69 to 86 per cent (10 to 15 per cent for DZ twins). We also find that he also changed the hospital diagnosis in the direction of schizophrenia in 14 cases. For the first time, the paper by Shields et al. allowed access to the crucial figures which had eluded critics for 21 years: only 50 per cent of the MZ co-twins of the schizophrenic index twins had a hospital diagnosis of schizophrenia themselves at the start of the study (DZ = 6 per cent).

A series of factors, it emerges, had combined to increase concordance rates, including diagnostic changes by Kallmann, diagnoses of schizophrenia on co-twins who had never previously been hospitalized or diagnosed, the inclusion of 'suspected schizophrenics', and the use of correction factors. The exaggerated rates were then represented as crucial evidence in the nature–nurture debate.

Shields and his co-authors also provided another answer to a question which had been concerning critics for 21 years: in what ways were diagnosis and zygosity determined? It does, in fact, seem that Kallmann *himself* determined both diagnosis and zygosity, and that this part of the study was not delegated to disinterested investigators. Yet Kallmann's method of zygosity determination, a crucial factor in such an investigation, was based largely upon visual assessment. Inevitably, Kallmann left himself open to the possibility of observer bias in this fundamental component of the research. It has already been shown that Kallmann had a strong belief in the genetic aetiology of schizophrenia long before his 1946 paper, and when this is considered in conjunction with his seriously flawed methodology and his use of arbitrary correction factors it is difficult to accept that his results throw any light on the complex issue of the aetiology of psychotic behaviour.

Other twin studies

Since Kallmann's work, there have, of course, been a number of further twin studies. Almost all the reports indicate that there is a statistically significant genetic component in the behaviour we term schizophrenia. Yet it would appear that the size of the component appears to be related to the quality of the research methodology. By and large the more carefully controlled studies, which attempt to take into account the difficulties inherent in twin studies, find lower concordance rates for both MZ and DZ twins. Thus, for example, three of the later twin studies found concordance rates of 25 per cent, 14 per cent, and 24 per cent for MZ twins and 7 per cent, 4 per cent, and 10 per cent for fraternal twins respectively (Kringlen 1967; Allen et al. 1972; Fischer 1973). Gottesman and Shields (1966) reported concordance rates of 42 per cent and 15 per cent for MZ and DZ twins respectively, but since then concordance rates seem to have been consistently lower.

Those who would caution against the acceptance of the major

genetic-component argument are often regarded as attempting to dismiss the genetic case. I have yet to come across any author who seriously advocates that we ignore genetic factors. There seems little doubt that inherited factors are relevant in any attempt to understand schizophrenia; the issue which is really under debate concerns the degree of this linkage. This issue is of major importance to our attitudes, understanding, and treatment of those whose conduct has led to a diagnosis of schizophrenia. It is my contention that the claims for a genetic stance result from an inflation of the evidence for a modest linkage. Gottesman and Shields (1982) assert that the variation in the liability to developing schizophrenia appears to be under a high degree of genetic control, and it is this tendency to emphasize the very high genetic contribution which appears to be unwarranted. I will therefore briefly attempt to outline the ways in which crucial evidence becomes distorted to fit what appears to be a predetermined notion of schizophrenia as a biological phenomenon.

As an illustration of this process, Marshall and Pettit (1985) examined the ways in which authorities in the field advocate how others should calculate concordance rates – the figures which determine hereditability calculations. We took as our example a study by Kringlen (1967). Kringlen included 55 pairs of MZ twins, at least one of each pair having been diagnosed as schizophrenic or suffering from a schizophreniform psychosis. His investigation revealed a concordance rate of 25 per cent (MZ). However, Gottesman and Shields, correctly note that if *borderline states* are included the concordance rate rises to 38 per cent. However, Gottesman and Shields then proceed to recalculate Kringlen's data using a quite different method. Instead of employing the traditional calculation, the *pairwise* concordance rate, they advocate a subtly different method – the *probandwise* concordance rate. If the concordance rate which includes the borderline states is recalculated the figure now jumps to 51 per cent. This, say the authors, puts Kringlen 'ironically within shouting distance of Kallmann's 69 per cent' (1982: 105). Thus, evidence which could not be said to have provided support for a large genetic component in schizophrenia now finds itself classified in the same numerical category as the results obtained by Kallmann, the arch-geneticist in the field. (Incidentally, it is rare for Kallmann's concordance figures to be reported as 69 per cent. This was, in fact, the concordance rate prior to the addition of an age-correction factor, which increased the rate to the more often quoted figure of 86 per cent.)

Thus, Kringlen's modest figures were increased by Gottesman and Shields, to a level which has quite different implications, by two methods. The first method, which will be referred to in more detail later, was by the inclusion of disorders other than schizophrenia. The second was by using a quite arbitrary method of calculating concordance rates. After considering this latter method in detail Marshall and Pettitt (1985) concluded that its arbitrariness makes it very unscientific. In the probandwise concordance some pairs are counted twice if both members of a pair are affected and if each affected pair was identified independently. 'Independently' refers to co-twins of index twins being netted in the trawl through records, rather than being located in the search for co-twins of known schizophrenic index twins.

To illustrate this procedure let us imagine that an investigator has dug through hospital records with the aim of finding schizophrenics who are also identical twins. Out of 100 pairs let us assume that he finds thirty pairs, both of whom are classified as schizophrenics. This, quite simply, represents a *pairwise* concordance of 30 per cent. In 70 per cent of cases where one member of an identical pair is considered schizophrenic the other is not. However, Gottesman and Shields assert that the calculation should be expressed as a *probandwise* concordance. This procedure runs as follows: suppose that our imaginary investigator found ten of the thirty co-twins independently – i.e. that they were discovered in their own right, rather than as a result of follow-up of a known schizophrenic twin. Now, say Gottesman and Shields, we have not 100 probands, but 100 + 10 = 110. The probandwise concordance rate would now be (30 + 10)/110 = 36 per cent. If all concordant pairs had been located independently then the probandwise concordance rate would rise to (30 + 30)/130 = 46 per cent. So by employing this method it is possible to increase the pairwise concordance rate by over half (30 to 46 per cent). Marshall and Pettit argued that principles of statistical science sensibly suggest that proband membership should have no effect on the statistical analysis of the data. Whether or not a twin pair happen to be in the same hospital is irrelevant from a statistical standpoint.

RICHARD MARSHALL

In fact the probandwise method begins to look even more odd if we switch the focus of our attention from concordance to discordance rates. If we were to apply the same statistical operations to the discordance rate of 70 per cent found in our imaginary study, then by using the probandwise method it would be possible to increase this figure to 82 per cent. It could then be argued that the *concordance* rate is negligible. Here we have an example of how the same original data could be used to support an extreme environmentalist or an extreme hereditarian position, simply by the introduction of the probandwise method. To my knowledge, however, this method of calculation has never been used when calculating of discordance rates. Other statistical methods are proposed by Gottesman and Shields (1972, 1982). They rely upon assertions of such authors as Smith (1970) that *low* concordance rates in MZ twins cannot be taken to prove that genetic factors are *not* important in the predisposition to a disorder: a concordance rate of 13 per cent is calculated as a hereditability rate of 50 per cent. In fact, Gottesman and Shields calculated hereditability indices for schizophrenia ranging up to 106 per cent, although they admit that values greater than 100 per cent are obvious signs that the method is subject to error.

It is interesting to note how quickly, and uncritically, the calculating methods described here become accepted practice. Kendler (1983), for example, in reviewing the results of twin studies, employs the probandwise method, and in a later paper (1987), presents a table of twin studies which not only employs solely probandwise measures, but makes no mention of the fact that the concordance rates represent broad concordance measures. The broad rates include as concordant cases those in which at least one twin is described as borderline schizophrenic or as suffering from a schizo-affective psychosis. Thus, for instance, Kendler subjects Kringlen's study mentioned above to recalculation based on the probandwise method and broad assessment. The concordance rate is now 45 per cent, an increase of 80 per cent on that originally reported by the author of the original paper. Similarly, Fischer's (1973) study which has a narrow concordance rate of 24 per cent is now reported by Kendler (1987) to indicate a concordance rate of 61 per cent. Next, employing concordance rates inflated in this way as the basic data, Kendler goes on to calculate the coefficient of genetic determination based upon these arbitrarily derived figures, and not surprisingly the coefficients are very high. 'There is', he writes, 'substantial agreement across the major twin studies of schizophrenia that the hereditability of schizophrenia is between 0·6 and 0·9. Twin studies consistently suggest that genetic factors play a major role in the familial transmission of schizophrenia. (p 8.)

It is difficult to avoid the impression that statistical manœuvres are being employed with the aim of increasing the heredity indices, making it more and more difficult for the reader of reviews and textbooks to gain insight into the *actual* pairwise concordance rates reported in the original studies. In fact, a team of French authors examined the relationship between the contents of original reports of genetic studies and subsequent reviews based upon these investigations. Their report should have a salutory impact upon those who tacitly accept the accuracy of scientific reporting in this particular area.

Cassou and his colleagues (1980) were not attempting to answer the question of whether or not there exists a genetic effect in schizophrenia. They sought to answer the question whether or not there exists a scientific proof for the existence of this effect within the original studies quoted in ten reviews by authors who are considered to be authoritative in their disciplines. These ten reviews were found to be unanimous in stating that the importance of genetic factors had been convincingly demonstrated.

On first consideration this project may appear to be rather odd, not to say unnecessary. The scientific community relies upon comprehensive and balanced summaries of research evidence. Only those who have the time, facilities, and knowledge to specialize in a particular field are suitably positioned to inform others who cannot hope to adequately evaluate the original research reports. Consequently, research reviews by those acknowledged as authoritative in their disciplines are quite crucial to the formation of knowledge bases which become established in a subject area. It is recognized (if somewhat embarrassingly so) that at times the writers of papers and textbooks do not always return to source material for their own work. (Harris 1979, for example, has illustrated the way in which J.B. Watson's report of his experiment on Little Albert became distorted over the years, so that later reports had very little in common with the original. The changes were not merely incidental, but were concerned with some of the fundamental aspects of learning theory and behaviour therapy.)

Even our recognition that distortion of evidence does occur would not have prepared us for the findings of Cassou et al. Having selected the ten reviews they went on to consider every relevant publication cited by at least one of the authors. These publications were subjected to a detailed methodological and statistical examination. Whereas the ten review papers had all arrived at a consensus view concerning the genetic aetiology of schizophrenia, Cassou et al. found that the original evidence just did not warrant this consensus conclusion. In fact, they asserted that 'after a meticulous and exhaustive re-evaluation, we therefore conclude that there is *no* evidence for a genetic effect in the schizophrenic process (Schiff et al. 1980 (English translation): 138, my emphasis).

Cassou et al. therefore concluded that the process through which a consensus is reached within academic circles, on multidisciplinary issues of great social importance, is, in itself, seriously problematic: 'The very existence of such contradictions shows the potential danger of relying on expert opinion on matters of social importance.' (ibid.: 139) I will return later to the significance of the findings of these French authors, but for the moment I would like to consider their review of the most quoted contemporary evidence for the genetic determination of schizophrenia – the Danish Adoption Studies.

Danish Adoption Studies

Although the case for assuming a genetic model of schizophrenia rests upon a variety of studies, most contemporary textbooks and literature reviews point to the Danish Adoption Studies (DAS) as providing definitive evidence for the role of heredity in schizophrenia.

The DAS consisted of a series of investigations, first reported in 1968, and are of two kinds. The first, with Kety as senior author, begins by finding those who became schizophrenic as adults, and who had been adopted in early life. The aim was to trace their biological relatives and to compare their mental health histories with the control biological relatives of adoptees who had not developed schizophrenia (Kety et al. 1968). Such a method is aimed at discovering whether the biological relatives of the schizophrenic adoptees (the index cases) display an increased incidence of schizophrenia despite the lack of a shared environment. The results of these reports (Kety et al. 1968, 1975) have been widely reported as providing evidence to support the genetic approach. Gottesman and Shields (1982), for instance, in their oft-quoted book, summarize the results of these studies as follows: 'Adoptive relatives of schizophrenic adoptees do not have significantly elevated rates of schizophrenia compared to the biological relatives of the adoptees, who do have high rates' (ibid.: 244). The DAS, write Gottesman and Shields, therefore provide strong confirmation of the importance of genetic factors in schizophrenia.

The second group of studies have either Rosenthal or Wender as their senior authors, and I will refer briefly to these after a more detailed examination of the first kind. It should be pointed out that all these studies have previously been critically reviewed by a number of authors. The US psychologists Sarbin and Mancuso (1980), for example, describe the Danish Adoption Studies as being of small value. More recently, a US psychiatrist and two psychologists have provided detailed critiques of the studies (Lidz et al. 1981: Lidz and Blatt 1983). They, too, conclude that careful examination of the evidence indicates that genetic influences may play only a limited role in the aetiology of chronic schizophrenia. The most recent evaluation of the DAS is provided by Rose et al. (1984), who conclude that the weaknesses of the studies are so obvious that it is difficult to understand how distinguished scientists could have regarded them as eliminating all the artefacts which beset family and twin studies of nature and nurture. Cassou et al. include the Danish studies in their detailed examination of all genetic studies.

In Kety et al.'s 1968 study the investigators located thirty-four adoptees who had been diagnosed as schizophrenic. Their 150 biological relatives were then traced, together with the 156 biological relatives of the controls. In fact there was only one 'chronic schizophrenic' amongst the first group. There was also one in the control group. This is less than would be anticipated in a sample of the general population. Lidz and Blatt therefore stress that the data do not provide evidence for the claim by Kety and his colleagues that the 10 per cent prevalence of schizophrenia in the families of naturally reared schizophrenics is a manifestation of genetic factors. Seemingly significant results were, however, obtained when Kety et al. widened their diagnostic criteria to include a schizophrenic spectrum of disorders, which included 'homosexual panic', 'inadequate personality', and 'uncertain borderline state'. With this wide-ranging definition 8·6 per cent of the biological relatives of the schizophrenic adoptees and 1·9 per cent of the relatives of the controls were considered to be within the spectrum. As Rose et al. point out, without the inclusion of such vague diagnoses as 'inadequate personality' and 'uncertain borderline schizophrenia', there would be no significant results in the Kety study.

From raw data supplied by Kety to Rose and his colleagues a clear selective adoptive placement effect was demonstrated. It is known that children of more highly educated mothers, when put up for adoption, are more likely to be placed selectively into homes characterized by higher socio-economic status. In fact, in Kety's study, in a quarter of the adopting families of the schizophrenic adoptees, one of the parents had been a patient in a mental hospital, whereas not one adoptive parent of a control adoptee had. Interestingly, even the biological parents of the schizophrenic adoptees had a low frequency of hospital admissions (6 per cent). Thus, the small difference between the two groups in the number of biological relatives falling in the spectrum (8·6–1·9 per cent) may be an artefact of selective placements. In other words, because the adoptee who becomes schizophrenic is more likely to originate from a biological family characterized by crime, alcoholism, and personal and social disturbance, he or she, when placed for adoption, is more likely to be placed in a similarly less-well-adjusted family. It should be remembered that this runs counter to our contemporary notions of adoption because recent changes have ensured that there are relatively few babies put up for adoption, and agencies are in a position to choose more suitable homes. The Kety study was based upon infants who had been adopted between 1924 and 1947 when there were many more children given up for adoption, and when agencies were not in the position to ascertain that all went to nurturing and integrated homes.

Lidz and Blatt also consider more recent publications by Kety and his co-workers in which the study was extended, but their detailed analysis does not lead them to change their conclusions.

However, out of the numerous methodological and statistical criticisms of the DAS which have been made by a variety of authors, the report of Rose et al. contains perhaps the most surprising. This particular point refers to the 1975 Kety publication in which the researchers attempted to track down relatives of adoptees and then interview them. These interviews were transcribed and diagnoses were arrived at blindly by the investigators. Once again there were more spectrum disorders found amongst relatives of the index cases. However, this time the diagnosis of 'inadequate personality' was excluded from the spectrum. It should be remembered that the 1968 results would not have been significant if it had not been for the inclusion of this category. In the 1975 study such diagnoses occurred with equal frequency in control and index groups; it appears that this led to their being excluded from the study.

Personal correspondence between Rose et al. and one of the authors of the Kety papers revealed that in several cases, when relatives were dead or unavailable, the psychiatrist prepared a 'pseudo-interview' from hospital records. This was then blindly rated by the investigators. One such subject of the study had been diagnosed as 'inadequate personality' in the 1968 study. She was the biological mother of a schizophrenic adoptee, and as this diagnosis was *inside* the 'schizophrenic spectrum of disorders' at that time she was one of the thirteen (8·6 per cent) relatives considered to be in the spectrum, and therefore as contributing to the genetic case. This same subject was, in 1975, considered to be a case of 'uncertain borderline schizophrenia'. This is, once again, *inside* the spectrum, whereas now 'inadequate personality' is outside the spectrum. Furthermore, personal correspondence between Rose et al. and the authors of the 1975 papers revealed that the woman was never interviewed, because she had committed suicide. She had, in fact, been diagnosed as manic depressive by the psychiatrists who had treated her. Rose and his co-authors express their surprise at this discovery which only came to light as a result of personal correspondence: 'We can only marvel at the fact that the American diagnosticians, analysing abstracts of these same records, were twice able to detect – without ever seeing her – that she really belonged within the shifting boundaries of the spectrum'. (Rose et al. 1984: 224-5)

The other Danish Adoption Studies (Rosenthal et al. 1968,

1971) have also been carefully evaluated by the same authors. These studies are concerned with the fate of children of schizophrenic parents who had given up their children for adoption. The aim is to discover whether such children, growing up in a different environment, will develop schizophrenia. The preliminary reports did claim to observe a barely significant tendency for spectrum disorders to be more frequent among the index cases (Rose et al. 1984). Lidz et al. (1981) concluded that, without the inclusion of parents with manic-depressive and indefinite diagnoses in the index group, there is no statistically significant difference between the number of offspring with schizophrenic spectrum diagnoses in the index and control groups.

Rose et al. (1984) further add that, when consensus diagnoses like those in the Kety study were reported for the first time in 1978, it developed that there was no significant tendency for spectrum cases to occur more frequently among index subjects. In any case, only one of the seventy-six (1·3 per cent) index adoptees had ever been hospitalized with the diagnosis of schizophrenia, a figure within the expectation for the general population rather than for the offspring of schizophrenic parents. As Lidz et al. conclude:

> Contrary to the claims of the investigators, their study of the adopted-away offspring of schizophrenic parents fails to provide definite or statistically significant evidence of a genetic factor in the etiology of schizophrenic disorders ....The investigators in this study, as well as in the study of the biological and adoptive relatives of adoptees who became schizophrenic, seem to consider the existence of a genetic factor in the etiology of schizophrenic disorders an axiom rather than a hypothesis.

AN AXIOM OR A HYPOTHESIS?

Those authors who have evaluated the Danish Adoption Studies all refer to the contrasting nature of the actual evidence and the inferences drawn from that evidence and reported widely. Lidz et al. (1981) make the elementary, yet often overlooked, point that it is important that we should understand exactly what is meant by the use of the term 'significant' in the context of the genetic studies.

Thus, for example, they consider Rosenthal's (1971) conclusion that heredity plays a significant role in the aetiology of schizophrenia spectrum disorders. Lidz et al. assume that Rosenthal is referring to statistical significance, but point out that this statement has been misinterpreted by many to mean that there is evidence of a highly clinically significant genetic factor. Even the authors of the DAS at times seem to overlook this distinction: for example, Wender et al. (1977) assert that adoption studies have demonstrated that genetic and not rearing factors play an aetiological role in schizophrenia. Such definitive statements then lead review writers to present conclusions which are hardly warranted from the actual evidence.

As Lidz et al. (1981) note, one of the main criticisms which might be levelled at investigators in the field is their apparent tendency to confuse axiom with hypothesis. To explain this we might begin by considering the source of publications in the field. Typically they emanate from institutions whose titles confirm their particular interest – for example, a department of psychiatric genetics. There would appear to be relatively few institutions whose avowed aim is to discover the role of environmental factors in psychological disorder. Furthermore, it is much more likely that research in the former type of institution will benefit from sponsorship by the pharmaceutical industry. This is not to imply that results of such studies will always be compromised. However, as research leads inevitably to publication so it is not unexpected that the large research resources available for biological psychiatry lead to a large number of biologically orientated publications which, in turn, have a large effect on the knowledge base.

It can hardly be held that the drug companies are acting in a disinterested way, because the establishment of a major genetic component to any psychological disorder is often regarded as justification for the administration of drugs. As Rose et al. (1984) point out:

> The logic, erroneous at every step, is as follows: The Danish adoption studies have shown that schizophrenia and a number of behavioural eccentricities are genetically produced. Since the genes influence biological mechanisms, it must follow that the most effective treatment for schizophrenia, and for behavioural eccentricity, is drug treatment. Focusing on social or environmental conditions

as a cause of disorderd behaviour would be fruitless.

(Rose et al. 1984: 227)

Rose et al. then argue that, even if schizophrenia were largely genetic in origin, it would in no way follow that drugs – or any biological, as opposed to social, treatment – would necessarily be the most effective therapy: 'Just as drugs change behaviour, so will altered behaviour imposed by talking therapies change brains.' (ibid.: 228)

Of course it is not denied that biological factors are of relevance, but it does seem that they are often overemphasized, so that, consequently, less attention is then paid to the damaging emotional effects of a wide range of environmental conditions: poverty, social estrangement, unemployment, low social status, powerlessness, degrading life experiences, low self-esteem, loneliness, social isolation, and social marginality. Cassell (1976) has shown that high risk for *all* kinds of pathology accompany all of these phenomena. Yet they are all too often completely ignored in schizophrenia research.

A recent book by Smail (1987) provides a framework in which we might consider the effects of such modes of living. For Smail, explanations of psychological disorder or distress which rely simply on concepts of malfunctioning or intransigence lead nowhere. Often, he argues, explainers and explained will collude in an illusory vision of a world which has no substance outside their own heads. Although Smail is concerned specifically with psychotherapy, his words, applying at least equally to genetic explanations, provide an apt conclusion to the present chapter:

> The explanation of our conduct is not to be sought in a psychological analysis of individuals, but in a socio-economic, historical analysis of relations between people, and of the ways these have shaped the world we have to live in.

(ibid.: 18)

EDITOR'S NOTE

Since this chapter was written there have been reports that a gene for schizophrenia has been identified using new techniques of molecular genetics. These claims are discussed briefly in the editor's concluding remarks at the end of this volume.

REFERENCES

Albee, G.W. (1982) 'The politics of nature and nurture', *American Journal of Community Psychology* 10.(1): 4–36.

Allen, M.G., Cohen, S., and Pollin, W. (1972) 'Schizophrenia in veteran twins: a diagnostic review', *Archives of General Psychiatry* 128: 939–45.

Bernal, J.D. (1965) *Science in History*, London: C.A. Watts.

Burt, C. (1909) 'Experimental tests of general intelligence', *British Journal of Psychology* 3: 94–177.

Cassell, J. (1976) 'The contribution of the social environment to host resistance', *American Journal of Epidemiology* 104: 107–23.

Cassou, B., Schiff, M., and Stewart, J. (1980) 'Génétique et schizophrénie: ré-évaluation d'un consensus', *Psychiatrie de l'Enfant*, 87–201.

Crow, T. and Deakin, B. (eds) (1987) *Transmission: Biological Psychiatry in Clinical Practice*. London: Education in Practice.

Dowbiggin, I. (1985) 'Degeneration and hereditarianism in French mental medicine 1840–90: psychiatric theory as ideological adaptation', in W.F. Bynum, R. Porter, and M. Shepherd (eds) *The Anatomy of Madness: Essays in the History of Psychiatry*, London: Tavistock.

Fischer, M. (1973) 'Genetic and environmental factors in schizophrenia: a study of schizophrenic twins and their families', *Acta Psychiatrica Scandinavica* Supp. 223.

Gergen, K.J. (1985) 'The social constructionist movement in modern psychology', *American Psychologist* 40: 266–75.

Gottesman, I.I. and Shields, J. (1966) 'Schizophrenia in twins: 16 years' consecutive admissions to a psychiatric clinic', *British Journal of Psychiatry* 112: 809–18.

— (1972) *Schizophrenia and Genetics*, London: Academic Press.

(1982) *Schizophrenia: The Epigenetic Puzzle*, Cambridge: Cambridge University Press.

Gould, S.J. (1981) *The Mismeasure of Man*, New York: W.W. Norton.

Harris, B. (1979) 'Whatever happened to Little Albert?', *American Psychologist* 34: 151–60.

Jackson, D.D. (1960) 'A critique of the literature on the genetics of schizophrenia', in D.D. Jackson (ed.) *The Etiology of Schizophrenia*, New York: Basic Books.

Kallmann, F.J. (1938) *The Genetics of Schizophrenia*, New York: J.J. Augustin.

— (1946) 'The genetic theory of schizophrenia', *American Journal of Psychiatry* 103: 309–22.

— (1953) *Heredity in Health and Mental Disorder*, New York: W.W. Norton.

Karon, B.P. and VandenBos, G.R. (1981) *Psychotherapy of Schizophrenia: The Treatment of Choice*, New York: Jason Aronson.

Kendler, K.S. (1983) 'Overview: a current perspective on twin studies of schizophrenia', *American Journal of Psychiatry* 140: 1413–25.

— (1987) 'The genetics of schizophrenia: a current perspective', in H. Meltzer (ed.) *Psychopharmacology: The Third Generation of Progress*, New York: Raven.

Kety, S.S., Rosenthal, D., Wender, P.H., and Schulsinger, F. (1968) 'The types and prevalence of mental illness in the biological and adoptive families of adopted schizophrenics', in D. Rosenthal and S.S. Kety (eds) *The Transmission of Schizophrenia*, Oxford: Pergamon.

Kety, S.S., Rosenthal, D., Wender, P.H., Schulsinger, F., and Jacobsen, B. (1975) 'Mental illness in the biological and adoptive families of adopted individuals who have become schizophrenic: a preliminary report based on psychiatric interviews', in R. Fieve, D. Rosenthal, and H. Brill (eds) *Genetic Research in Psychiatry*, Baltimore: Johns Hopkins University Press.

Kringlen, E. (1967) *Heredity and Environment in the Functional Psychoses*, London: Heinemann.

Laing, R.D. (1976) 'A critique of Kallmann's and Slater's genetic theory of schizophrenia', in R.I. Evans (ed.) *R.D. Laing: The Man and his Ideas*, New York: E.P. Dutton.

Lidz, T. and Blatt, S. (1983) 'Critique of the Danish-American studies of the biological and adoptive relatives of adoptees who became schizophrenic', *American Journal of Psychiatry* 140: 426–431.

— and Cook, B. (1981) 'Critique of the Danish-American adoption studies of the adopted-away offspring of schizophrenic parents', *American Journal of Psychiatry* 138: 1063–8.

Luxenburger, H. (1928) 'Vorläufiger bericht über psychiatrische serienuntersuchungen an zwilligen', *Zeitschrift für die gesamte Neurologie und Psychiatrie* 116: 295–326.

McDonald, M. (1984) 'Exploring the myths of nervous breakdown', *Psychology Today* October: 141–6.

Marshall, J.R. (1984) 'The genetics of schizophrenia revisited', *Bulletin of the British Psychological Society* 37: 177–81.

— (1985) 'Schizophrenia and the need for a critical analysis of information', in J.M. Brittain (ed.) *Consensus and Penalties for Ignorance in the Medical Sciences*, London: Taylor Graham.

— (1986) 'A critical review of the genetics of schizophrenia', in N. Eisenberg and D. Glasgow (eds) *Current Issues in Clinical Psychology*, Aldershot: Gower.

— and Pettit, A.N. (1985) 'Discordant concordant rates', *Bulletin of the British Psychological Society* 38: 6–9.

Mayer-Gross, W., Slater, S., and Roth, M. (1974) *Clinical Psychiatry*, London: Cassell.

Myrdal, G. (1944) *An American Dilemma: The Negro Problem and Modern Democracy*, New York: Harper & Brothers.

Pastore, N. (1949a) *The Nature-Nurture Controversy*, New York: Columbia University Press.

— (1949b) 'The genetics of schizophrenia: a special review', *Psychological Bulletin* 46: 285–302.

Rose, S., Kamin L.T., and Lewontin, R.C. (1984) *Not in Our Genes*, London: Penguin.

Rosenthal, D. (1971) 'Two adoption studies of heredity in schizophrenic disorders', in M. Bleuler and J. Angst (eds) *The Origins of Schizophrenia*, Bern: Huber.

— Wender, P.H., Kety S.S., Welner, J., and Schulsinger, F. (1971) 'The adopted-away offspring of schizophrenics', *American Journal of Psychiatry* 128: 307–11.

Rosenthal, D., Wender, P.H., Kety, S.S., Schulsinger, F., Welner, J., and Ostergaard, L. (1968) 'Schizophrenics' offspring reared in adoptive homes', in D. Rosenthal and S.S. Kety (eds) *The Transmission of Schizophrenia*, Oxford: Pergamon.

Sarbin, T.R. and Mancuso, J.C. (1980) *Schizophrenia: Medical Diagnosis or Moral Verdict?*, Oxford: Pergamon.

Schiff, M., Cassou, B., and Stewart, J. (1980) *Genetics and Schizophrenia: The Reconsideration of a Consensus*. Unpublished English version of the 1980 French monograph by Cassou, Schiff, and Stewart (1980).

Shields, J., Gottesman, I., and Slater, E. (1967) 'Kallmann's 1946 schizophrenic twin study in the light of new information', *Acta Psychiatrica Scandinavica* 43: 385–96.

Slater, E. and Cowie, V. (1971) *The Genetics of Mental Disorders*, London: Oxford University Press.

Smail, D. J. (1987) *Taking Care: An Alternative to Therapy*, London: Dent.

Smith, C. (1970) 'Heritability of liability and concordance in monozygous twins', *Annals of Human Genetics* 34: 85–91.

Strauss, J.S. (1969) 'Hallucinations and delusions as points on continua functions', *Archives of General Psychiatry* 21: 581–6.

Szasz, T.S. (1976) 'Schizophrenia: the sacred symbol of psychiatry', *British Journal of Psychiatry* 129: 308–16.

Wender, P.H. Rosenthal, D., 'Schizophrenics' adopting parents', *Archives of General Psychiatry*, 34: 777–84.

Zerbin-Rudin, E. (1967a) 'Schizophrien', in P.E. Becker (ed.) *Humangenetik, Vol. 2*, Stuttgart: Thieme.

— (1967b) 'Endogene psychosen', in P.E. Becker (ed.) *Humangenetik, Vol. 2*, Stuttgart: Thieme.

Chapter Five

ARE THERE BIOLOGICAL MARKERS OF SCHIZOPHRENIA?

HOWARD F. JACKSON

GENERAL CONSIDERATIONS

A myriad of competing, conflicting, and contradictory theories and findings have arisen from nearly a century of medical, psychological, and socio-political endeavour towards an understanding of schizophrenia. Most reviews of this literature have not been able to resist the temptation to conclude in favour of one or more of these theories and in so doing dismiss potentially important and relevant findings related to those conditions currently held under the umbrella term 'schizophrenia'. No single theory of schizophrenia is advocated here. Indeed, it will be apparent that to do so would destroy the core of the present argument. The emphasis is deliberately placed on the uncritical appreciation of the biological findings. Where criticism of particular theories or findings is made, it is done so not with the aim of discrediting these theories but, simply to restrict the sometimes false attributions awarded to them.

The biological role

There can be little doubt that a biological account of schizophrenia has been the predominant view adopted during nearly a century of schizophrenia research. Indeed, as Kety (1980) noted, both Kraepelin and Bleuler explicitly held the view that there was a common morbid process which formed the basis from which the common features of schizophrenia sprang. In his descriptions of dementia praecox, Kraepelin (1919) included those cerebral lesions mentioned earlier by Alzheimer (1897). Similarly, Bleuler (1911/1950) suggested that mental factors may play a role in the symptoms of schizophrenia but that the cause of the 'disease' was psychobiological, and even went so far as to suggest that there was a schizotoxin.

However, even the most ardent defender of the biological theories today would dismiss the notion that there was a simple relationship between a biochemical or neurological system and schizophrenia such that one would expect to find a universal lesion or biological abnormality amongst all schizophrenics. Neither could it be argued that a single abnormality would be an adequate explanation for a disorder which varies greatly between individuals (see Chapter 2 by Bentall in this volume) and within the same individual across time (see Chapter 3 by Barham and Hayward in this volume). Further, it would be difficult to maintain that any current biological account would be an adequate explanation (even if the notion of numerous subtypes were entertained) without reference to the functional relationship between the hypothesized biological abnormality and the phenomenology of the disorder. Simply finding differences between schizophrenics and non-schizophrenics on any measure, in the absence of an understanding of how those differences influence the expression of the disorder or the functional significance of the biological agents involved, is clearly insufficient. This interface between psychology and biology is extremely difficult to make and yet is most important for a full understanding of both the phenomena of schizophrenia and the processes from which they arise.

Some authors have suggested, rather pessimistically, that psychology is impossible to reduce or translate to physiology. Philosophers, even those with a materialistic bent, have also argued that it may be impossible to identify a simple relationship between mental states and brain states. Davidson (1968), for example, has argued for a form of 'anomalous monism' in which mind states are equivalent to brain states but in which, none the less, psychological laws cannot be reduced to neurophysiological relationships. To a large extent, this apparent dichotomy between biology and psychology underpins many of the objections to biological approaches to schizophrenia. Siminov (1986) provides an illustration of this problem:

> Let us imagine that there appeared on Earth an investigator from another planet completely without the sensation of

pain. As a result of his experiments, he found that, by amplifying various mechanical, thermal, sonic, and other such stimuli, at a given moment he could elicit a number of characteristic, objectively recorded shifts in the human organism...even to changing the activity of nerve cells in certain sections of the brain. We can say that such a highly intelligent extraterrestrial might leave the Earth thinking, what is pain but a subjective reality of experience? Of course this is impossible. We comprehend the pain of another exclusively because of our own capacity to experience the sensation of pain.

(ibid.: 6)

Kety (1975) provides a similar example of a hypothetical future society, scientifically sophisticated, but illiterate, attempting to make sense of a book. Physical or chemical examination of the structure or constituents of the book will not provide any insight into the story-line, or other semantic content. The point to be recognized is that a certain level of information 'carries sets of meanings which are given by personal history, culture, social and economic circumstances and are not reducible to the mere motion of molecules' (Rose 1984: 352). It might be argued that the phenomena of schizophrenia are entirely in the domain of existential or experiential levels of information and biologically orientated approaches are therefore irrelevant. This argument, of course, ignores the indivisible relationship between brain and experience.

Before the old philosophical chestnut of dualism emerges, it is important to note that, like Pavlov (1973), the present author does not consider that there are fundamental differences between a neurological event and a psychological event. Pavlov wrote: 'How could we separate from one another what the physiologist calls the temporal connection and what the psychologist calls association? In this case, the one is completely merged, completely absorbed by and identified with the other'. (ibid.: 489) Ultimately, all experience and action are phenomena of the brain. However, this does not mean that schizophrenic phenomena are amenable to reductionist biological investigations which make reference only to the individual differences in brain functioning and the complexity of interacting neural systems. A compromise position between psychological and organic interpretations of psychotic phenomena, inherent in the early writings of Griesinger (1845) and Bleuler (1911/1950), is available. Although Griesinger even more than Bleuler believed in a single neuropathology for madness, both writers suggested that psychological overlays to a neurological abnormality may account for the variance found in symptomatology, course of the disorder, and response to treatment found in the psychotic population. This two-stage, organic-psychological model has been advocated by Maher (1974) with respect to delusions but may be applicable to other forms of psychotic symptoms such as attentional deficits. Indeed, it is possible to imagine a number of strategies which an individual may invoke as a form of compensation which could promote a variety of information-processing dysfunctions or maladaptive attributions leading to psychotic phenomena.

The model has important implications for the neurobiological approach to schizophrenia research. First, it suggests the necessary involvement of a neurological event which acts as an initiator for further elaboration. However, the possible transient nature of this event would suggest that it may not be detectable in any but the acute stages of onset: it might also be found in those who do not go on to develop psychotic symptoms perhaps due to greater resilience or a more favourable environment (see Chapter 6 by Claridge in this volume). This model would clearly support Csernansky et al.'s (1983) contention that biochemical investigations should be concerned with the variability of presentation across the course of schizophrenic disorders rather than assuming a static, trait-like model.

Frith (1979) presented a similar dualistic interpretation of delusions, suggesting that these phenomena arose from the schizophrenic's application of normal reasoning in order to accommodate an abnormal increase in information arriving at consciousness. This notion presents a slightly different picture in that it assumes a continuing, and implicitly organic, abnormal process in selective attention which 'floods' consciousness. In this model, ongoing rather than transient biological factors play an important role in the schizophrenic disorder.

A particular weakness of the dual-process model of schizophrenia is that, despite the common occurrence of posttraumatic psychotic symptoms following head injury for example (Levin et al. 1982), very few of such cases actually develop a full-blown psychosis which extends beyond the acute stages of recovery from injury. Indeed, the available evidence would suggest that very few first-episode schizophrenics evidence a primary organic disorder. Johnstone et al. (1987) reported that, out of a population of 268 cases of first-episode schizophrenia, only fifteen patients (less than 6 per cent) were found to have an organic disease which appeared to be relevant to their mental states. Similar percentages have been reported by earlier investigations (McClelland et al. 1966; Small et al. 1966). Without denying the potential importance of organic factors in certain cases, the evidence suggests that organic dysfunction is neither necessary nor sufficient to account for the emergence of schizophrenic symptoms. Rather, if the dual-process model is to survive, it will have to accommodate the notion that organic pathology must have a subtle effect on those processes involved with the interpretation of the self and the world and that these processes may also be affected in a similar way by non-organic forces.

Multiple cause – multiple effect

Much of the brain's functioning is not hard-wired but is the consequence of experience. Differences in the neural substrates of behaviour and experience across individuals may therefore reflect genetic differences in both the hard-wired brain systems as well as the soft-programming arising through previous experience. Thus, stimulation of a particular part of the brain may produce markedly different psychological phenomena in different individuals and for the same individual at different times and under different settings or environmental conditions. Studies of brain stimulation in animals (for example, Delgado 1966), which demonstrated differing reactions to stimulation or lesioning of discrete neuronal areas, are evidence that it would be naïve to consider a simple, universal one-to-one relationship between neurological activity at specific loci and the psychological experience of that activity. Similarly, it has long been known that the majority, if not all, psycho-active drugs may produce different behavioural effects dependent upon the rate of the behaviour (Dews 1958; Kelleher and Morse 1964), the schedule of reinforcement (Dews 1958; Cook and Kelleher 1962, 1963), and the action of relevant discriminative stimuli, be they interoceptive or exteroceptive (Dews 1955; Overton 1966).

With respect to psychiatric phenomena, Cutting (1985) cites the findings of Caine and Shoulson (1983) undermining those biochemical theories of schizophrenia which assume a generalized cortical or subcortical basis for the condition. Caine and Shulson interviewed thirty patients with Huntington's chorea and found that twenty-four of them had one or more of seven different psychiatric disorders according to DSM-III criteria, including three with schizophrenia. Since Huntington's chorea is a disorder of known unitary biological pathology which gives rise to heterogeneous psychiatric disorders, Cutting (1985) argued that the search for a single biological abnormality in one of these disorders is likely to prove fruitless. It is clear that Luria's (1973) arguments concerning the holistic functioning of the brain are important here. It is not possible to consider the effects of an alteration at a specific point within a system without also considering the resulting changes in the rest of the system. The brain is a system with only part localization of functioning. It is only at a theoretical level that one may consider isolating one subsystem from the whole. On the other hand, whereas it is possible to agree with Cuttings's critique of endeavours to identify a *single* biochemical abnormality (which inevitably promotes the discarding of potentially important factors in favour of others which are more 'in vogue'), this does not imply that biochemical research into schizophrenia should be abandoned altogether as Cutting seems to argue. Simply because a particular biochemical abnormality has a non-specific effect it should not be assumed that such an abnormality is not important for an overall understanding of schizophrenic symptomatology.

In contrast to a single cause–multiple effect model are models that assume that a single effect may have multiple causes. In other words, it is possible that what appears to be a unitary phenomenon in terms of presentation may vary in aetiology and functional significance. This is especially so where the phenomenon is complex in nature. It may be assumed that the more complex the psychological functions involved, the greater the number of theoretical brain subsystems that come into play. It would therefore be possible for a distortion in a high-level cognitive function of a particular type to be the result of disruptions at any point within the system. In more concrete terms, a single well-defined psychological phenomenon may appear to be the same across different individuals but the aetiology of that phenomenon may be vastly different. Consider intelligence as measured by an individual's score on an IQ test. This is clearly a high-order concept. Many different neural subsystems are likely to be involved in achieving a good IQ score and a dysfunction of any one of these subsystems may cause an IQ deficit.

Of course, schizophrenia is particularly likely to fit such a model, not only because it involves psychological factors such as thought, perception, emotion, and social behaviour, but more importantly because schizophrenia is not a single, well-defined disorder. Heterogeneity abounds amongst the schizophrenic population to the extent that a permutation of symptoms is required in order to preserve the integrity of the psychiatric diagnosis. Furthermore, in the present author's view (Bentall et al. 1988, see also Chapter 2 by Bentall in this volume), there is little valid or scientific reason to suggest that the symptoms pertinent to such permutations are in any way fundamentally related. Under these conditions, it would not be surprising if schizophrenic symptoms arise from a number of disparate sources of influence. Heterogeneity of cause may even be attributable to a single symptom such as hallucinations, paranoid delusions, social withdrawal, or blunting of affect. Each of these phenomena may arise for many different reasons in the same way that a runny nose may be due to influenza, hay fever, sneezing powder, or a blast of cold air.

It is clear that researchers must accept that there are likely to be many-to-many correspondences between brain events and mental states rather than one-to-one or one-to-many as often assumed by many contemporary investigators (cf. Rose 1984). It is also apparent that nosological strategies aimed at identifying more homogeneous subtypes of schizophrenia based upon overt symptomatology may be misleading since the aetiology of even a single symptom is likely to be variable.

Biological interactions

The search for the 'schizotoxin' has taken researchers along many diverse paths of investigation, each resulting in claim and counter-claim with the assumption that biological theories are mutually exclusive and contradictory to each other. As a consequence, not only have potentially important biochemical agents been ignored, but so also has the importance of the interaction between them. There have for example been several reports of a potentially important interaction between dopamine and cholinergic agents. Thus, it has been claimed that the therapeutic effects of neuroleptics is reversed in some schizophrenics following adminstration of anticholinergics (given to combat the effects of neuroleptic side-effects) such as benztropine (Singh and Kay 1975a) and trihexyphenidyl (Singh and Kay 1975b). Johnstone et al. (1983) found that the adverse effects of anticholinergic drugs were specific only to the positive symptoms (delusions and hallucinations) and not to negative symptoms (anhedonia, social withdrawal, blunting of affect). Recently, Singh et al. (1987) reanalysed their data on forty-seven schizophrenic patients obtained from previous studies, thereby contrasting symptom ratings during the anticholinergic treatment against the preceding and following periods during which neuroleptics were administered alone. These analyses confirmed the specificity of the anticholinergic–neuroleptic interaction for positive symptoms, in that only the positive-symptom patients deteriorated significantly during anticholinergic treatment. The lack of an effect on negative symptoms might seem hardly surprising considering that, on both theoretical (Crow 1980) and empirical (for example, Csernansky et al. 1986) grounds, neuroleptics would not be expected to have a therapeutic effect on negative symptoms, although this point is debatable (see below).

These arguments, highlighting the complexity of the relationships between different neurochemical systems and between neurochemistry and phenomenology, indicate the major problems confronting biological research into psychosis. Some of these have been elucidated previously by Slater et al. (1963) in relation to the syndrome of schizophrenia, but they also hold for each symptom contributing to the diagnosis. When an association between a central-nervous-system abnormality and schizophrenic symptomatology is discovered there are several possibilities:

(1) The association may simply be fortuitous.
(2) The CNS abnormality may cause the symptom directly. This would suggest a direct relationship such that, for example,

excessive dopaminergic activity in the left temporal lobe produces auditory hallucinations. Here fluctuations in the symptom or symptoms would mirror fluctuations in the underlying pathology.

(3) The CNS abnormality may precipitate the symptoms. This is the more traditional stance of Bleuler (1911/1950) which demands the action of another factor (biological or psychological) to account for the symptom's occurrence.

(4) The CNS abnormality may be a symptom of a separate disease or psychological process which has no causal influence on schizophrenic phenomena (for example, acetylecholine abnormalities are associated with memory dysfunctions which are often observed in schizophrenics as a side-effect of the drugs given to combat the side-effects of neuroleptic medication).

(5) The CNS abnormality may be associated with a symptom but bear no functional relationship with it. This possibility suggests a potential correlation between CNS activity and schizophrenic symptoms, but no causal relationship, for example when the brain exhibits signs of distress consequent on the emotional trauma involved in psychotic breakdown.

With respect to the last of these possibilities, it is important not to lose sight of the multitude of peripheral effects of a distressing mental state, such as disturbances in mood, arousal, activity level, and so on, which may not be considered central to the schizophrenic disorder but which may have significant neurochemical consequences.

Although the above theoretical points may appear somewhat laboured, they merit consideration, not only in order to dismiss dualist arguments against biological factors in schizophrenia, but also to lay seed for a more positive interpretation of the numerous biological factors found to be associated with such mental states. The difficulties facing researchers today attempting to assimilate the vast amount of often contradictory evidence may not lie within problems of biological methodology but more at the feet of a loosely defined concept of schizophrenia which is clearly heterogeneous, not only in terms of expression but also in terms of aetiology. There is a pressing need to adopt a more holistic view of these mental states, one which permits variability and individual differences. This is not to say that all the biological facets which have been associated with schizophrenic symptomatology are valid.

Indeed, some are clearly more pertinent than others. Perhaps even more important is the idea that certain biological factors are more related than others to specific expressions of psychosis. The following sections briefly and selectively review these possibilities.

STRUCTURAL ABNORMALITIES

Although the connection between structural abnormalities and schizophrenic symptomatology can only be through the effect those abnormalities have on complex and distributed brain functions, it is nevertheless of value to consider the evidence for the influence of localized lesions in schizophrenia. Since at least some aspects of function are localized in the brain, structural abnormalities may provide some indication of the processes underlying particular manifestations of schizophrenic phenomena. It is possible that such structural abnormalities may induce a vulnerability to certain 'schizophrenic' experiences which act as a catalyst for later elaboration by otherwise normal cognitive processes. More importantly, structural abnormalities may reflect biases in the way that schizophrenics process information or abnormalities in more fundamental processes such as arousal (Venables 1964, 1977), attention (Allen 1982) or responsiveness to reward (Mason 1984; Crow and Deakin 1985; McKenna 1987). As already noted, it is important to recognize that the extent of the neural areas under investigation determines the level of psychological processes that can be considered. Simply put, the greater the extent of the brain regions involved, the higher and more sophisticated the corresponding psychological processes. For this reason, Wexler (1980) has claimed that cerebral-laterality studies are of great value since they reflect high-level functional organization, with each hemisphere of the brain acting as a separate functional subunit. Of course, with greater complexity comes greater uncertainty regarding the specificity of the relationships between organic disorder, cognitive processes, and psychiatric phenomena.

Indices of global neural dysfunction

A number of early autopsy studies have noted a decrease in the number of cortical cells and nerve fibres in schizophrenic patients (Weinstein 1954). Cortical atrophy in schizophrenics has been found more recently by several investigators (Reider et al. 1979; Weinberger et al. 1979b; Golden et al. 1981; Brown et al. 1986). Equally, schizophrenic subjects have been shown to exhibit cerebellar atrophy upon CAT scan (Weinberger et al. 1979a; Weinberger and Wyatt 1982) and Luchins et al. (1980) found the area of the anterior cerebellar vermis to be smaller than normal in five out of twelve schizophrenics. Enlarged ventricles under pneumoencephalography (PEG) investigations (Storey 1966; Huag 1962) or CAT scan (Johnstone et al. 1976; Golden et al. 1980; Andreasen et al. 1982; Golden et al 1982; Nasrallah et al. 1982) have also been associated with schizophrenia. Luchins and Meltzer (1986) found larger ventricular size in forty-five schizophrenics and twenty-two patients with affective disorder compared to sixty-two controls. Also, those affective patients who evidenced larger ventricles tended to be diagnosed as psychotic more often than those with smaller ventricles.

There have been a number of negative findings in this area as well. Jernigan, Zatz, Moses, and Berger (1982) could find no evidence of cortical atrophy or enlarged ventricles in their sample of schizophrenics. Similarly, Trimble and Kingsley (1978) found normal ventricular sizes. Schlesinger (1950), in a study of a large series of cerebellar tumours, produced no case which mimicked a functional psychosis, and Cutting (1976) suggested that cases of psychotic patients exhibiting cerebellar atrophy resembled chronic mania rather than schizophrenia. Even sympathetic reviews of the literature (Seidman 1984) estimate that only 20–30 per cent of schizophrenics suffer from such gross organic impairment, and some researchers (for example, Tatetsu 1964) have pointed out that similar structural abnormalities have also been found in the brains of non-psychotic war victims, executed criminals, and mentally healthy individuals with acute illness. Trimble and Kingsley (1978) have suggested that cerebral atrophy in schizophrenics may be an artefact of diet, institutionalization, neuroleptic drugs, convulsion therapies, and so on. Further, Reveley (1985) reported that ventricle enlargement was related to lifetime dosage of phenothiazines. However, Huag (1962) noted that neural atrophy was highest in those schizophrenics with an acute, catastrophic course of schizophrenia rather than those presenting with a steady progressive disease process. Similarly,

Weinberger et al. (1979a, b) found that cortical atrophy did not correlate with age, length of illness, or length of hospitalization. Indeed, in Weinberger's sample 29 per cent of the chronic and 32 per cent of the first-episode schizophrenics had CAT scan abnormalities. Thus, it seems unlikely that these findings are purely artefact. However, gross neural abnormalities do not appear to be primarily or necessarily related to schizophrenic symptoms. The most that could be maintained on the basis of these positive results is that structural abnormalities of the brain somehow induce a vulnerability to schizophrenic symptoms, but are neither necessary nor sufficient to induce such symptoms.

More importantly, these studies fail to provide any insight into the process of schizophrenia. If the structural abnormalities were localized to a specific neural region then some indications of the functional significance of these abnormalities could be found. The problem with research in this area is that very many brain loci have been implicated, albeit some more so than others.

Subcortical abnormalities

Disorders of the brain stem may suggest an abnormality of arousal in schizophrenia. Lidsky et al. (1979) outlined a theoretical argument linking basal ganglia abnormalities to the catatonic, affective, and attentional features of schizophrenia. Fishman (1975) autopsied the brains of eight schizophrenics and ten non-mentally ill controls. Six of the schizophrenics had encephalitic-like lesions in the area of the brain stem whereas only one control had this type of lesion. Interestingly, no other lesions were detected. Francis (1979) reported a case of a whole family with calcification of the basal ganglia associated with schizophrenia. In contrast, Hankoff and Peress (1981) found only one patient out of a sample of twenty-seven schizophrenics with brain-stem pathology. Cutting (1985) argued that the descriptions of patients found to suffer from pathology of the brain stem or basal ganglia appear to fit affective rather than schizophrenic profiles. However, it is difficult to determine exactly how one would dissociate such affective components from schizophrenia in the light of research which indicates that psychological stress plays an important part in the emergence of certain positive schizophrenic symptoms such as hallucinations (Slade and Bentall 1988) and

129

given the difficulties of differential diagnosis between schizophrenic and affective disorders (Bentall et al. 1988).

The functional connection between basal ganglia and schizophrenic symptoms is rather tenuous and based largely on findings of chorea- and athetosis-like disorders in some schizophrenics even without a history of neuroleptic treatment (Owens et al. 1982; Rogers 1985). However, McKenna (1987) has recently argued that these movement disorders reflect a volitional motor disturbance. It is this cognitive impairment of 'volition', leading to motivational disturbances and impaired exploration, which seems to bear the greatest functionally significant relationship between basal-ganglia pathology and schizophrenia.

Ingvar (1980) postulated that schizophrenia was related to a malfunction of subcortico-cortical projection systems involving the thalamus and basal ganglia. Nielsen (1958) previously considered that lesions in the limbic system (mammillary bodies, anterior and mesial thalamic nuclei, anterior cingulate gyri, and hippocampi) were involved in schizophrenic symptomatology. Torrey and Peterson (1974) suggested that abnormalities of the limbic system could induce an attentional disorder which would promote schizophrenic symptoms. There is certainly a strong association between the limbic system and emotions (cf. Siminov 1986) which may potentially underlie certain negative symptoms (Andreasen 1982; Crow 1980) or schizo-affective disorders. Similarly, Mesulam and Geschwind (1978) claimed that disruption of the connections between the neocortex and the limbic system could create pathological attentional and emotional processes leading to schizophrenic symptoms.

In a report of eighteen autopsied patients exhibiting limbic tumours, Malamud (1967) reported that the two patients with lesions in the cingulum were diagnosed as schizophrenic. Similarly, Escobar and Chandel (1977) cited a case of nuclear symptoms of schizophrenia following cingulectomy. These findings are somewhat surprising when one considers recent evidence which indicates increased vertical axon projections in the cingulate cortex of schizophrenics (Benes et al. 1987). Taken together, these findings would suggest that both hypo- and hyper-connections between the limbic system and the cortex may be relevant to schizophrenia. Unfortunately, these studies do not report the phenomenological features of their schizophrenic samples adequately enough to permit an examination of possible schizophrenic subtypes.

Perhaps the most convincing evidence for limbic system involvement relates pathology of the hippocampus to schizophrenia. Bogerts et al. (1985), for example, found evidence of volume reduction in the parahippocampal cortex and hippocampal formation of schizophrenics. Other investigators have detected a similar volume reduction in the parahippocampal system (Brown et al. 1986; Jacob and Beckmann, 1986; Colter et al. 1987). However, there are several cases of post-encephalitic amnesia who have clearly suffered extensive hippocampal injury without developing schizophrenic symptoms.

There are several possible functional relationships between schizophrenic symptoms and hippocampal pathology. The hippocampal formation appears to play a significant role in discriminating between salient and irrelevant stimuli (Gray 1982; Siminov 1986). Hippocampal dysfunctioning could invoke attributions of salience to irrelevant stimuli, thereby disrupting attentional processes and promoting certain positive schizophrenic symptoms such as pressure of thought, hallucinations, and delusions. The hippocampal formation is also thought to be involved in the process of computing expectancies and making predictive judgements (for example, Siminov 1986). A dysfunction in these processes may result in abnormal belief systems and impairment of the processes required for falsification or verification of beliefs, thereby leaving the sufferer open to delusional or hallucinatory symptoms. These hypotheses are clearly speculative but are proposed to demonstrate the possible relationships that may exist between neurological pathology and schizophrenic symptoms.

Cortical abnormalities

Virtually all of the lobes of the cortex have been implicated in schizophrenia. Ramani (1981) describes a single case of schizophrenia due to frontal lobe sclerosis from Schilder's disease. Luchins et al. (1979, 1982) found that some schizophrenics had larger left than right frontal areas and larger right than left occipital areas than controls, although these patients presented with relatively mild forms of schizophrenia and there is some doubt regarding the validity of the diagnosis. On the other hand, Torrey (1980) found no structural frontal abnormalities on CAT scan investigation.

Conversely, studies of cerebral metabolism strongly implicate the frontal lobes in schizophrenia (Ingvar 1976; Mathew et al. 1981). Despite the small samples currently employed, all the relevant PET scan studies (for example, Farkas et al 1980; Buchsbaum et al. 1982) have reported lower frontal activation in schizophrenics. The absence of structural changes in the frontal lobes of schizophrenics, together with the abnormalities in more functional measures such as cerebral blood flow, glucose distribution (Buchsbaum et al. 1982), and neurological soft signs (for example, Cox and Ludwig 1979), tend to support Goldstein's (1975) hypothesis that it is the schizophrenics 'non-use' (as part of a protective mechanism against the dangers of catastrophe and anxiety) rather than their inability to utilize frontal functions which underlies their symptomatology.

Interestingly, a recent study by Taylor (1987) failed to detect any indications of frontal-lobe dysfunction on a number of neuropsychological tests (Wisconsin Card Sort Test, Benton Verbal Fluency Test, and so on) in violent or non-violent chronic schizophrenics, which is contrary to other studies (for example, Bourne et al. 1977; Goldberg et al. 1987). Frontal lobe pathology in humans has long been known to induce behavioural and cognitive changes such as excessive inertia, highly concrete and overinclusive thinking, impaired abstraction and sequencing functions, and 'stimulus bound', impulsive behaviour which is resistant to negative feedback (cf. Stuss and Benson 1985). Such deficits have clear implications for the genesis of both negative symptoms and delusions associated with schizophrenia. The very low incidence of schizophrenic symptoms following closed head injury (which almost invariably disrupts frontal-lobe functioning) suggests that these 'frontal-type' deficits are unlikely to be a primary cause of schizophrenic symptoms. However, this does not negate the possibility that frontal lobe dysfunction is either a consequence of schizophrenia or that such deficits add to the vulnerability of the individual towards schizophrenic symptoms.

There are more reports of schizophrenic-like phenomena following lesions to the parietal lobes, which is perhaps not surprising considering the important role that these areas play in perception. Lance (1976) described a number of patients with well-formed visual hallucinations and lesions confined to the right parieto-occipital region. Mesulam et al. (1976) reported three patients with acute infarcts in the right inferior parietal lobe who developed delirium. Similarly, Levine and Finklestein (1982) found eight patients who had suffered right temporo-parietal lesions and who presented with schizophrenic-like psychoses.

Finally, the temporal lobes have been most implicated in schizophrenia largely because of their involvement in linguistic and associative processes and because of the overt behaviour observed during temporal lobe epilepsy (TLE). Inappropriate bizarre behaviour, delusions, paranoia, hallucination, explosiveness of affect, complex states of unreality, distortions of perception of the self, and dreamy states have all been associated with TLE (Bear and Fedio 1967; Williams 1968). Investigation by the present author of psychotic patients in a maximum-security hospital indicate that temporal lobe epileptics are more likely to be diagnosed as suffering from a mental illness than either psychopathic disorder or mental impairment, whereas other epileptics are more likely to be diagnosed as mentally impaired (Jackson et al. 1988). This relationship has not been observed by all authors, however. Gibbs (1951) reported a TLE–schizophrenia relationship in a sample of 163 patients with focal epilepsy, but only 17 per cent of those with TLE exhibited psychotic symptoms. This finding was echoed in the studies of Parnas et al. (1982), who found that only five out of twenty-nine patients diagnosed with epileptic psychoses met Bleuler's criteria for schizophrenia and that a further two met the criteria for pseudoneurotic schizophrenia. It is worthy of note that three of these seven patients did not suffer from TLE. However, sixteen of the epileptics presented with a paranoid hallucinatory state and five evidenced paranoid psychosis. It is clear that TLE is neither a necessary nor sufficient explanation for schizophrenic phenomena, even though it may play an indirect role in the genesis of paranoid and hallucinatory symptoms.

Relative dysfunction

As mentioned above, it would be naïve to consider the brain as anything other than a holistic unit. In this sense, simple mapping of schizophrenic phenomena to particular brain locations without considering the influence of other intact (and possibly potentiated) neural functions may be misleading. There have been a number of attempts to consider the relative impact of a specific brain dysfunction in relation to other intact functions. This approach underlies much of the work surrounding hemisphere-imbalance theories. These theories have implied that schizophrenia results from either a left-hemisphere dysfunction, a right-hemisphere dysfunction (or overactivation), or a callosal transfer deficit.

Callosal-transfer theories were first hypothesized to underlie schizophrenia by Beaumont and Dimond (1973), who argued that schizophrenics resemble split-brain patients who have undergone surgical transection of the corpus callosum (a bundle of neural fibres connecting the two hemispheres of the brain). Pathological evidence (Rosenthal and Bigelow 1972; Nasrallah 1982; Bigelow et al. 1983) suggests that the corpus callosum is thicker than normal in chronic schizophrenics. Nasrallah and McChesney (1981) did find psychiatric symptoms in five cases of callosal tumour; however, three of these patients were dementing and two had a functional type of psychosis.

In contrast to Beaumont and Dimond's original hypothesis, which suggests a reduction in communication between the hemispheres, physiological studies have suggested that there is excessive communication along the corpus collosum such that the delay observed between the electrically evoked potential recorded at the stimulated hemisphere and that recorded at the contralateral hemisphere is considerably shortened in schizophrenic patients (Tress et al. 1979; Jones and Miller 1981; Gulman et al. 1982). These findings also contradict Galin's (1976) hypothesis that the degree of interhemispheric communication is excessively inhibited in schizophrenics, but favour Randall's (1980) notion of an exaggerated connection and communication between hemispheres in schizophrenics. Unfortunately, neuro-psychological studies (for example, Green 1978, Green et al 1979, 1983; Weller and Kluger 1979; Carr 1980) report poor performance on interhemispheric tasks, suggesting an impairment of communi-cation between hemispheres. The current status of interhemis-pheric-transference theories is thus confused and contradictory, with evidence for both reduced and enhanced interhemisphere communication. Indeed, neither interhemisphere-transference theory has been supported by more recent studies (Shagass et al. 1983; Sheldon and Knight 1984).

This situation becomes no clearer when one considers hemisphere-imbalance theories. Left-hemisphere dysfunction has been suggested from neurosychological investigations (for example, Flor-Henry and Yeudall 1979; Taylor et al. 1981); CAT scan (for example, Luchins et al. 1979; Golden et al. 1981); electroencephalogram (EEG) studies (Flor-Henry 1976; d'Elia et al. 1977), and pathology studies (for example, Davison and Bagley 1969). However, others have failed to confirm these findings (for example, Etevenson et al. 1979; Luchins et al. 1981; Jernigan, Zatz, Moses and Cardellins 1982), and some researchers have suggested left-hemisphere overactivation in schizophrenics (for example, Gur 1978). It is worthy of note that left-hemisphere dysfunction has been implicated in a number of psychiatric groups other than schizophrenics such as those with personality disorder, affective disorders, autistic children, and so on (Merrin 1981). Furthermore, Pritchard et al. (1980) report a relationship between left-sided TLE foci and other psychological complications.

The possibility of an overactive left hemisphere in schizophrenics has led to the hypothesis that the important functional abnormality consists of the inhibition or dysfunctioning of the right hemisphere (Gur 1979; Cutting 1985). There is some evidence to support this contention. First schizophrenic symptomatology is more often found in those patients with right rather than left parietal or tempero-parietal lesions (Lance 1976; Mesulam et al. 1976; Levine and Finklestein 1982), and second, there is some evidence to suggest that TLE patients diagnosed as psychotic predominantly suffer from left-hemisphere epileptic foci (Flor-Henry 1969). Of course, this latter finding has not gone unchallenged, and some researchers have been unable to find a significant relationship between the side of TLE foci and schizophrenia (Taylor 1975; Kristensen and Sindrup 1978).

This raises the possibility that all the above neurological abnormalities may be associated with schizophrenic disorder. This hypothesis can take two forms. The first of these is that neurological dysfunction may create a form of general vulnerability which, non-specifically, gives rise to a number of psychiatric problems, schizophrenia among them but that no specific brain locus is likely to be associated with schizophrenia directly. In this sense, the notion of a common morbid process, organic in nature, purported by Kraepelin (1919) and Bleuler (1911/1950) would have to be abandoned. The alternative analysis proposes that different forms of schizophrenia are associated with different types of neurological impairment.

Regarding the second of these suggestions, Gruzelier (1981) claimed that there are two neuropsychological syndromes associated with schizophrenia. In one there is a left-hemisphere overactivation resulting in paranoid, over-inclusive, and hyperactive motor symptoms whereas in the other there is left-hemisphere underactivation eliciting non-paranoid, negative symptoms. However, as Cutting (1985) points out, right-hemisphere-injured patients frequently present with an exaggeration of emotion (for example, emotional lability, euphoria, incongruent affect, and so on). Magaro and Chamrad (1983) have suggested a similar correspondence between paranoid and non-paranoid subtypes with right- and left-hemisphere dysfunction respectively. Increased left-hemisphere EEG variability has been associated with acute and paranoid schizophrenics (Rochford et al. 1970) but not hebephrenic patients. Parnass et al. (1982) reported that in their sample only paranoid and paranoid-hallucinating patients evidenced left TLE. Davison and Bagley (1969) reported that primary delusions and catatonia were strongly associated with left-cerebral lesions.

Unfortunately, all the available data are not consistent. Levine and Grek (1984) found delusions to be associated more with right-hemisphere lesions in patients with severe diffuse brain atrophy only. No major effects were noted for either the size or location of the lesion. They suggested that a right-hemisphere lesion superimposed on a diffusely atrophied brain seemed to be a cause of delusions. Normal cerebral blood-flow (Hoyer and Oesterreich 1975) and minimal or absent cerebral damage has been associated with paranoid symptomatology (Mirsky 1969; Malec 1978). Huag (1962) found that cortical or subcortical atrophy were not associated with any schizophrenic subtype. Disturbances in left-hemisphere functioning have been noted with both hallucinating (Bazhin et al. 1975) and non-hallucinating (Alpert et al. 1976) schizophrenics, and such abnormalities have also been associated with milder forms of disorder (Boklage 1977; Luchins et al. 1979, 1982; Wyatt et al. 1981). Seidman's (1984) review points out that there is an apparent strong relationship between negative features of schizophrenia and poor performance on cognitive tests sensitive to cortical injury. However, statistically significant differences in neuropsychological test performance between schizophrenic patients presenting with positive or negative symptoms have not been found (Opler et al. 1984).

To conclude this section, there can be no doubt that organic factors play an important part in the presentation of schizophrenic symptomatology but the nature of this role is highly equivocal. The interaction between neurological and psychological factors has been largely ignored. The investigation of biological factors alone is likely to prove fruitless. Indeed, as Wexler (1980: 289) points out:

> extensive changes in brain structure in neurological illness often lead to little change in behaviour...persistent surgical and biochemical lesions in experimental animals often lead to only temporary changes in behaviour...despite gross recurrent and persistent behavioural changes in psychiatric illness, accompanying disorders of brain function and structure have thus far eluded description.

BIOCHEMICAL MARKERS OF SCHIZOPHRENIA

There are obvious parallels to be drawn between the current status of biochemical theories of schizophrenia and that of the neuroanatomical theories described above. First, numerous neurochemicals have been implicated in schizophrenia: dopamine, noradrenaline, serotonin, acetylcholine, prostoglandin, neuropeptides, GABA, and so on. Second, none have been specifically and uniquely associated with schizophrenic phenomena. Third, the introduction or lesioning of these chemicals in the brain has failed to induce in normals the range of symptoms associated with schizophrenia, although some compounds such as amphetamine (for example, Janowsky et al. 1973), LSD (Green and Costain, 1981), mescaline, psilocybin, and delta-THC (Siegel and Jarvik 1975) promote experiences not entirely dissimilar to some aspects of schizophrenic symptomatology. To take one example of the complex way in which neurochemicals have been found to affect schizophrenic symptoms, amphetamine (which may elicit paranoid delusions in normal subjects) has been found to exacerbate some symptoms in some schizophrenic patients (Janowsky et al. 1973), whilst in others there has been no response (for example, Kornetsky 1976) or even slight improvement (Angrist et al. 1980).

Perhaps the major source of interest in neurochemical theories has been the reported success and widespread use of anti-psychotic, neuroleptic medication for schizophrenic patients. It has been argued that a major benefit of these drugs is the prevention of relapse (Leff and Wing 1971; Davis 1975). A recent publication from a series of studies carried out at Northwick Park Hospital (Crow et al. 1986) clearly indicated the value of prophylatic neuroleptic treatment. However, only 16 per cent of first-episode schizophrenics appeared to benefit over and above placebo and nearly half those on active medication relapsed within the first 2 years. An interesting finding was that relapse was positively related to the delay between onset and first intervention, a finding contradictory to the results of other research (Carpenter et al. 1977; Rappaport et al. 1978). This raises the possibility (mentioned previously) that schizophrenic phenomena may in part result from a psychological reaction to temporally discrete biological (or possibly psychological) events. In this case, early intervention with neuroleptic medication may arrest the processes following the initial disturbance and thereby reduce the long-term consequences.

More importantly, Crow et al. were unable to determine subgroups of patients who would do well or fair worse with neuroleptic medication. It has long been known that many schizophrenic patients are neuroleptic resistant (for example, Nasrallah et al. 1979). Crow (1980) postulated that responsivity to neuroleptic medication could be determined by reference to positive and negative symptomatology and that negative-symptom schizophrenics were unlikely to benefit. However, studies relating these syndromes to drug responsivity have produced mixed results. Angrist et al. (1980) compared positive- and negative-symptom schizophrenics in terms of their response to amphetamine and neuroleptic medication. They reported significant worsening of all symptoms on amphetamine whereas neuroleptics improved positive, but not negative, symptoms. However, emotional withdrawal, an aspect of negative symptomatology, actually improved significantly in the same way as the positive symptoms. Kay and Opler (1987), in a more recent interpretation of the positive–negative dichotomy, have postulated developmental dual processes which correspond to the negative and positive components. The first is a neuroleptic-resistant component observed predominantly, they claim, in hebephrenic and nuclear types of schizophrenia. The second is a neuroleptic-responsive component seen mainly in catatonic and schizophreniform types. It is worthy of note that some workers (for example, Cutting 1985) have argued that catatonic symptoms should not be considered a feature of schizophrenia. Furthermore, it is curious that Kay and Opler (1987) also report that both the neuroleptic Pimozide (with dopamine-blocking properties) and Sinemet (which augments levels of dopamine and noradrenaline) were highly effective in the treatment of negative symptoms.

It is the effectiveness of neuroleptics and their known action on the catecholeamines which has focused attention on dopamine as a potential agent in schizophrenic disorders. The most convincing evidence for this theory is the finding that dopamine-receptor density is elevated in schizophrenics compared to controls, especially in the caudate, putemens, nucleus accumbens (Owen et al. 1978) and substantia nigra (Owen et al. 1984). However, this result has not been reported by some authors (Reynolds et al. 1980, 1981). In those studies yielding positive results, there is a notably high degree of overlap between the schizophrenic and normal samples, and some researchers have suggested that the specificity of the receptors in question to dopamine is debatable (Lechin et al. 1983).

Other measures of dopamine activity are far less convincing. Generally, no consistent differences in dopamine levels have been found between drug-free schizophrenics and normals. Similarly, many studies have been unable to find elevated levels of dopamine metabolites which would indicate greater dopamine activity and some (Berger et al 1978; van Kammen 1979) have found lower levels of the dopamine metabolite homovanillic acid. Drugs which increase dopamine activity, such as levadopa, bromocriptine, benzotropine, amantodine, and apomorphine very rarely induce schizophrenic-like reactions (Goodwin et al. 1971; Lieberman et al. 1979). In addition, there are a number of reports of patients with long-standing Parkinson's disease developing schizophrenic-like psychoses despite degeneration of dopamine neurons in these patients (Rastogi et al. 1981).

More detailed critical analyses of the dopamine hypothesis are available elsewhere (Csernansky et al. 1983; Carlton and Manowitz 1984; Jackson 1986). Suffice to say that dopamine is unlikely to prove the basic biochemical abnormality underlying all forms of schizophrenia although it may play a fundamental role in some schizophrenics. However, the nature of this role is highly equivocal. It is likely to involve a more dynamic process than has generally been assumed. Csernansky et al. (1983) suggest that an overactivity or underactivity in one part of a neurochemical system may bring about changes in other areas or within the same area, thus bringing about a functional equilibrium. Indeed, the pathological process may not lie with dopamine but with some related chemical system. Furthermore, the importance of dopamine may vary within the same individual across the course of the disorder. Theodorau et al. (1981), for example have pointed out that dopamine antagonism is unlikely to be responsible for the continued anti-psychotic effects of the neuroleptics since long-term administration has been shown to increase rather than decrease dopamine-receptor activity.

In recent years other neurochemicals have been largely dismissed with respect to schizophrenia. However, their activity may be relevant to symptom variation across schizophrenics. Noradrenaline has been strongly implicated as a potential factor in schizophrenia (Lechin et al. 1983), and it also appears to have significant interactions with dopamine, as evidenced from a number of animal studies (Deutch et al. 1985). Hornykiewicz (1982) suggested that increased noradrenergic functioning in some schizophrenics results in a chronic overactivity of the brain-stem reticular formation. Sternberg et al. (1981) reported that three of their schizophrenic sample (9 per cent) had unusually elevated noradrenaline levels in their cerebral spinal fluid, and Glazer et al. (1987) reported a notable dysphoric-arousal reaction in some schizophrenics following administration of yohimbine (an α-2 adrenergic receptor antagonist which increases noradrenergic function).

The indoleamine, serotonin (5-hydroxytryptamine; 5HT) has also been implicated in schizophrenia, not least because of its association with psychedelic drugs such as LSD. However, there are conflicting findings again. It has been suggested that blood platelets provide an adequate model of neural activity (Sneddon

1973; Stahl 1977). Some studies have noted that the maximal uptake rate for 5HT in blood platelets is significantly lower in drug-free schizophrenics (for example, Lingjaerde 1983), and elevated platelet concentrations of serotonin have also been found (Garelis et al. 1975). However, negative findings have also been reported (for example, Post et al. 1975; Joseph et al. 1979).

Serotonin is also known to interact with dopamine so that some neuroleptics (for example, haloperidol) and other antidopaminergic drugs can block the effects of the 'serotonin syndrome' (a distinct set of stereotypic behaviours) induced by the 5HT precursor 5HTP (5-hydroxytryptophan) or paraglyine (for example, Silbergeld and Hruska 1979).

There are relatively isolated reports of the therapeutic effects of tryptophan (a precursor to 5HTP), 5HTP, and parachlorophenylalanine (a tryptophan hydroxylase inhibitor which reduces, relatively specifically, brain 5HT) on schizophrenic symptoms (Wyatt et al. 1972; Nasrallah et al. 1979). Wyatt et al. (1972), for example, found 5HTP to have therapeutic effects in six out of seven chronic undifferentiated schizophrenic and one of four chronic paranoid patients who were resistant to phenothiazine treatment. Interestingly, two of the paranoid patients worsened following 5HTP treatment. The finding of a clinical effect of 5HTP in a case of paranoia is particularly surprising since this phenomenon has been especially linked to dopaminergic overactivity (because amphetamine, which increases brain dopamine activity, can induce a paranoid-like psychosis in normal subjects). These, and other findings, led Nasrallah et al. (1979) to suggest that there are two distinct subtypes of schizophrenia relating to either an overactivity or an underactivity of serotonin and which correspond to symptomatology closely resembling current concepts of positive and negative symptoms. Serotonergic overactivity was favoured as an explanation of schizophrenia by Bender (1976), who also suggested that anti-psychotics may have their clinical effect by blockage of serotonergic receptors.

The initial enthusiasm for 5HT has withered in recent years. Perhaps its demise has come about partly as a result of the scientific community's eagerness to embrace the dopamine hypothesis, partly because of a number of negative findings (for example, Lucas et al. 1971) and partly because 5HT abnormalities have been closely linked with other psychiatric disorders such as depression (cf. Toumisto et al. 1979; Cowan and Charig 1987), Down's syndrome (cf. Coleman 1978), and, more recently, obsessive–compulsive disorder (cf. Zohar et al. 1987). Serotonergic overactivity (along with dopaminergic overactivity) has been associated with Huntington's chorea (Aminoff et al. 1974; McLean and Nihei 1977) which in turn has been linked to schizophrenic-like symptoms (for example, Heathfield 1967). It is nevertheless the case that, to date, few other neurochemical candidates have been implicated specifically in the apparent primary perceptual abnormalities found in some schizophrenics.

Prostaglandin (Feldberg 1976), GABA (Lingjaerde 1982), and other neurochemicals, on current evidence, are less clearly associated with schizophrenic symptomatology than dopamine, serotonin, or noradrenaline, yet they may play more indirect roles in certain cases of schizophrenia. Thus, for example, despite the absence of a clear and reproducible GABA disturbance in schizophrenics (Garbutt and van Kammen 1983), Lingjaerde (1982) reported a general clinical improvement and a reduction in the frequency of hallucinations following combined treatment with estrazolam (a benzodiazepine) and a neuroleptic in chronic schizophrenics who had previously proved resistant to neuroleptics alone. Lingjaerde therefore postulated a potential GABA–dopamine interaction in some schizophrenics.

The above review of the biological factors potentially associated with schizophrenia is necessarily selective. However, the main objective has been to expose the marked variability within schizophrenia and across the schizophrenic subtypes in terms of biological indices. The review is deliberately uncritical; despite this, it should be clear that the current knowledge does not easily lend itself to drawing any conclusions concerning the nature of the relationship between biological factors and schizophrenic phenomena.

THE FUTURE OF SCHIZOPHRENIA

It is clear that schizophrenia is not a unitary clinical or biological entity, but involves very divergent and autonomous features. The rush to identify homogeneous subgroups in terms of positive–negative, chronic–acute dichotomies, or more traditional nosologies has not met with much success. The evidence suggests that it is highly unlikely that neuroanatomical, neurochemical, or neurofunctional factors will reveal discrete subtypes of schizophrenics who exhibit divergent symptomatology, at least in the way that the range of schizophrenic symptoms are currently defined. It is possible that clearer and more precise definitions of these symptoms would permit a greater understanding of the role played by biological factors. McKay et al. (1981), for example, noted that left-frontal lobe impairment, as indicated by performance on the Luria–Nebraska Neuropsychological Battery, was specific to auditory-hallucinating patients and not to visual-hallucinating and non-hallucinating psychiatric patients.

A number of authors, including Bannister (1968), Persons (1986), and Bentall et al. (1988) have advocated the abandonment of research into syndromes (however refined by a process of subdivision) and have argued that investigators should channel their efforts into single-symptom research. Of course, it is to be expected that similar problems of definition will arise even using more precise descriptions of the phenomena under investigation. However, because of the imposition of more stringent criteria for sampling and the resultant increase in group homogeneity, such an approach will be less likely to eliminate potentially important factors and more likely to improve our understanding of the underlying processes relating organic abnormalities to schizophrenic phenomena. Currently, the study of schizophrenic subjects who exhibit grossly diverse symptomatology leads to difficulties in determining whether the organic factor under investigation is related to a specific symptom, an underlying process, or is an artefact.

Investigations of function and structure should go hand in hand. The investigation of structure alone gives little indication of the significance of findings to the emergence of psychotic phenomena. Conversely, the identification of neurofunctional abnormalities may reflect the non-use rather than the inability to use these functions. It is possible that the variability in symptoms between schizophrenics even with the same aetiology is caused not by the primary neurological deficit or information-processing dysfunction, but by the variety of ways in which individuals attempt to compensate or cope with the primary dysfunction. For these and other reasons, consideration of the developmental course of the phenomena of schizophrenia is essential.

Psychological and social investigations should be carried out together with biological studies. Taking into account the waxing and waning of symptoms (and other factors relating to clinical state), the process of onset, family and medical histories, and life experiences would permit the investigation of the relationship between neurogenic and psychogenic factors, primary and secondary processes of schizophrenic phenomena, and would lead to more reliable and valid criteria for grouping both symptoms, processes, and biological factors.

The past century of research has led to increased sophistication in the techniques and methods available for the investigation of psychopathology. It has identified many important factors in psychosis (although it may have dismissed many more prematurely). The question now facing researchers is not *which* factors are important but *how* these factors are important. To answer this question, a major reconstruction of our conceptualization of both research methodology and the schizophrenias is required.

REFERENCES

Allen, H.A. (1982) 'Dichotic monitoring and focused versus divided attention in schizophrenia', *British Journal of Clinical Psychology* 21: 205–12.

Alpert, M., Rubenstien, H., and Kesselman, M. (1976) 'Asymmetry of information processing in hallucinators and non-hallucinators', *Journal of Nervous and Mental Disease* 162: 258–65.

Alzheimer, A. (1897) 'Beitrage zur pathologischen Anatomie der Hirnrinde und zur anatomoschin Grundlage einiger Psychosen', *Monatsschrift für Psychiatrie und Neurologie* 2: 82–119.

Aminoff, M.J., Trenchard, A., Turner, P., Wood, W.G., and Hills, M. (1974) 'Plasma uptake of dopamine and 5-hydroxytryptamine and plasma-catecholamine levels in patients with Huntington's chorea', *Lancet* ii: 1115–16.

Andreasen, N.C. (1982) 'Negative symptoms in schizophrenia', *Archives of General Psychiatry* 36: 1315–30.

— Smith M.R., Jacoby, C.G., Dennert, J.W., and Olsen, S.A. (1982) 'Ventricular enlargement in schizophrenia: definition and prevalence', *American Journal of Psychiatry* 139: 297–301.

Angrist, B., Rostrosen, J., and Gershon, S. (1980) 'Differential effects of amphetamine and neuroleptics on negative and positive symptoms in schizophrenia', *Psychopharmacolgy* 72: 17–19.

Bannister, D. (1968) 'The logical requirements of research into schizophrenia', *British Journal of Psychiatry* 132: 293–5.

Bazhin, E.F., Wasserman, L.I., and Tonkongii, I.M. (1975) 'Auditory hallucinations and temporal lobe pathology', *Neuropsychologia* 13: 481–7.

Bear, D.M. and Fedio, J. (1967) 'Quantitative analysis of interictal behaviour in temporal lobe epilepsy', *Archives of Neurology* 34: 454–67.

Beaumont, J. and Dimond, S. (1973) 'Brain disconnection in schizophrenia', *British Journal of Psychiatry* 123: 661–2.

Bender, D.A. (1976) 'Tryptophan and serotonin in schizophrenia', *Lancet* 21: 427.

Benes, F.M., Majocha, R., Bird, E.D., and Marotta, C.A. (1987) 'Increased vertical axon numbers in cingulate cortex of schizophrenics', *Archives of General Psychiatry* 44: 1017–21.

Bentall, R.P., Jackson, H.F., and Pilgrim, D. (1988) 'Abandoning the concept of "schizophrenia": some implications of validity arguments for psychological research into psychotic phenomena', *British Journal of Clinical Psychology* 27: 303–24.

Berger, P.A., Elliot, G.R., and Barchas, J.D. (1978) 'Neuroregulators and schizophrenia', in M.A. Lipton, A. Dimascio, and K.F. Killam (eds) *Psychopharmacology: A Generation of Progress*, New York: Raven Press, pp. 1071–82.

Bigelow, L.B., Nasrallah, H.A., and Rauscher, F.P. (1983) 'Corpus callosum thickness in chronic schizophrenia', *British Journal of Psychiatry* 142: 284–7.

Bleuler, E. (1911) *Dementia Praecox or the Group of Schizophrenias*, translated 1950, New York: International University Press.

Bogerts, B., Meertz, E., and Schonefeldt-Bausch, R. (1985) 'Basal ganglia and limbic system pathology in schizophrenia', *Archives of General Psychiatry* 42: 784–91.

Boklage, C.E. (1977) 'Schizophrenia brain asymmetry development, and twinning: cellular relationship with etiology and possible prognostic implications', *Biological Psychiatry* 12: 19–35.

Bourne, L.E., Justesen, D.R., Abraham, T., Beeker, C., Brauchi, J.T., Whitaker, L.C., and Yaroush, R.A. (1977) 'Limits to conceptual rule-learning by schizophrenic patients', *Journal of Clinical Psychology* 33: 324–34.

Brown, R., Colter, N., Corsellis, J.A.N., Crow, T.J., Frith,' C.D., Jagoe, R., Johnstone, E.C., and Marsh, L. (1986) 'Postmortem evidence of structural changes in schizophrenia', *Archives of General Psychiatry* 43: 36–42.

Buchsbaum, M.S., Ingvar, D.H., Kessler, R., Waters, R.N., Cappelletti, J., van Kammen, D.P., and others (1982) 'Cerebral glucography with positron tomography', *Archives of General Psychiatry* 39: 251–9.

Caine, E.D. and Shoulson, I. (1983) 'Psychiatric syndromes in Huntington's disease', *American Journal of Psychiatry* 140: 728–33.

Carlton, P.L. and Manowitz, P. (1984) 'Dopamine and schizophrenia: an analysis of the theory', *Neuroscience and Biobehavioural Reviews* 8: 137–51.

Carpenter, W.T., McGlashan, T.H., and Strauss, J.S. (1977) 'The treatment of acute schizophrenia with drugs: an investigation of some current assumptions', *American Journal of Psychiatry* 134: 14–20.

Carr, S.A. (1980) 'Interhemispheric transfer of sterognostic information in chronic schizophrenics', *British Journal of Psychiatry* 136: 53–8.

Coleman, M. (1978) 'The effects of 5-hydroxytryptophan in Down's syndrome and other diseases of the central nervous system', in D.J. Boullin (ed.) *Serotonin in Mental Abnormalities*, New York: Wiley.

Colter, N., Battal, S., Crow, T.J., Johnstone, E.C., Brown, R., and Bruton, C. (1987) 'White matter reduction in the parahippocampal gyrus of patients with schizophrenia', *Archives of General Psychiatry* 44: 1023.

Cook, L. and Kelleher, R.T. (1962) 'Drug effects on the behavior of animals', *New York Academy of Science* 96: 315–35.

— (1963) 'Effects of drugs on behavior', *Annual Review of Pharmacology* 3: 205–22.

Cowan, P.J. and Charig, E.M. (1987) 'Neuroendocrine responses to intravenous tryptophan in major depression', *Archives of General Psychiatry* 44: 958–66.

Cox, S.M. and Ludwig, A.M. (1979) 'Neurological soft signs and psychopathology', *Journal of Nervous and Mental Disease* 167: 161–5.

Crow, T.J. (1980) 'Molecular pathology of schizophrenia: more than one disease process?', *British Medical Journal* i: 66–8.

— and Deakin, J.F. (1985) 'Neurohumoral transmission, behaviour and mental disorder', in M. Shepherd (ed.) *Handbook of Psychiatry, Vol. 5. The Scientific Foundation of Psychiatry*, Cambridge: Cambridge University Press.

Crow, T.J., MacMillan, J.F., Johnson, A.L., and Johnstone, E.C. (1986) 'The Northwick Park study of first episode schizophrenics: II. A randomised controlled trial of prophylactic neuroleptic treatment', *British Journal of Psychiatry* 148: 120–7.

Csernansky, J.G., Brown, K., and Hollister, L.E. (1986) 'Is there drug treatment for negative schizophrenic symptoms?', *Hosp. Formul.* 21: 790–2.

Csernansky, J.G., Holman, C.A., and Hollister, L.E. (1983) 'Variability and the dopamine hypothesis of schizophrenia', *Schizophrenia Bulletin* 9: 325–6.

Cutting, J.C. (1976) 'Chronic mania in childhood: case report of a possible association with a radiological picture of cerebellar disease', *Psychological Medicine* 6: 635–42.

— (1985) *The Psychology of Schizophrenia*, Edinburgh: Churchill Livingstone.

Davidson, D. (1968)) 'Actions, reasons and causes', in A.R. White (ed.) *The Philosophy of Action*, Oxford: Oxford University Press.

Davis, J.M. (1975) 'Overview: maintenance therapy in psychiatry. I. Schizophrenia', *American Journal of Psychiatry* 132: 1237–45.

Davison, K. and Bagley, C.R. (1969) 'Schizophrenia-like psychoses associated with organic disorders of the central nervous system: a review of the literature', in R.N. Herrington (ed.), *Current Problems in Neuropsychiatry*, Ashford, Kent: Headley Bros.

Delgado, J.M.R. (1966) 'Aggressive behavior evoked by radio stimulation in monkey colonies', *American Zoologist* 6: 669–81.

d'Elia, G. Jacobsen, L., von Knorring, L., and others (1977) 'Changes in psychopathology in relation to EEG variables and visual average evoked responses (V. AER) in schizophrenic patients with penfluridol or thiothinene', *Acta Psychiatrica Scandinavica* 55: 309–18.

Deutch, A.Y., Tam, S-Y., and Roth, R.H. (1985) 'Footshock and conditional stress increase DOPAC in the ventral tegmental area but not the substantia nigra', *Brain Research* 333: 143–6.

Dews, P.B. (1955) 'Studies on behavior. I. Differential sensitivity to phenobarbital of pecking performance in pigeons depending on schedule of reward', *Journal of Pharmacology and Experimental Therapeutics* 113: 393–401.

— (1958) 'Studies on behavior. IV. Stimulant action of methamphetamine', *Journal of Pharmacology and Experimental Therapeutics* 122: 137–47.

Escobar, J.I. and Chandel, V. (1977) 'Nuclear symptoms of schizophrenia after cingulectomy: a case report', *American Journal of Psychiatry* 134: 1394–405

Etevenson, P., Pidoux, B., Rious, P., Peron-Magnan, P., Verdeaux, G., and Deniker, P. (1979) 'Intra- and interhemispheric EEG differences quantified by spectral analysis', *Acta Psychiatrica Scandinavica* 60: 57–8.

Farkas, T., Reivich, M., Alavi, A., Greenberg, J.H., Fowler, J.S., MacGregor, R.R., Christman, D.R., and Wolf, A.P. (1980) 'The application of ^{18}F-deoxy-2-fluoro-D-glucose and positron emission tomography in the study of psychiatric conditions', in J.V. Passonneau, R.A. Hawkins,W.D. Lust, and F.A. Welsh (eds) *Cerebral Metabolism and Neural Function*, Baltimore: Williams & Wilkins.

Feldberg, W. (1976) 'Possible association of schizophrenia with a disturbance in prostaglandin metabolism: a physiological hypothesis', *Psychological Medicine* 6: 359–69.

Fishman, M. (1975) 'The brain stem in psychosis', *British Journal of Psychiatry* 126: 414–22.

Flor-Henry, P. (1969) 'Schizophrenic-like reactions and affective psychosis associated with temporal lobe epilepsy: aetiological factors', *American Journal of Psychiatry* 126: 400–4.

— (1976) 'Lateralised temporal-limbic dysfunction and psychopathology', *Annals of the New York Academy of Science* 280: 777–97.

— and Yeudall, L.T. (1979) 'Neuropsychological investigation of schizophrenia and manic-depressive psychosis', in J. Gruzelier and P. Flor-Henry (eds) *Hemispheric Asymmetries of Function in Psychopathology*, Amsterdam: Elsevier, pp.341–62.

Francis, A.F. (1979) 'Familial basal ganglia calcification and schizophreniform psychosis', *British Journal of Psychiatry* 135:360–2.

Frith, C.D. (1979) 'Consciousness, information processing and schizophrenia', *British Journal of Psychiatry* 134: 225–35.

Galin, D. (1976) 'Hemispheric specialization: implications for psychiatry', in R.G. Grenell and S. Gabay (eds) *Biological Foundations of Psychiatry, Vol.1.*, New York: Raven Press, pp.145–76.

Garbutt, J.C. and van Kammen, D.P. (1983) 'The interaction between GABA and dopamine: implications for schizophrenia', *Schizophrenia Bulletin* 9: 336–53.

Garelis, E., Gillan, J.C., and Wyatt, R.J. (1975) 'Elevated blood serotonin concentrations in unmedicated chronic schizophrenic patients: a preliminary study', *American Journal of Psychiatry* 132: 184–6.

Gibbs, F.A. (1951) 'Ictal and nonictal psychiatric disorders in temporal lobe epilepsy', *Journal of Nervous and Mental Disease* 113: 522–8.

Glazer, W.M., Charney, D.S., and Heninger, G.R. (1987) 'Noradrenergic function in schizophrenics', *Archives of General Psychiatry* 44: 898–904.

Goldberg, T.E. Weinberger, D.R., Berman, K.F., Pliskin, N.H., and Podd, M.H. (1987) 'Further evidence for dementia of the prefrontal type in schizophrenia', *Archives of General Psychiatry* 44: 1008–14.

Golden C.J., Graber, B., Coffman, J., Berg, R.A., Newlin, D.B., and Bloch, S. (1981) 'Structural brain deficits in schizophrenia: identification by computed tomographic scan density measurements', *Archives of General Psychiatry* 38: 1014–17.

Golden, C.J., McInnes, W.D., Ariel, R.N., Reudrich, S.L., Chu, C-C., Coffman, J.A., and others (1982) 'Cross validation of the ability of the Luria-Nebraska neuropsychological battery to differentiate between chronic schizophrenics with and without ventricular enlargement', *Journal of Consulting and Clinical Psychology* 50: 87–95.

Golden, C.J., Moses, J.A., Zelazowski, R., Graber, B., Zatz, L., Hovarth, T., and Berger, P. (1980) 'Cerebral ventricular size and neuropsychological impairment in young chronic schizophrenics', *Archives of General Psychiatry* 37: 619–23.

Goldstein, K. (1975) 'Functional disturbances in brain damage', in M.F. Reisser (ed.) *American Handbook of Psychiatry IV. Organic Disorder and Psychosomatic Medicine. 2nd Edition*, New York: Basic Books.

Goodwin, F.K., Murphy, D.L., Brodie, H.K.H., and Bunney, W.E. Jr. (1971) 'Levadopa: alterations in behaviour', *Clinical Pharmacology Therapy* 12: 383–96.

Gray, J.A. (1982) *The Neuropsychology of Anxiety: an Enquiry into the Functions of the Septo-hippocampal System*, Oxford: Oxford University Press.

Green, A.R. and Costain, D.W. (1981) *Pharmacology and Biochemistry of Psychiatric Disorders*, London: John Wiley.

Green, P. (1978) 'Interhemispheric transfer in schizophrenia', *Behavioural Psychotherapy* 6: 105–10.

— Glass, A. and O'Callaghan, M.A.J. (1979) 'Some implications of abnormal hemispheric interaction in schizophrenia', in J.H. Gruzelier and P. Flor-Henry (eds) *Hemispheric Asymmetries in Psychopathology*, London: Macmillan Press.

Green, P., Hallett, S., and Hunter, M. (1983) 'Abnormal hemispheric specialisation in schizophrenics and high-risk children', in P. Flor-Henry and J. Gruzelier, (eds) *Laterality and Psychopathology*, Amsterdam: Elsevier.

Griesinger, W. (1845) *Mental Pathology and Therapeutics*, translated 1867, London: New Sydenham Society.

Gruzelier, J. (1981) 'Hemispheric imbalance masquerading as paranoid and non-paranoid syndromes?', *Schizophrenia Bulletin* 7: 662–73.

148

Gulman, N.C., Wildschiodtz, G., and Orbaek, K. (1982) 'Alterations in interhemispheric conduction through the corpus callosum in chronic schizophrenia', *Biological Psychiatry* 17: 585–94.

Gur, R.E. (1978) 'Left hemisphere dysfunction and left hemisphere overactivation in schizophrenia', *Journal of Abnormal Psychology* 87: 226–38.

— (1979) 'Cognitive concomitants of hemispheric dysfunction in schizophrenia', *Archives of General Psychiatry* 36: 269–74.

Hankoff, L.D. and Peress, N.S. (1981) 'Neuropathology of the brain stem in psychiatric disorders', *Biological Psychiatry* 16: 945–52.

Heathfield, K.W.G. (1967) 'Huntington's chorea', *Brain* 90: 203–32.

Hornykiewicz, O. (1982) 'Brain catecholamines in schizophrenia: a good case for noradrenaline', *Nature* 299: 484–6.

Hoyer, S. and Oesterreich, K. (1975) 'Blood flow and oxidative metabolism of the brain in patients with schizophrenia', *Psychiatria Clinica* 8: 304–13.

Huag, J.O. (1962) 'Pneumoencephalographic studies of mental disease', *Acta Psychiatrica Scandinavica* Supplement 165.

Invar, D.H. (1976) 'Functional landscapes of the dominant hemisphere', *Brain Research*, 107: 181–97.

— (1980) 'Abnormal distribution of cerebral activity in chronic schizophrenia: a neuropsychological interpretation', in C. Baxter and T. Melnechuk (eds) *Perspectives in Schizophrenia Research*, New York: Raven Press, pp.107–25.

Jackson, H.F. (1986) 'Is there a schizotoxin?: a critique of the evidence for the major contender – dopamine', in N. Eisenberg and D. Glasgow (eds) *Current Issues in Clinical Psychology, Vol. 5*, Aldershot: Gower.

— Law, J.B., and Ashcroft, J.B. (1988) 'Neurological disorder and Mental Health Act diagnostic classification in mentally abnormal offenders', Moss Side Hospital, UK: unpublished hospital document.

Jacob, H. and Beckmann, H. (1986) 'Prenatal developmental disturbances in the limbic allocortex in schizophrenics', *Journal of Neural Transmission* 65: 303–26.

Janowsky, D.S., El-Yousef, M.K., Davis, J.M., and Sekerke, H.J. (1973) 'Provocation of schizophrenic symptoms by intravenous administration of methyl phenidate', *Archives of General Psychiatry* 28: 181–5.

Jernigan, T.L., Zatz, L.M., Moses, J.A., and Berger, P.A. (1982) 'Computed tomography in schizophrenics and normal volunteers: I. Fluid volume'. *Archives of General Psychiatry* 39: 765–70.

Jernigan, T.L., Zatz, L.M., Moses, J.A., and Cardellins, J.P. (1982) 'Computed tomography in schizophrenics and normal volunteers. II. Cranial asymmetry', *Archives of General Psychiatry* 39: 771–3.

Johnstone, E.C., MacMillan, F., and Crow, T.J. (1987) 'The occurrence of organic disease of possible or probable aetiological significance in a population of 268 cases of first episode schizophrenia', *Psychological Medicine* 17: 371–9.

Johnstone, E.C. Frith, C.D., Crow, T.J., and others (1976) 'Cerebral ventricular size and cognitive impairment in chronic schizophrenia', *Lancet* 2: 924–6.

Johnstone, E.C., Crow, T.J., Ferrier, I.N., Frith, C.D., Owens, D.G.C., Bourne, D.C., and others (1983) 'Adverse effects of anticholinergic medication on positive schizophrenic symptoms', *Psychological Medicine* 13: 513–27.

Jones, G.H. and Miller, J.J. (1981) 'Functional tests of the corpus callosum in schizophrenia', *British Journal of Psychiatry* 139: 553–7.

Joseph, M.H., Frith, C.D., and Waddington, J.L. 'Dopaminergic mechanisms and cognitive deficit in schizophrenia', *Psychopharmacology* 63: 273–80.

Kay, S.R. and Opler, L.A. (1987) 'The positive–negative dimension in schizophrenia: its validity and significance', *Psychiatric Developments* 2: 79–103.

Kelleher, R.T. and Morse, W.H. (1964) 'Escape behavior and punished behavior', *Federal Proceedings* 23: 808–17.

Kety, S.S. (1975) 'A biologist examines the mind and behaviour', in T. Milton (ed.) *Medical Behavioural Science*, Philadelphia: W.B. Saunders Co.

— (1980) 'The syndrome of schizophrenia: unresolved questions and opportunities for research', *British Journal of Psychiatry* 136: 421–36.

Kornetsky, C. (1976) 'Hyporesponsivity of chronic schizophrenic patients to dextroamphetamine', *Archives of General Psychiatry* 33: 1425–8.

Kraepelin, E. (1919) *Dementia Praecox and Paraphrenia*, Edinburgh: Livingston.

Kristensen, O. and Sindrup, E.H. (1978) 'Psychomotor epilepsy and psychosis I: physical aspects', *Acta Neurologica Scandinavica* 57: 361–9.

Lance, J.W. (1976) 'Simple formed hallucinations confined to the area of specific visual field defect', *Brain* 99: 719–34.

Lechin, F.J., van der Dijs, B., Gomez, F., Lechin, E., Oramas, O. and Villa, S. (1983) 'Positive symptoms of acute psychosis: Dopaminergic or noradrenergic overactivity', *Research Communications in Psychology, Psychiatry and Behaviour* 8: 23–54.

Leff, J.P. and Wing, J.K. (1971) 'Trial of maintenance therapy in schizophrenia', *British Medical Journal* 3: 599–604.

Levin, H.S., Benton, A.L., and Grossman, R.G. (1982) *Neurobehavioral Consequences of Closed Head Injury*, New York: Oxford University Press, pp. 172–88.

Levine, D.N. and Finklestein, S. (1982) 'Delayed psychosis after right temporoparietal stroke or trauma', *Neurology* 32: 267–73.

Levine, D.N. and Grek, A. (1984) 'The anatomical basis of delusions after right cerebral infarction', *Neurology* 34: 577–82.

Lidsky, T.I., Weinhold, P.M., and Levine, F.M. (1979) 'Implication for basal ganglionic dysfunction for schizophrenia', *Biological Psychiatry* 14: 3–12.

Lieberman, A., Neophytides, A., Kupersmith, M., Casson, I., Durso, R. Foo, S.H., Khayali, M., Tartaro, T., and Goldstein, M. (1979) 'Treatment of Parkinson's disease with dopamine agonists: a review', *American Journal of Medical Science* 278: 65–78.

Lingjaerde, O. (1982) 'Effects of the benzodiazepine derivative estrazdam in patients with auditory hallucinations: a multicentre double-blind cross-over study', *Acta Psychiatrica Scandinavica* 63: 339–54.

— (1983) 'Serotonin uptake and efflux in blood platelets from untreated and neroleptic-treated schizophrenics', *Biological Psychiatry* 18: 1345–56.

Lucas, A.R., Warner, K., and Gottlieb, J.S. (1971) 'Biological studies in childhood schizophrenia: serotonin uptake by platelets', *Biological Psychiatry* 3: 123–8.

Luchins, D.J. and Meltzer, H.Y. (1986) 'A comparison of CT findings in acute and chronic ward schizophrenics', *Psychiatry Research* 17: 7–14.

Luchins, D.J., Bigelow, L.B., and Wyatt, R.J. (1980) [cited in Seidman, L.J. (1984)] 'Schizophrenia and brain dysfunction: an integration of recent neurodiagnostic findings', *Psychological Bulletin* 94: 195–238.

Luchins, D.J., Weinberger, D.R., and Wyatt, R.J. (1979) 'Schizophrenia: evidence for a subgroup with reversed cerebral asymmetry', *Archives of General Psychiatry* 36: 1309–11.

— (1982) 'Schizophrenia and cerebral asymmetry detected by computed tomography', *American Journal of Psychiatry* 139: 753–7.

Luchins, D.J., Morihisa, J.M., Weinberger, D.R., and Wyatt, R.J. (1981) 'Cerebral asymmetry and cellular atrophy in schizophrenia: a controlled post-mortem study', *American Journal of Psychiatry* 138: 1501–3.

Luria, A.R. (1973) *The Working Brain*, New York: Basic Books.

McClelland, H., Roth, M., and Neubauer, H. (1966) 'Some observations on a case material based on patients with certain common schizophrenic symptoms', *paper presented at the World Congress of Psychiatry*, Madrid.

McKay, S.E., Golden, C.J., and Scott, M. (1981) 'Neuropsychological correlates of auditory and visual hallucinations', *International Journal of the Neurosciences* 15: 87–94.

McKenna, P.J. (1987) 'Pathology, phenomenology, and the dopamine hypothesis of schizophrenia', *British Journal of Psychiatry* 151: 228–301.

McLean, D.R. and Nihei, T. (1977) 'Uptake of dopamine and 5-hydroxytryptamine by platelets from patients with Huntington's chorea', *Lancet* i: 249–50.

Magaro, P.A. and Chamrad, D.L. (1983) 'Information processing and lateralisation in schizophrenia', *Biological Psychiatry* 18: 29–44.

Maher, B.A. (1974) 'Delusional thinking and perceptual disorder', *Journal of Individual Psychology* 30: 98–113.

Malamud, N. (1967) 'Psychiatric disorder with intracranial tumours of the limbic system', *Archives of Neurology* 17: 113–23.

Malec, J. (1978) 'Neuropsychological assessment of schizophrenics versus brain damage: a review', *Journal of Nervous and Mental Disease* 166: 507–16.

Mason, S.T. (1984) *Catecholamines and Behaviour*, Cambridge: Cambridge University Press.

Mathew, R.J., Meyer, J.S., Francis, D.J., Schoolan, J.C., Weinman, M., and Mortell, K.F. (1981) 'Regional cerebral blood flow in schizophrenia: a preliminary report', *American Journal of Psychiatry* 138: 112–13.

Merrin, E.L. (1981) 'Schizophrenia and asymmetry. An evaluation of evidence for dominant lobe dysfunction', *Journal of Nervous and Mental Disease* 169: 405–16.

Mesulam, M.M. and Geschwind, N. (1978) 'On the possible role of neocortex and its limbic connections in attention and schizophrenia', in L.C. Wynne, R.L. Cromwell, and S. Matthysse (eds) *The Nature of Schizophrenia*, New York: J. Whiley, Ch.14, pp.161–6.

Mesulam, M.M., Waxman, S.G., Geschwind, N., and Sabin, T.D. (1976) 'Acute confusional states with right middle cerebral artery infarction', *Journal of Neurology, Neurosurgery and Psychiatry* 39: 84–9.

Mirsky, A.F. (1969) 'Neuropsychological bases of schizophrenia', Annual Review of Psychology 20: 321–48.

Nasrallah, H.A. (1982) 'Laterality and hemispheric dysfunction in schizophrenia', in F.A. Henn and H.A. Nasrallah (eds) *Schizophrenia as a Brain Disease*, New York: Oxford University Press, Ch. 13, pp. 273–94.

— and McChesney, C.M. (1981) 'Psychopathology of corpus callosum tumours', *Biological Psychiatry* 16: 663–9.

Nasrallah, H.A., McCalley-Witters, M., and Kuperman, S. (1982) 'Neurological differences between paranoid and non-paranoid schizophrenics: pt 1. Sensory-motor lateralisation', *Journal of Clinical Psychiatry* 43: 305–6.

Nasrallah, H.A., Risch, S.C., and Fowler, R.C. (1979) 'Reserpine, serotonin and schizophrenia', *American Journal of Psychiatry* 136: 856–7.

Nielsen, J.M. (1958) 'Cerebral localization and the psychoses', *Research Publication of Association for Research in Nervous and Mental Diseases* 36: 467–77.

Opler, L.A., Kay, S.R., Rosado, V., and Lindenmayer, J.P. (1984) 'Positive and negative syndromes in chronic schizophrenic inpatients', *Journal of Nervous and Mental Disease* 172: 317–25.

Overton, D.A. (1966) 'State-dependent learning produced by depressant and atropine-like drugs', *Psychopharmacologia* 10: 6–31.

Owen, F., Cross, A.J., Crow, T.J., Longden, A., Poulter, M., and Riley, G.J. (1978) 'Increased dopamine receptor sensitivity in schizophrenia', *Lancet* ii: 223–8.

Owen, R., Owen, F., Poulter, M., and Crow, T.J. (1984) 'Dopamine D2 receptors in substantia nigra in schizophrenia', *Brain Research* 299: 152–4.

Owens, D.G.C., Johnstone, E.C., and Frith, C.D. (1982) 'Spontaneous involuntary disorders of movement: their prevalence, severity and distribution in chronic schizophrenics with and without treatment with neuroleptics', *Archives of General Psychiatry* 39: 452–61.

Parnas, J., Korsgaard, S., Krautwald, O., and Jensen, P.S. (1982) 'Chronic psychosis and epilepsy', *Acta Psychiatrica Scandinavica* 66: 282–93.

Pavlov, I.P. (1973) *Lectures on Conditioned Reflexes*, New York: International Publishers Co.

Persons, J.B. (1986) 'The advantages of studying psychological phenomena rather than psychiatric diagnosis', *American Psychologist* 41: 1252–60.

Post, R.M., Fink, E., Carpenter, W.T., and Goodwin, F.K. (1975) 'Cerebrospinal fluid amine metabolites in acute schizophrenia', *Archives of General Psychiatry* 32: 1063–9.

Pritchard, P.B. III, Lombrosko, C.T., and McIntyre, M. (1980) 'Psychological complications of temporal lobe epilepsy', *Neurology* 30: 227–32.

Ramani, S.V. (1981) 'Psychosis associated with frontal lobe lesions in Schilder's cerebral sclerosis: a case report with C.T. scan evidence', *Journal of Clinical Psychiatry* 42: 250–2.

Randall, P.L. (1980) 'A neuroanatomical theory on the aetiology of schizophrenia', *Medical Hypotheses* 6: 645–58.

Rappaport, M., Hopkins, H.K., Hall, K., Belleza, T., and Silverman, J. (1978) 'Are there schizophrenics for whom drugs may be unnecessary or contra-indicated?', *International Journal of Pharmacopsychiatry* 13: 110–11.

Rastogi, R.B., Radhey, L., Lapierre, S., and Lapierre, I.D. (1981) 'Effects of short and long-term neuroleptic treatment on brain serotonin synthesis and turnover: focus on the serotonin hypothesis of schizophrenia', *Life Science* 29: 735–41.

Reider, R. Donelly, E., Herdt, J., and Waldman, I. (1979) 'Sulcal prominence in young chronic schizophrenic patients: CT scan findings associated with impairment on neuropsychological tests', *Psychiatry Research* 1: 1–8.

Reveley, D.A. (1985) 'CT scans and schizophrenia', *British Journal of Psychiatry* 146: 367–71.

Reynolds, G.P., Riederer, P., Jellinger, K., and Gabriel, E. (1981) 'Dopamine receptors and schizophrenia: the neuroleptic drug problem', *Neuropharmacology* 20: 1319–20.

Reynolds, G.P., Reynolds, L.M., Riederer, P., Jellinger, K., and Gabriel, E. (1980) 'Dopamine receptors and schizophrenia: drug effect or illness', *Lancet* ii: 1251.

Rochford, J.M., Detre, T., Tucker, G.J., and Harrow, M. (1970) 'Neuropsychological impairments in functional psychiatric diseases', *Archives of General Psychiatry* 22: 114–19.

Rogers, D. (1985) 'The motor disorders of severe psychiatric illness: a conflict of paradigms', *British Journal of Psychiatry* 1457: 221–32.

Rose, S.P. (1984) 'Disordered molecules and diseased minds', *Journal of Psychiatric Research* 18: 351–9.

Rosenthal, R. and Bigelow, L.B. (1972) 'Quantitative brain measurements in chronic schizophrenia', *British Journal of Psychiatry* 121: 259–64.

Schlesinger, B. (1950) 'Mental changes in intracranial tumours', *Confinia Neurologica* 10: 225–63.

Seidman, L.J. (1984) 'Schizophrenia and brain dysfunction: an integration of recent neurodiagnostic findings', *Psychological Bulletin* 94: 195–238.

Shagass, C., Josiassen, R.C., Roemer, R.A., Straumanis, J.J., and Slepner, S.M. (1983) 'Failure to replicate evoked potential observations suggesting corpus callosum dysfunction in schizophrenia', *British Journal of Psychiatry* 142: 471–6.

Sheldon, E.J. and Knight, R.G. (1984) 'Inter-hemispheric transmission times in schizophrenics', *British Journal of Clinical Psychology* 23: 227–8.

Siegel, R.K. and Jarvik, M.E. (1975) 'Drug-induced hallucinations in animal and man', in R.K. Siegel and I..J. West (eds) *Hallucinations: Behavior, Experience and Theory*, London: Wiley.

Silbergeld, E.K. and Hruska, R.E. (1979) 'Lisuride and LSD: dopaminergic and serotonergic interactions in the "serotonin syndrome"', *Psychopharmacology* 65: 233–7.

Siminov, P.V. (1986) *The Emotional Brain*, New York: Plenum Press.

Singh, M.M. and Kay, S.R. (1975a) 'A comparative study of haloperidol and chlorpromazine in terms of clinical effects and therapeutic reversal with benztropine in schizophrenia: theoretical implications for potency differences amongst neuroleptics', *Psychopharmacologia* 43: 103–13.

— (1975b) 'A longitudinal therapeutic comparison between two prototypic neuroleptics (haloperidol and chlorpromazine in matched groups of schizophrenics. Non-therapeutic interaction with trihexyphenidyl. Theoretical implications for mode of action', *Psychopharmacologia* 43: 115–23.

— and Opler, I..A. (1987) 'Anticholinergic–neuroleptic antagonism in terms of positive and negative symptoms of schizophrenia: implications for psychobiological subtyping', *Psychological Medicine* 17: 39–48.

Slade, P.D. and Bentall, R.P. (1988) *Sensory Deceptions: Toward a Scientific Analysis of Hallucinations*, London: Croom Helm.

Slater, E., Beard, A.W., and Glithero, E. (1963) 'The schizophrenic-like illness of epilepsy', *British Journal of Psychiatry* 109: 95–150.

Small, J.G., Small, I.F., Field, S.P., and Hayden, M.P. (1966) 'Organic cognates of acute illness', *American Journal of Psychiatry* 122: 790–7.

Sneddon, J.M. (1973) 'Blood platelets as a model for monoaminergic-containing neurons', *Progress in Neurobiology* 1: 151–98.

Stahl, S.M. (1977) 'The human platelet: a diagnostic and research tool for the study of biogenic amines in psychiatric and neurological disorders', *Archives of General Psychiatry* 34: 509–16.

Sternberg, D.E., van Kammen, D.P., Lake, C.R., Ballenger, J.C., Marder, S.R., and Bunney, W.E. (1981) 'The effect of pimozide on CSF norepinephrine in schizophrenia', *American Journal of Psychiatry* 138: 1045–51.

Storey, P.B. (1966) 'Lumbar air encephalography in chronic schizophrenia: a controlled experiment', *British Journal of Psychiatry* 112: 135–44.

Stuss, D.T. and Benson, D.F. (1985) *The Frontal Lobes*, New York, Raven Press.

Tatetsu, S. (1964) 'A contribution to the morphological background of schizophrenia: with special reference to the findings in the telencephalon', *Acta Neuropathologica* 3: 558–71.

Taylor, D.C. (1975) 'Factors influencing the occurrence of schizophrenic-like psychosis in patients with temporal lobe epilepsy', *Psychological Medicine* 5: 249–54.

Taylor, J. (1987) 'Frontal lobe dysfunction in chronic schizophrenic offenders', Presented at the Annual General Meeting of the Special Hospital Psychologists Advisory Group, Park Lane Hospital, Maghull, England.

Taylor, M.A., Redfield, J., and Abrams, R. (1981) 'Neuropsychological dysfunction in schizophrenia and affective disease', *Biological Psychiatry* 16: 467–78.

Theodorau, A., Gommeren, W., Clow, A., Leysen, J., Jenner, P., and Marsend, C.D. (1981) 'Chronic neuroleptic treatment specifically alters the number of dopamine receptors in rat brain', *Life Science* 28: 1621–7.

Torrey, E.F. (1980) 'Neurological abnormalities in schizophrenic patients', *Biological Psychiatry* 15: 381–8.

— and Peterson, M.R. (1974) 'Schizophrenia and the limbic system', *Lancet* ii: 942–6.

Toumisto, J., Tukiainen, E., and Ahlfors, U.G. (1979) 'Decreased uptake of 5-hydroxytryptamine in blood platelets from patients with endogenous depression', *Psychopharmacology* 65: 141–7.

Tress, K.H., Kugler, B.T., and Caudrey, D.J. (1979) 'Interhemispheric integration in schizophrenia', in J. Gruzelier and P. Flor-Henry (eds) *Hemisphere Asymmetries of Function in Psychopathology*, Amsterdam: Elsevier, pp.449–62.

Trimble, M. and Kingsley, D. (1978) 'Cerebral ventricular size in chronic schizophrenia', *Lancet* i: 278–9.

Van Kammen, D.P. (1979) 'The dopamine hypothesis of schizophrenia revisited', *Psychoneuroendocrinology* 4: 37–9.

Venables, P.H. (1964) 'Input dysfunction in schizophrenia', in B.A. Maher (ed.) *Progress in Experimental Personality Research*, vol. 1, New York: Academic Press, pp. 1–56.

— (1977) 'Input dysfunction in schizophrenia', in B. Maher (ed.) *Contributions to the psychopathology of schizophrenia*, New York, Academic Press, pp. 1–56.

Weinberger, D.R. and Wyatt, R.J. (1982) 'Brain morphology in schizophrenia: in vivo studies', in F.A. Henn and H.A. Nasrallah (eds) *Schizophrenia as a Brain Disease*, New York: Oxford University Press, Ch. 8, pp. 148–75.

Weinberger, D.R., Torrey, E.F., Neophytides, A.N., and Wyatt, R.J. (1979a) 'Lateral cerebral ventricular enlargement in chronic schizophrenia', *Archives of General Psychiatry* 36: 735–9.

— (1979b) 'Structural abnormalities in the cerebral cortex of chronic schizophrenic patients', *Archives of General Psychiatry* 36: 935–9.

Weinstein, M.R. (1954) 'Histopathological changes in the brain in schizophrenia: a critical review', *A.M.A. Archives of Neurology and Psychiatry* 71: 539–53.

Weller, M. and Kluger, B. (1979) 'Tactile discrimination in schizophrenic and affective psychoses', in J. Gruzelier and P. Flor-Henry (eds) *Hemispheric Asymmetries of Function in Psychopathology*, Amsterdam: Elsevier, pp. 463–74.

Wexler, B.E. (1980) 'Cerebral laterality and psychiatry: a review of the literature', *American Journal of Psychiatry* 137: 279–91.

Williams, D. (1968) 'Man's temporal lobe', *Brain* 91: 639–54.

Wyatt, R.J., Vaughan, T., Galanter, M., Kaplan, J., and Green, R. (1972) 'Behavioural changes of chronic schizophrenic patients given 1-5-hydroxytryptophan', *Science* 177: 1124–6.

Wyatt, R.J., Potkin, S.G., Kleinman, J.E., Weinberger, D.R., Luchins, D.J., and Jeste, D.V. (1981) 'The schizophrenic syndrome: examples of biological tools for subclassification', *Journal of Nervous and Mental Disease* 169: 110–12.

Zohar, J., Mueller, E.A., Insel, T.R., Zohar-Kadouch, R.C., and Murphy, D.L. (1987) 'Serotonin responsivity in obsessive–compulsive disorder: comparison of patients and healthy controls', *Archives of General Psychiatry* 44: 946–51.

Chapter Six

CAN A DISEASE MODEL OF SCHIZOPHRENIA SURVIVE?

GORDON CLARIDGE

DISEASE: SOME THEORETICAL ISSUES

The title of this chapter poses a question which, in the heady Laingian days of the 1960s, many would have regarded as merely rhetorical. For most of that decade – and a little while beyond – schizophrenia seemed about to shake off its medical strait-jacket for good and be reconstructed as a form of suffering having its origins, not in a diseased brain, but in the social and psychological circumstances of victimized or labelled individuals. That such a formulation should fail was inevitable since, like all protest movements, the alternative psychiatry of the day overstated its case and stubbornly refused to see anything of worth in the professional Establishment's perspective on, and management of, schizophrenia. More seriously, they failed their patients and in retrospect it is not – for all its insights and intellectual brilliance – Laing's (1960) *The Divided Self* that makes the greater impact; rather it is David Reed's (1977) *Anna*, the tragic story of an individual schizophrenic who was persuaded by a Laingian doctor to face up to her madness without drugs and whose slow, painful death from self-inflicted burns symbolizes in the most awful way the end of an era in psychiatry.

The subsequent backlash in orthodox psychiatry was such that it has now entered an even more vigorous phase of organic explanation, revitalized by fresh discoveries in biochemistry (Haracz 1982), psychiatric genetics (Gottesman and Shields 1982), and neuropathology, including the newly developed science of brain imaging (Weinberger et al. 1983). Nevertheless, the exact nature and causes of psychotic behaviour remain as mysterious as ever and this revived optimism – that schizophrenia will indeed turn out to be a disease of the nervous system – has not gone unchallenged. As several chapters in this volume reveal, criticism continues to come from a fresh wave of protest that has again taken up some of the themes and arguments of the 1960s.

Another challenge to current medical thinking about schizophrenia – and the one to be developed here – takes a very different form, resting on theoretical considerations and experimental observations that have largely remained outside the more publicized disagreements between psychiatry and antipsychiatry about the relevance of the disease model to schizophrenia. To anticipate somewhat, it will be argued here that it is possible to trace a path between the polarized positions of the two major protagonists in that debate – in short, to propose a model for schizophrenia that recognizes in it some features of disease, but which at the same time calls into question certain assumptions made about the condition by contemporary organic psychiatry. The crux of the argument lies in the nature of disease itself. It is therefore instructive to begin by examining how the term 'disease' has been defined, both by those who have defended and by those who have opposed its use in psychiatry. The first point to be made is, ironically perhaps, best brought out in the writings of the most vehement critic of the notion of 'mental disease': the American psychiatrist, Thomas Szasz (1974, 1976, 1987).

As is well known, for many years Szasz has waged an impassioned campaign against the 'medicalization' of deviant behaviours and forms of suffering that he regards as 'problems in living', rather than as signs of psychiatric disease. Among such conditions he has included schizophrenia; indeed, the latter has regularly formed a major focus for his arguments. In the most recent return to his theme Szasz (1987) recapitulates and enlarges on the reasons why he thinks it is wrong to regard schizophrenia (and other 'functional' psychoses) as diseases. Szasz defines disease or illness (he uses the terms synonymously) quite uncontroversially, as 'a structural or functional abnormality of cells, tissues, organs, or bodies'. He then goes on to attack orthodox psychiatry with his familiar 'seduction' argument: that having had some success in the past in discovering a physical basis for one disorder of the mind (i.e. neurosyphilis as a cause of General Paralysis of the Insane (GPI), psychiatry has since laboured under the delusion that, with advances in science, schizophrenia will yield up a comparable secret; despite the fact that after nearly 100 years of intensive research it has failed to do so. He calls this self-deception the 'historical transformation of suspected diseases into proven diseases'.

Up to this point Szasz's argument is, if not conclusive, at least persuasive. However, it is important to note that it is only so because of the definition of 'disease' he chooses to adopt; for this allows him to conclude that, if schizophrenia *were* to be a disease, it would necessarily have to be a *neurological* disease, after the fashion of, say, Huntington's chorea, Alzheimer's disease, or, indeed, GPI. In other words, he limits his definition to the classic 'lesion' notion of disease, in which there is a demonstrable pathophysiology and a discrete cause. (It is interesting to note in passing that, to help make his case, Szasz commits his own subtle transformation of terminology when he quickly substitutes 'lesion' for the broader term, 'functional abnormality', in his own definition of disease. This shift is actually quite significant because it excludes other and, as argued later, more appropriate applications of the concept to schizophrenia.)

If Szasz restricts his terms of reference for debating the place of the disease concept in psychiatry, then he is, to be fair to him, merely meeting those he is criticizing on their own ground. For it is in fact true that the organic psychiatry he attacks *is* still largely wedded to a traditional neurological or lesion model of schizophrenia; as witness, for example, very recent attempts to revive an old-fashioned theory that it is due to a virus (Crow 1984).

By confining their debate to a particular, limited meaning of 'disease', both conventional psychiatry and its critics in the radical-psychiatry movement have each, in their albeit different ways, excluded a proper discussion of the disease concept itself; and particularly of two related and very important issues which, we shall argue here, bear closely on our understanding of schizophrenia and on its possible status as a disease. These concern, first, the exact nature of the contribution that *biological* factors might make to the causation of mental disorder, and second, the question of *discontinuity* between function and dysfunction in disease.

Because of its commitment to a neurological model for

schizophrenia, organic psychiatry has assumed that the condition is in all respects entirely discontinuous with healthy functioning: that is to say, explaining it can necessarily have no reference point in normal behaviour. In attacking that view the anti-disease lobby has, equally justifiably, pointed out that many of the features of schizophrenia *are* understandable in terms of the psychology of the individual, making a discrete brain lesion an unlikely explanation. Yet its own preferred alternative is also unsatisfactory, for it fails to take any account of the fact that, even to a casual observer, the psychotic state is accompanied by what appears to be a gross disturbance of brain function. Thus, Szasz makes almost no reference except dismissively, to *biological* factors in mental illness, couching his explanation purely in social and sociological terms. Likewise, the Laingian account and its derivatives are fashioned from an existentialist philosophy that pays little or no attention to brain processes.

The evident failure of both sides in this debate to resolve their differences entirely derives from the fact that each has seen incompatibilities where none exist. Conventional psychiatry, for its part, has assumed that a disease view of schizophrenia necessarily precludes a degree of continuity between health and sickness. On the other hand, antipsychiatry and radical psychiatry, while recognizing such continuity, have gone on to reach the wrong conclusions: that schizophrenia cannot therefore have any qualities ascribable to disease, and that studying its biology is irrelevant to our understanding of it. It will be argued here that these confusions stem, in turn, from both sides having debated the question of schizophrenia as disease around an inappropriate version of the medical model. However, before presenting a more viable alternative, it is first necessary to introduce a third viewpoint on the issues discussed so far – one that comes closer than the other two to resolving their common dilemma and which provided a jumping-off ground for the ideas to be presented here.

The view in question is historically and ideologically quite distinct from those of the antipsychiatry and radical-psychiatry movements, but like the latter – and around the same time – it also challenged medical orthodoxy about psychological disorder. I am referring, of course, to Eysenck's equally vehement dismissal of the notion of psychiatric disease (Eysenck 1960). Unlike the more populist anti-disease lobby, however, Eysenck based his attack on statistical and experimental evidence, making two proposals. One was that mental 'illnesses' merely form the end-points of continuously variable behavioural dimensions. The other was that these dimensions have a substantial biological basis, grounded in naturally occurring individual variations in brain functioning. This second postulate was derived historically from the Pavlovian theory of 'nervous types': that temperamental or personality differences partly reflect differences in the underlying properties of the central nervous system (Pavlov 1928; Gray 1964).

The details and subsequent history of Eysenckian theory are too well known to detain us long here. Suffice it to say that it has evolved into a flourishing school of biological personality psychology, with several applications to less serious forms of psychological abnormality (for example, Zuckerman 1979; Gray 1982). In the present context the crucial point is that Eysenck established an important principle, unrecognized by his uneasy bedfellows in the anti-disease camp – *viz.*, that the assumption of an inextricable connection between normal and abnormal does not rule out the importance of biological factors in causation. By joining these two themes together, Eysenck therefore cut through many of the difficulties intrinsic to the debate between psychiatry and its sociologically minded critics.

Even so, Eysenck's formulation was not without its own ambiguities. As an opponent of the disease concept in psychiatry and as an adherent of a *totally* dimensional view, he, in turn, failed to recognize that almost all psychological abnormality involves some *discontinuity* of function – the appearance of symptoms or other rare, or transient, signs of aberration. In other words, he neglected to make the distinction that Foulds (1965) had drawn between enduring traits as descriptors of personality and symptoms as indicators of illness. Nevertheless, in Eysenckian theory a potential (biological) connection between the two could be discerned, opening the way for a perspective on mental disorder that accepts neither the traditional organic model nor the exclusively non-biological view, but which instead attempts to combine certain features of both. Elsewhere (Claridge 1985) I have developed such a theory as a general paradigm for mental disorder and more recently (Claridge 1987) as the model for schizophrenia reproduced below.

Figure 6.1 Hypothetical model for schizophrenia, drawing parallel with hypertension-related disease. Features to be noted in both cases include: continuum of normal functioning describing dimension of vulnerability; arbitrarily definable borderline state of malfunction; and full-blown disease as interaction between exogenous and endogenous factors.

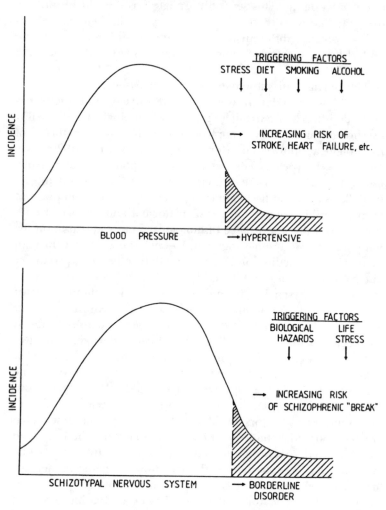

A MODEL FOR SCHIZOPHRENIA

The proposed model is based on a comparison between schizophrenia and what in physical medicine are recognized as the *systemic diseases*. Unlike the infectious diseases and the major gene disorders which, as seen earlier, psychiatrists can be legitimately criticized for having used as their model for mental illness, the systemic diseases have a number of features which, it can be argued, closely parallel those found in schizophrenia. These can be illustrated by reference to an example of a commonly quoted set of systemic disorders, namely, the hypertension-related diseases (see Figure 6.1, upper half).

The first important feature of systemic disease is that it originates in bodily mechanisms which, in their normal condition, perform perfectly healthy adaptive functions, but which are nevertheless capable of bringing about a state of *dysfunction*. Quite explicit in systemic disease, therefore, is the idea of *continuity*, an inescapable connection between illness and health. This continuity can be looked at from two points of view. One is that it merely describes a degree of *normal individual variation* that can be observed in the population on the characteristic relevant to the disease – in this case blood pressure. Another view is as *predisposition to disease:* other things being equal, those with high natural blood pressure will be at greater risk for the systemic diseases associated with it. In these diseases, therefore, continuity refers, at one and the same time, to *both* natural biological variation *and* liability to illness, and knowledge of the mechanisms responsible for the normal state is an essential prerequisite for an understanding of their aberrant functioning.

A second important feature of systemic disease to be noted is that in its mild form or early stages the definition of illness is by no means clear-cut. In the case of essential hypertension this is decided by some arbitrary cut-off point on a quantitative scale of blood pressure, thus giving rise to a spectrum or continuum of dysfunction, rather than a sharply definable, all-or-none, state. At the same time, the further up this continuum of mild disorder the person is, the more likely it is that he or she will suffer the clear discontinuity or catastrophe of severe illness: in this case diseases such as stroke or heart failure.

Finally, as to cause, systemic diseases are almost always multiply determined, coming about through an interaction between the underlying disposition and a range of developmental, accumulating life-load, and short-term triggering factors which combine to push the individual beyond the threshold for clearly recognizable disease.

As illustrated in the lower half of Figure 6.1, I have argued, on the basis of evidence shortly to be discussed, that schizophrenia shows almost identical features, with respect to causation, clinical form, and the dimensional nature of its underlying disposition. The last of these qualities is referred to in Figure 6.1 as the 'schizotypal nervous system': to denote an assumption that the relevant variations will prove to have a biological basis – in the sense in which, in earlier forms of the theory (Claridge 1967, 1972), I proposed that there is a normal 'nervous type' associated with schizophrenia, comparable to those underlying other individual-difference traits that predispose to other psychological disorders. As argued in the second of those earlier papers, at a behavioural level such traits will be observable as cognitive and personality variations which, in moderate degree, are perfectly healthy, adaptive characteristics. In more extreme form, however, they put the individual at increasing risk for biological and psychological *dysfunction,* occurring in some cases as the 'catastrophe' of acute psychotic illness.

It should be emphasized at this point that, in one form or another, almost all of the ideas contained in the model just described have been available in the psychological and/or clinical literature for many years. However, its central feature – the proposed continuity between the normal and the schizophrenic – has recently benefited from a resurgence of interest among clinical and personality psychologists. More detailed consideration of that aspect, including a summary of the current experimental evidence, will be taken up in the next section. Discussion here will be confined to some other observations that support the model.

One feature that deserves further comment is the assumption, based on the parallel drawn here with the physical systemic diseases, that mild or subclinical varieties of schizophrenia can occur. Slow to be accepted in Britain, the notion of schizophrenia as a *spectrum* of disorders is now well-established in US psychiatry; though, in fact, the idea goes back at least far as the descriptions of schizophrenia itself and later emerged in psychoanalysis as the notion of 'borderline' states. Over the past decade these border-line states have received considerable attention from US researchers (*Schizophrenia Bulletin* 1979, 1985; Stone 1980) and formal criteria for diagnosis established (Spitzer et al. 1979). Of the two borderline conditions included in DSM-III (American Psychiatric Association 1980), the most relevant to schizophrenia is that of 'schizotypal personality disorder', the defining features of which are very much those of the full-blown illness, occurring in mild form. Furthermore, there is now good evidence (Kety 1985) that schizotypal disorder and schizophrenia are genetically related, suggesting that the former is a partial expression of similar underlying traits. The genetic evidence in general about schizophrenia also supports the model proposed here. The precise role of genetic factors in the disorder is still problematical and their exact mode of transmission is unknown. What is most likely, however, is that it is the *dispositional* aspects that are inherited, as is true of many other human traits. This conclusion would certainly be consistent with the most plausible theory of the genetics of schizophrenia – namely, the polygenic, diathesis/stress model proposed some 20 years ago by Gottesman and Shields (1968) and reaffirmed in their 1982 book. Their theory readily incorporates the idea of a graded continuum of liability to schizophrenia that can manifest itself as mild disorder or as schizophrenic-like traits existing without signs of overt illness.

It is interesting to note that antedating that theory both Meehl (1962) and Rado (1953) – who first coined the term 'schizotypy' – had already formulated similar genetic models of schizophrenia. Thus, Meehl argued for a biological continuum which he labelled 'schizotaxia', a genetic dimension predisposing to schizophrenia but capable of being expressed in some odd, but otherwise healthy, individuals as 'schizotypy'.

The general idea of a continuum stretching from clinical psychosis right back into normal personality is much older, however, being first represented in Kretschmer's (1925) suggestion that some traits associated with both schizophrenia and manic-depressive psychosis can be used to describe normal temperamental differences. Indeed, it was Kretschmer's proposal for a continuum of 'schizothymia-cyclothymia' that inspired Eysenck's (1952) early contribution to the thinking behind the ideas presented here. Eysenck's own proposal, of course, has been for a *general* personality

on of 'psychoticism' encompassing all forms of psychosis,
...an for a continuum specifically confined to schizophrenia.
.evertheless, his theorizing has been very influential in stimulating
attempts to measure psychotic traits in normal individuals.

PSYCHOTIC TRAITS IN NORMAL PEOPLE

Over the past decade or so experimental and clinical psychologists
have shown considerable interest in the measurement of those
aspects of individual variation which theories such as that
described here suggest have a reference point in clinical psychosis,
especially schizophrenia. Part of the impetus for this work has
been the attempt to identify individuals who may be vulnerable to
psychotic breakdown: as such there is a close convergence (to
which we will return) on similar efforts in the field of longitudinal
high-risk research, described elsewhere in this volume by Peter
Venables (Chapter 7).

The work to be discussed here differs from the longitudinal
approach in two respects. First, it has so far concentrated on *adult*
populations; and second, instead of focusing on individuals already
indentifiable as at risk (for example, according to genetic
criteria), it concentrates on the study of behavioural features that
appear to be definably psychotic. The research in question has
proceeded in two stages or, looked at another way, at two levels of
analysis. The first has been through the use of appropriately
designed questionnaires; the second through the laboratory
investigation of the correlates of such scales, applying one or
other relevant experimental paradigm drawn from the
schizophrenia literature. Research on both of these aspects has
recently been reviewed elsewhere (Claridge 1988), and the
present account will simply attempt to draw together some of the
main themes in the field. It will also serve to update evidence in
what has turned out to be a rapidly accelerating output of
research studies.

As shown in Table 6.1, a large number of questionnaire scales
have now been developed for measuring psychotic-like traits in
normal subjects. These have differed considerably with respect to
the label attached to them, their item content, and the point of
departure which inspired their construction. Nevertheless, they
all have in common the attempt to sample the domain of

Table 6.1 Psychotic trait scales

Scales	Reference(s)	Remarks
Schizotypy	Golden & Meehl (1979)	Items drawn from MMPI[a]
Chapman scales Perceptual aberration	Chapman et al. (1978)	
Magical ideation	Eckblad and Chapman (1983)	Derived from sympto-matology of psychosis, mainly schizophrenia
Social & physical anhedonia	Chapman et al. (1976)	
Hypomanic personality	Eckblad and Chapman (1986)	
STQ	Claridge and Broks (1984)	
Schizotypal personality (STA)		Modelled on DSM-III criteria for 'schizotypal personality disorder'
Borderline personality (STB)		and 'borderline personality disorder'
Predisposition to hallucination	Launay and Slade (1981) Bentall and Slade (1985b)	Perceptual item content
Schizophrenism	Nielsen and Petersen (1976)	Attention/thought-process items
Schizoid cognitions	Rust (1987)	Derived from multiscale inventory of psychotic cognition
Psychoticism (P-scale)	Eysenck and Eysenck (1975)	Part of Eysenck Personality Questionnaire (EPQ)

Note: a. MMPI = Minnesota Multiphasic Personality Inventory.

psychotic – and usually more specifically schizophrenic – character-istics. Their success in doing so has varied but, taken as a whole, the results obtained put beyond reasonable doubt the existence of psychotic characteristics as traits widely distributed in the general population. The questions that remain to be answered, therefore, concern not *whether* such traits occur, but how best to describe them, how they map on to the clinical symptomatology of psychotic disorder, and the extent to which various scales measure common, or different, features. Interest in the last of these questions has very recently led to a small spate of factor-analytic studies that have explored the relationships, either among the different scales shown in Table 6.1 or, in some cases, individual items drawn from them.

It can be stated at the outset that the results of these analyses all agree in suggesting that the term 'schizotypy' – which is being used here as a shorthand descriptor for the traits under consideration – already appears too global and too restrictive. This became clear even in the first of such studies to be reported, that by Muntaner et al. (1988) who factor analysed a small number of the scales, including several of those developed by Chapman and his colleagues, The Eysenck Personality Questionnaire, and a schizotypy questionnaire devised by the present author, the STQ. Muntaner et al. identified three components: 'cognitive', concerned with aberrant perception and thinking; 'affective', specifically anhedonia; and 'antisocial nonconformity', defined by the Eysenck P-scale.

Two other studies of rather different type replicated the results of that analysis, either exactly or in important respects. The first, carried out by Faily and Venables (1986), found precisely the same three factors: notably, these authors chose to factor analyse, not scales, but a large, representative pool of 'schizotypy' *items*. The other analysis – of a limited set of *scales* by Raine and Allbutt (1989) – failed to demonstrate the 'antisocial behaviour' factor, but did identify two major 'cognitive' and 'anhedonia' components, similar to those reported by Muntaner et al.

The most comprehensive analysis to date, however, is one recently carried out as a joint exercise between the Oxford and Liverpool groups and reported by Bentall et al. (1989). The first part of this study utilized eleven psychotic trait scales, together with the remaining three scales from Eysenck's EPQ. Three components were identified, one of which was clearly that of 'anhedonia', previously reported by other workers. The other two factors were both broadly 'cognitive' in nature, but referring to different aspects, not clearly separated out in earlier studies. One was a factor of manifestly perceptual aberration; the other of more general cognitive disorganization associated with anxiety (it had high loadings on Eysenck's neuroticism scale).

Additional evidence for statistically separable components of the cognitive aspects of schizotypy has also come from a recent study by Hewitt and Claridge (1989). They have now analysed the items in the present author's 'schizotypal personality scale' (STA), one of the measures included in the Oxford/Liverpool analysis and found these to be loaded on *both* of the cognitive factors identified by Bentall et al. Consistent with its performance when analysed alongside other scales, it appears that the STA contains different sets of items referring, on the one hand, to unusual perceptual experiences and, on the other, to anxiety-related thinking disorganization, such as paranoid ideation.

In a second stage of their joint study Bentall et al. conducted another factor analysis that included four further scales which had also been administered to their subjects. The scales in question were four delusions measures taken from Foulds's Delusions Symptoms States Inventory (Foulds and Bedford 1975). They were not therefore strictly trait measures; they were designed rather to assess the presence of active symptomatology and, as such, they showed heavily skewed distributions. Nevertheless, their inclusion extended the findings of the earlier analysis in some interesting ways.

In this second analysis *four* factors appeared, one of which was the asocial or antisocial component reported by other workers but not seen in Bentall et al.'s earlier three-factor solution. Otherwise, the factor structure was left largely unchanged by inclusion of Foulds's scales, the three components of anhedonia, cognitive disorganization, and perceptual aberration still being identifiable. The most striking feature was the very high loadings of all four delusions scales on the perceptual aberration factor. In other words, the presence of delusional symptomatology – even in normal subjects – appeared to be closely linked to those (cognitive) traits of schizotypy having the most obvious 'psychotic' content. This last result, together with other evidence from the factor analyses described, suggests that different components of 'schizotypy' might map in sensible ways on to different features of schizophrenia, representing at the trait or dispositional level the heterogeneity of the clinical phenomena.

The varied manifestation of schizophrenic symptomatology has long been a cause for debate and research and several ways of conceptualizing it have been suggested. In an early publication (Claridge 1967), for example, I proposed, on the basis of psychophysiological evidence, a distinction between 'active' and 'retarded' types of psychosis, the former being characterized by florid symptomatology and the latter by poverty of expression. It is tempting to see some parallel between that grouping and the, respectively, cognitive and anhedonia components of 'schizotypy' consistently found in the trait analyses reviewed here. What makes this especially convincing – given my early observation that retarded psychosis was associated, in the personality domain, with *introversion* – is the finding now that the latter does indeed seem to be a strong constituent of anhedonia when measured in normal individuals (Muntaner et al. 1988; Bentall et al. 1989).

There is an obvious link, too, with the very similar distinction currently made by some psychiatrists between so-called 'positive' and 'negative' schizophrenic symptoms (Crow 1980). In fact, this is explicitly stated in the Bentall et al. study, though the authors also point out that a simple positive/negative symptom dichotomy may be incomplete. Here they quote from a recent factor-analytic study of symptom data collected on schizophrenic patients by Liddle (1987). He has argued for *three* psychotic syndromes, two of which correspond to the traditional positive and negative categories, the third being associated with cognitive disorganization. Bentall et al. note that the last of these might be aligned with the second of the cognitive components identified in their own analysis of psychotic traits.

As mentioned earlier, in parallel with their studies at the questionnaire level, many investigators have undertaken experimental research, designed to throw light on the underlying nature of schizotypy. The usual strategy has been to take some objective feature of schizophrenia and then try to map it across into normal samples selected according to scores on particular psychotic trait scales.

It should be said that, compared with the questionnaire studies, a less coherent picture has emerged. There are probably two reasons for this. First, researchers have almost always used just one scale of 'schizotypy' or 'psychoticism' to select their subjects of study; and, as I have just argued, different scales are certainly tapping different aspects of what can no longer be regarded as a single global trait. Second, the experimental paradigms chosen as guidelines for the research have varied considerably: these have included psychophysiological, cognitive, and neuropsychological approaches to the problem, and, even within these broad areas, different paradigms have been adopted.

Table 6.2 Summary of experimental approaches to schizotypy

A. Psychophysiological		
Anhedonia	Electrodermal Hyporesponsiveness	Simons (1981, 1982)
Schizophrenism	Electrodermal hyperresponsiveness	Nielsen and Petersen (1976)
Psychoticism	Electrodermal hyporesponsiveness	Robinson and Zahn (1985)
Psychoticism	Physiological 'dissociation'	Claridge and Birchall (1978)
B. Neuropsychological		
Schizotypal personality	Hemisphere asymmetry differences	Broks (1984) Rawlings and Claridge (1984) Broks et al. (1984)
Schizoid personality	Ditto	Raine and Manders (1988)
C. Cognitive		
Perceptual aberration	Idiosyncratic word association	Miller and Chapman (1983)
Psychoticism	Divergent thinking	Woody and Claridge (1977)
Hallucinatory predisposition	Altered reality testing (Signal detection)	Bentall and Slade (1985a)
Schizotypy	Slow processing (backward masking)	Steronko and Woods (1978) Nakano and Saccuzzo (1985)
Psychoticism	Weak cognitive inhibition (semantic priming)	Bullen and Hemsley (1984)
Schizotypal personality	Ditto (negative priming)	Beech and Claridge (1987) Beech et al. (1989)

Nevertheless, as the studies summarized in Table 6.2 demonstrate, out of this work has come a considerable amount of empirical evidence for the model of schizophrenia proposed in this chapter. Mirroring observations made on schizophrenic

171

patients, normal subjects high in schizotypal or more general psychotic traits have been found to resemble their clinical counterparts in a variety of ways: profiles of psychophysiological response, modes of information processing, and patterns of hemisphere organization.

If a single theme to explain such differences has yet to be discovered, then that is no less true of the comparable data obtained in the patient research from which the normal studies derive. In both cases there is a clear need to find some unifying construct or set of constructs that can explain variations crossing such different domains of behaviour as those sampled in current experimental research on schizotypy and schizophrenia. It could be argued that all three types of approach referred to in Table 6.2 have some advantages and disadvantages in that respect. Psychophysiological models certainly remain close to the biological processes which I have argued here define the 'nervous typological' dispositions to schizophrenia; but the theoretical constructs of such models make it difficult to visualize the actual mechanisms of clinical symptomatology. Cognitive paradigms fare better in that respect, but the language of the 'black box' in which they are couched leave them distant from the nervous system. The neuropsychological approach – i.e. hemisphere studies – might seem to combine the advantages of both, especially in view of the interest it has generated in the field of patient research (Wexler 1980; Walker and McGuire 1982; Gruzelier 1983). Its current drawback, however, is that hemisphere research has a weak base in normal individual-differences psychology. This is in marked contrast with the cognitive and psychophysiological approaches, which have the benefit of being able to draw generously on data and theory about normal individual variations.

An encouraging feature of the research on adult schizotypy is the sharpening convergence between questionnaire-based studies of the kind referred to here and those starting with the investigation of biologically at-risk children. Thus, workers in both fields of enquiry are adopting identical paradigms, for example from hemisphere research (Green et al. 1983; Hallett et al. 1986); while reviews of the experimental literature on, for example, the cognitive mechanisms of schizophrenia reveal a blurred distinction between the two topic areas (Nuechterlein and

Dawson 1984) In other words, the aims of longitudinal high-risk research are increasingly being defined not as the search for a single cause of schizophrenia, but as the description of multiple traits of individual variation which, while not unhealthy in themselves, make some children vulnerable to later psychotic breakdown. Bearing in mind the model for schizophrenia proposed here, it is therefore interesting to note some recent remarks by Watt (1984), summarizing two decades of high-risk research. Paraphrasing the conclusions of Mednick, a pioneer in the field, he notes:

> High-risk samples, of course, include relatively few future schizophrenics, so the conceptual significance of findings may change as psychological outcomes unfold. For the present, Mednick concludes that there may be no monolithic schizophrenic disorder that follows predictable rules of genetic transmission, as phenylketonuria and Huntington's chorea do. Consequently, he recommends that we look for 'degrees of schizophrenicity' or schizophrenic vulnerability, which obviously calls for subtle and complex conceptions of the disorder.
>
> (ibid.: 593)

FURTHER OBSERVATIONS

The construction of schizophrenia offered here accepts neither the traditional view of organic psychiatrists, nor that of their critics in antipsychiatry. It proposes, instead, that schizophrenia is essentially a *psychobiological* disturbance of function, arising out of an interaction between a disposition to react to events in a particular way and the impact of those events on a vulnerable individual. In considering the form of the underlying disposition, particular stress has been placed on its biological qualities. There are good reasons for this, stemming from theoretical arguments, empirical evidence to which I have referred, and the appearance of the psychotic state itself.

This emphasis on biological aspects should not be taken to mean, however, that formulations at other levels of description are invalid. On the contrary, as noted in the previous section, ideas drawn, for example, from cognitive psychology – which currently has minimal underpinning in neurophysiology – may be extremely useful in conceptualizing the transition from disposition to active symptomatology: for many of the central symptoms of schizophrenia are cognitive in form and it is entirely appropriate that attempts to understand them should make use of what is already known about normal information processing. The more important point, at the present stage of knowledge, is the principle that disorder and health in schizophrenia are not entirely separable domains, psychosis being an aberration of mechanisms responsible for normal functioning. The level at which those mechanisms are studied – and therefore the terminology in which particular explanations are cast – are likely to remain, for the moment at least, as varied as those adopted in general psychology.

There is, however, one particular – and in some quarters still controversial – sense in which the issue of a biological element in schizophrenia is crucial to our understanding. This concerns the influence of genetic factors. Some authors, even quite recently, have challenged the opinion that such factors play any part in schizophrenia (Rose et al. 1984) – despite considerable evidence to the contrary and including, incidentally, the unique success (compared with other methods) with which longitudinal high-risk studies have used genetic criteria to identify vulnerable individuals.

The extreme position adopted by critics of genetics research stems, I believe, from the same misunderstandings as those which, at the beginning of this chapter, I argued accounted for their outright rejection of a disease model of schizophrenia: that is to say, they have assumed that the only possibility available is of schizophrenia as a single, or major, gene disorder. Yet I have shown here that even many geneticists have reached a different conclusion, proposing a *continuum* of genetic effects which may have varying phenotypic expression and which no longer demand a view of schizophrenia as disease in the sense in which the critics have insisted. In terms of the model presented here, genetic influences would therefore be seen as having exactly the same status as they have in determining other quantitatively variable human charcteristics, such as extraversion, anxiety-proneness, intelligence – and blood pressure.

Of course, some commentators would even wish to deny an

inheritable component in *any* human psychological differences, whether these refer to healthy variations or to pathology. That, however, is to fly in the face of numerous investigations in psychogenetics research – including, incidentally, a very recent biometrical study of schizotypal traits in normal subjects, demonstrating a significant degree of heritability (Claridge and Hewitt 1987). To reject such evidence is also to make an absurd assumption: that the nervous system – which is after all the biological vehicle for psychological processes – constitutes the only system in the body immune to genetic influences. As described elsewhere (Claridge 1985), there are many nervous 'properties', which themselves relate to temperamental or personality variations, that are under some genetic control. It would be unlikely if 'schizotypy' were an exception.

There is, of course, an understandable fear by the anti-genetics school that admission of a role for inherited factors in, say, personality is to give in to a naïve determinism; that, extrapolated to schizophrenia, it removes the need to consider other influences on the emergence of the disorder, the psychotic person then merely being seen as a passive victim of his or her genes. It is possible to construe the matter differently, however, for the following reasons.

As Watt, from whom I quoted earlier, intimates, it is well documented in high-risk research that many heavily genetically vulnerable children do *not* proceed to psychotic breakdown in later life: on the contrary, they frequently go on to achieve a perfectly adequate, or even superior, adult adjustment (Bleuler 1984). These observations have recently led to a different perspective being placed on high-risk data and a growing interest in so-called 'invulnerable children' who, despite an unfavourable beginning (frequently social as well as biological) nevertheless remain well (Anthony and Cohler 1987).

This varying outcome for children 'at risk' – which is of course entirely predictable from the model proposed here – raises many interesting questions about the precise manner in which genetic vulnerability, life experience, and immediate social influences interact in schizophrenia. At the biological end, a crucial issue concerns the exact quality of the 'schizotypal nervous system' that makes it abnormally receptive to those events that precipitate schizophrenic breakdown; or, alternatively, able to flourish in favourable environments. In the social domain it is equally important to ask what the vital elements are that make the environment pathological or benign.

Here I have deliberately avoided such questions, concentrating instead on addressing not what causes schizophrenia, but what kind of disorder it might be. However, it is worth making some brief general observations on the former point. I am thinking here of recent work, in social psychiatry, on the influence of 'expressed emotion' in families on the course of schizophrenia (Leff and Vaughn 1985; see also Chapter 10 by Tarrier in this volume). It seems increasingly probable that the quality of interpersonal interaction in the family setting – as revealed in expressed-emotion research – is also an important factor contributing to the *emergence* of schizophrenia; not as a sole cause of the disorder, but because it is peculiarly pathogenic for certain 'schizotypal' individuals. Thus, the latter's nervous typological characteristics can readily be understood as contributing to the effect: that is to say, ambiguous, critical, or otherwise emotion-laden communications from others might have a greater than normal impact on the vulnerable family member, precisely because he or she is unduly sensitive to, or more likely to distort, their meaning.

Several of the experimental paradigms for schizotypy discussed in the previous section point to possible ways in which, on the receiver's side, this interplay between social influences and the individual's 'nervous type' might be mediated. These include poorly modulated arousal, weakly regulated controls at certain stages of cognitive analysis, and, in the neuropsychological domain, an unusual form of interhemispheric organization, particularly with respect to the processing of perceptual, affective, and linguistic information. It is not difficult to visualize, in general terms, how any of these features could put the schizotypal person at disadvantage in the complex settings of social interaction, especially those of an emotionally distressing nature.

The problem for experimentalists in schizotypy research is to understand such mechanisms in detail and to find a common principle that could account for the results of studies based on quite different paradigms. Elsewhere (Claridge 1987) I have noted that many investigators, working from quite different points of view, have made explicit use of the idea that schizophrenia (and hence schizotypy) might involve a relative weakening of some aspect of the *inhibitory* mechanisms which, at all levels of the nervous system, regulate its activity. The merit of this formulation is that it might be well placed to explain many of the central features of schizophrenia and, by extrapolation, of schizotypy. Thus, on the clinical side it would be consistent with Frith's (1979) argument that schizophrenia is essentially a 'failure to limit the contents of consciousness'. Similarly, Venables (1974), offering an interpretation of his psychophysiological data, has suggested that some schizophrenics may show an unduly 'open' mode of attention to the environment, a characteristic also inferred from comparable findings obtained in high-risk children (Venables et al. 1978). Interestingly, the latter authors, noting that such children also indulge in an unusual amount of creative play, speculate that their openness to stimulation might be a vehicle either for positive intellectual development or for pathology, depending on circumstances (see also Claridge et al. for a detailed discussion of this relationship between creativity and psychosis).

In considering the above suggestions I have of course blurred over the evidence, referred to in the previous section, that 'schizotypy' – like the set of disorders on to which it maps – is almost certainly not a unitary dimension. It is therefore unlikely that any single biological characteristic can account for the variety of the normal trait or the heterogeneity of the clinical condition; or, if it could, then it is of such a form that current theories have so far failed to capture its quality. Nevertheless, from work carried out to date it is possible to reach at least a minimum, but important, conclusion (as yet largely unrecognized by the medical Establishment): that present research on schizotypy is on the right general lines, in establishing that the study, in *normal* subjects, of the mechanisms underlying schizophrenia is vital to an understanding of the illness itself. Indeed, it is highly probable that in the absence of the former the latter will entirely elude us.

Turning now to a quite different consequence of the view of schizophrenia presented here, it has to be admitted that the comparison with physical systemic disease on which it is based is necessarily imperfect. This is not merely because the brain is biologically more complicated than, say, the cardiovascular system, but because it is, in a more profound sense, unique. As the organ of mind, the brain has properties that transcend its physiological features and it would be to trivialize schizophrenia to argue that the person suffering a psychotic 'break' is – to pursue the analogy with hypertensive disease – merely having a 'psychological stroke'.

There is also another way in which the analogy with physical disease is incomplete. Aberrations of brain function, unlike those of local bodily systems, have consequences in the disturbed behaviour of the *whole person*. Furthermore, except in the case of those (neurological) disorders where such behaviour can be quickly assigned to recognizable organic disease, decisions about its abnormality inevitably involve shifting social criteria. What in one context is regarded as a sign of madness will, in another, be taken as evidence of originality of thought or spiritual revelation. It is precisely this arbitrariness about the definition of insanity that has troubled those who have rejected disease views of schizophrenia in the past and the model suggested here does nothing to solve that problem. If anything it exacerbates it, in recognizing a genuine spectrum of disorders the milder forms of which fall on the borderline between extreme personality variation and psychopathology, and where subtle gradations of deviance – whether defined socially or biologically – are possible.

Ultimately, then – returning finally to the question from which this chapter started – whether a disease model of schizophrenia can survive might depend more on its pragmatic value as a guide to research than on its clinical usefulness in judging individual people. In the former case, there is no doubt that certain disease constructions of mental illness have in the past seriously hampered some kinds of research on schizophrenia. (More worryingly, they continue to do so: a very recent multi-authored 'state of the art' review of schizophrenia research (Crow 1987) makes no mention of the kind of experimental data referred to here, and promotes an entirely misleading conclusion that the psychoses are very near to being established as organic brain diseases, in the narrow neurological sense.) On the other hand, as I have shown, there are observations about schizophrenia that can be readily incorporated into a *modified* disease theory. In that respect it does seem that the disease concept continues to have some value, at least as a working model for those researchers out of sympathy with the current *Zeitgeist* in organic psychiatry, yet unpersuaded by the counter-arguments of neo-Szaszism.

In the clinical domain, too, crude organic disease theories have certainly blinkered past attempts at full understanding, as well as therapeutic policies. At the same time, unlike the antipsychiatric perspective, they have helped to keep in focus the fact that psychotic breakdown can bring about a serious impairment of mental health that is often only manageable by medical intervention. There, in order to avoid a foreclosing of opinion, it is possible that a distinction could usefully be made between *illness* and disease – despite Szasz's insistence on using the two terms synonymously. It is surely uncontroversial that many people reporting schizophrenic symptoms are ill (in the sense of suffering a profound loss of well-being) and to regard them as such pays due regard to their need for care and treatment, sometimes by pharmacological means. However, medical practitioners also need to be reminded of the fact that psychological experiences indistinguishable in form from the 'psychotic' can also be found in many whom we would hesitate to consider either ill or diseased: the mystic, the highly creative, the religiously or politically fanatical, and others happy in their fixed and deviant, but socially contained, beliefs. The slight shift in terminology proposed – from 'disease' to 'illness' – could at least allow all of those involved with schizophrenia to keep an open mind about the nature of that most inscrutable of human conditions.

REFERENCES

American Psychiatric Association (1980) *Diagnostic and Statistical Manual of Mental Disorders (DSM-III)*, *3rd edn*, Washington, DC: APA.

Anthony, E.J. and Cohler, B.J. (eds) (1987) *The Invulnerable Child*, New York: The Guilford Press.

Beech, A.R. and Claridge, G.S. (1987) 'Individual differences in negative priming: relations with schizotypal personality traits', *British Journal of Psychology* 78: 349–56.

Beech, A.R., Baylis, G.C., and Claridge, G.S. (1989) 'Individual differences in schizotypy as reflected in measures of cognitive inhibition', *British Journal of Clinical Psychology* 28: 117–29.

Bentall, R. and Slade, P. (1985a) 'Reality testing and auditory hallucinations: a signal detection analysis', *British Journal of Clinical Psychology* 24: 159–69.

— (1985b) 'Reliability of a scale measuring disposition towards hallucinations: a brief report', *Personality and Individual Differences* 6: 527–9.

Bentall, R.P., Claridge, G.S., and Slade, P.D. (1989) 'The multidimensional nature of schizotypal traits: a factor analytic study with normal subjects', *British Journal of Clinical Psychology* 28:363–75.

Bleuler, M. (1984) 'Different forms of childhood stress and patterns of adult psychiatric outcome', in N.F. Watt, J. Anthony, L.C. Wynne, and J.E. Rolf (eds) *Children at Risk for Schizophrenia. A Longitudinal Perspective*, Cambridge: Cambridge University Press.

Broks, P. (1984) 'Schizotypy and hemisphere function – II. Performance asymmetry on a verbal divided visual-field task', *Personality and Individual Differences* 5: 649–56.

— Claridge, G.S., Matheson, J., and Hargreaves, J. (1984) 'Schizotypy and hemisphere function – IV. Story comprehension under binaural and monaural listening conditions', *Personality and Individual Differences* 5: 665–70.

Bullen, J.G. and Hemsley, D.R. (1984) 'Psychoticism and visual recognition thresholds', *Personality and Individual Differences* 5: 735–9.

Chapman, L.J., Chapman, J.P., and Raulin, M.L. (1976) 'Scales for physical and social anhedonia', *Journal of Abnormal Psychology* 85: 374–82.

— (1978) 'Body-image aberration in schizophrenia', *Journal of Abnormal Psychology* 87: 399–407.

Claridge, G.S. (1967) *Personality and Arousal*, Oxford: Pergamon.

— (1972) 'The schizophrenias as nervous types', *British Journal of Psychiatry* 112: 1–17.

— (1985) *Origins of Mental Illness*, Oxford: Blackwell.

— (1987) '"The schizophrenias as nervous types" revisited', *British Journal of Psychiatry* 151: 735–43.

— (1988) 'Schizotypy and schizophrenia', in P. McGuffin and P. Bebbington (eds) *Schizophrenia: The Major Issues*, London: William Heinemann.

— and Birchall, P.M.A. (1978) 'Bishop, Eysenck, Block, and psychoticism', *Journal of Abnormal Psychology* 87: 664–8.

— and Broks, P. (1984) 'Schizotypy and hemisphere function – I. Theoretical considerations and the measurement of schizotypy', *Personality and Individual Differences* 5: 633–48.

— and Hewitt, J.K. (1987) 'A biometrical study of schizotypy in a normal population', *Personality and Individual Differences* 8: 303–12.

— Pryor, R., and Watkins, G. (in press) *Sounds from the Bell Jar: Ten Psychotic Authors*, London: Macmillan.

Crow, T.J. (1980) 'Positive and negative schizophrenic symptoms and the role of dopamine', *British Journal of Psychiatry* 137: 383–6.

— (1984) 'A re-evaluation of the viral hypothesis: is psychosis the result of retroviral integration at a site close to the cerebral dominance gene?', *British Journal of Psychiatry* 145: 243–53.

— (ed.) (1987) *Recurrent and Chronic Psychoses*, Edinburgh: Churchill Livingstone.

Eckblad, M. and Chapman, L.J. (1983) 'Magical ideation as an indicator of schizotypy', *Journal of Consulting and Clinical Psychology* 51: 215–25.

— (1986) 'Development and validation of a scale for hypomanic personality', *Journal of Abnormal Psychology* 95: 214–22.

Eysenck, H.J. (1952) 'Schizothymia-cyclothymia as a dimension of personality. II. Experimental', *Journal of Personality* 20: 345–84.

— (1960) 'Classification and the problem of diagnosis', in H.J. Eysenck (ed.) *Handbook of Abnormal Psychology*, 1st ed, London: Pitman.
— and Eysenck, S.B.G. (1975) *Manual of the Eysenck Personality Questionnaire*, London: Hodder & Stoughton.
Faily, S. and Venables, P.H. (1986) 'The structure of schizotypy', unpublished manuscript, Department of Psychology, University of York.
Foulds, G.A. (1965) *Personality and Personal Illness*, London: Tavistock.
— and Bedford, A. (1975) 'Hierarchy of classes of personal illness', *Psychological Medicine* 5: 181–92.
Frith, C.D. (1979) 'Consciousness, information processing and schizophrenia', *British Journal of Psychiatry* 134: 225–35.
Golden, R.R. and Meehl, P.E. (1979) 'Detection of the schizoid taxon with MMPI indicators', *Journal of Abnormal Psychology* 88: 217–33.
Gottesman, I.I. and Shields, J. (1968) 'In pursuit of the schizophrenic genotype', in S.G. Vandenberg (ed.) *Progress in Human Behaviour Genetics*, Baltimore: Johns Hopkins University Press.
— (1982) *Schizophrenia: The Epigenetic Puzzle*, Cambridge: Cambridge University Press.
Gray, J.A. (1964) *Pavlov's Typology*, Oxford: Pergamon.
— (1982) *The Neuropsychology of Anxiety*, Oxford: Oxford University Press.
Green, P., Hallett, S., and Hunter, M. (1983) 'Abnormal inter-hemispheric integration and hemispheric specialisation in schizophrenics and high-risk children', in P. Flor-Henry and J. Gruzelier (eds) *Laterality and Psychopathology*, Amsterdam: Elsevier/North-Holland.
Gruzelier, J.H. (1983) 'A critical assessment and integration of lateral asymmetries in schizophrenia', in M. Myslobodsky (ed.) *Hemisyndromes. Psychobiology, Neurology, Psychiatry*, New York: Academic Press.
Hallett, S., Quinn, D., and Hewitt, J. (1986) 'Defective inter-hemispheric integration and anomalous language lateralisation in children at risk for schizophrenia', *Journal of Nervous and Mental Disease* 174: 418–27.
Haracz, J.L. (1982) 'The dopamine hypothesis: an overview of studies with schizophrenic patients', *Schizophrenia Bulletin* 8: 438–69.
Hewitt, J. and Claridge, G.S. (1989) 'The factor structure of schizotypy in a normal population', *Personality and Individual Differences* 10: 323–9.
Kety, S.S. (1985) 'Schizotypal personality disorder: an operational definition of Bleuler's latent schizophrenia', *Schizophrenia Bulletin* 11: 590–4.
Kretschmer, E. (1925) *Physique and Character*, translated by W.J.H. Sprott, London: Kegan, Trench, & Trubner.
Laing, R.D. (1960) *The Divided Self*, London: Tavistock.
Launay, G. and Slade, P. (1981) 'The measurement of hallucinatory predisposition in male and female prisoners', *Personality and Individual Differences* 2: 221–34.
Leff, J. and Vaughn, C. (1985) *Expressed Emotion in Families*, New York: The Guilford Press.
Liddle, P.F. (1987) 'The symptoms of chronic schizophrenia: a re-

GORDON CLARIDGE

examination of the positive-negative dichotomy', *British Journal of Psychiatry* 151: 145–51.

Meehl, P.E. (1962) 'Schizotaxia, schizotypy, schizophrenia', *American Psychologist* 17: 827–38.

Miller, E.N. and Chapman, L.J. (1983) 'Continued word association in hypothetically psychosis-prone college students', *Journal of Abnormal Psychology* 92: 468–78.

Muntaner, C., Garcia-Sevilla, A.F., and Torrubia, R. (1988) 'Personality dimensions, schizotypal and borderline personality traits and psychosis-proneness', *Personality and Individual Differences* 9: 257–68.

Nakano, K. and Saccuzzo, D.P. (1985) 'Schizotaxia, information processing and the MMPI 2-7-8 code type', *British Journal of Clinical Psychology* 24: 217–18.

Nielsen, T.C. and Petersen, N.E. (1976) 'Electrodermal correlates of extraversion, trait anxiety, and schizophrenism'. *Scandinavian Journal of Psychology* 17: 73–80.

Nuechterlein, K.H. and Dawson, M.E. (1984) 'Information processing and attentional functioning in the developmental course of schizophrenic disorders', *Schizophrenia Bulletin* 10: 160–203.

Pavlov, I.P. (1928) *Lectures on Conditioned Reflexes*, translated by W.H. Gantt, New York: Liveright Publishing Corporation.

Rado, S. (1953) 'Dynamics and classification of disordered behaviour', *American Journal of Psychiatry* 110: 406–21.

Raine, A. and Allbutt, J. (1989) 'Factors of schizoid personality', *British Journal of Clinical Psychology* 28: 31–40.

Raine, A. and Manders, D. (1988) 'Schizoid personality, interhemispheric transfer and left hemisphere overactivation', *British Journal of Clinical Psychology* 27: 333–48.

Rawlings, D. and Claridge, G.S. (1984) 'Schizotypy and hemisphere function – III. Performance asymmetries on tasks of letter recognition and local-global processing', *Personality and Individual Differences* 6: 657–63.

Reed, D. (1977) *Anna,* Harmondsworth: Penguin.

Robinson, T.N. Jr, and Zahn, T.P. (1985) 'Psychoticism and arousal: possible evidence for a linkage of P and psychopathy', *Personality and Individual Differences* 6: 47–66.

Rose, S., Kamin, L.J., and Lewontin, R.C. (1984) *Not in Our Genes,* Harmondsworth: Penguin.

Rust, J. (1987) 'The Rust Inventory of Schizoid Cognitions (RISC): a psychometric measure of psychoticism in the normal population', *British Journal of Clinical Psychology* 26: 151–2.

Schizophrenia Bulletin (1979) 6 (1) (whole issue).

— (1985) 11 (4) (whole issue).

Simons, R.F. (1981) 'Electrodermal and cardiac orienting in psychometrically defined high-risk subjects', *Psychiatry Research* 4: 347–56.

— (1982) 'Physical anhedonia and future psychopathology: an electrodermal continuity?', *Psychophysiology,* 19: 433–41.

182

Spitzer, R.L., Endicott, J., and Gibbon, M. (1979) 'Crossing the border into borderline personality and borderline schizophrenia: the development of criteria', *Archives of General Psychiatry* 36: 17–24.

Steronko, R.J. and Woods, D.J. (1978) 'Impairment in early stages of visual information processing in nonpsychotic schizotypic individuals', *Journal of Abnormal Psychology* 87: 481–90.

Stone, M.H. (1980) *The Borderline Syndromes*, New York: McGraw-Hill.

Szasz, T.S. (1974) *The Myth of Mental Illness*, New York: Harper & Row.

— (1976) *Schizophrenia*, Oxford: Oxford University Press.

— (1987) *Insanity: The Idea and its Consequences*, New York: Wiley.

Venables, P.H. (1974) 'The recovery limb of the skin conductance response in "high-risk" research', in S.A. Mednick, F. Schulsinger, J. Higgins, and B. Bell (eds) *Genetics, Environment and Psychopathology*, Amsterdam: Elsevier/North Holland.

Mednick, S.A., Schulsinger, F., Raman, A.C., Bell, B., Dalais, J.C., and Fletcher, R.P. (1978) 'Screening for risk of mental illness', in G. Serban (ed.) *Cognitive Defects in the Development of Mental Illness*, New York: Brunner/Mazel.

Walker, E. and McGuire, M.D. (1982) 'Intra- and interhemispheric information processing in schizophrenia', *Psychological Bulletin* 92: 701–25.

Watt, N.F. (1984) 'In a nutshell: the first two decades of high-risk research in schizophrenia', in N.F. Watt, J. Anthony, L.C. Wynne, and J.E. Rolf (eds) *Children at Risk for Schizophrenia. A Longitudinal Perspective*, Cambridge: Cambridge University Press.

Weinberger, D.R., Wagner, R.L., and Wyatt, R.J. (1983) 'Neuropathological studies of schizophrenia: a selective review', *Schizophrenia Bulletin* 9: 193–212.

Wexler, B.E. (1980) 'Cerebral laterality and psychiatry: a review of the literature', *American Journal of Psychiatry* 137: 279–91.

Woody, E.Z. and Claridge, G.S. (1977) 'Psychoticism and thinking', *British Journal of Social and Clinical Psychology* 16: 241–8.

Zuckerman, M. (1979) *Sensation Seeking*, New York: Wiley.

Chapter Seven

LONGITUDINAL RESEARCH ON SCHIZOPHRENIA

PETER H. VENABLES

INTRODUCTION

Over the past 20 years the pattern on research on schizophrenia has changed from a concentration on the study of the adult patient in hospital, to one which now encompasses a wider spectrum of investigation. Because of a movement away from a view of the disorder emphasizing a categorical distinction between the schizophrenic patient *qua patient* and the rest of the population, work has looked for some of the characteristics to be found in patients in those in remission, in the pre-morbid state, in normal relatives of patients, and in members of the general public thought of displaying 'schizotypic' characteristics. Thus, there has been a move from a categorical to a dimensional point of view. The clear distinction between the 'mad' and the 'sane' is no longer drawn (see Chapter 6 by Claridge in this volume).

This change of emphasis is in no small measure due to Meehl (1962). In his seminal paper on 'Schizotaxia, schizotypy and schizophrenia', he put forward the model that 'schizotaxia' (a 'neural integrative defect', 'all that can properly be spoken of as inherited') may predispose an individual to develop schizophrenia if he or she encounters adverse environmental circumstances. However, if the circumstances in which the individual grows up are benign, then he or she may develop personality characteristics which suggest that he or she may be thought of as a schizotypic. If the behaviour of the schizotypic person never exhibits characteristics which his or her peers think of as grossly abnormal, then that person will not be referred to psychiatric agencies and achieve 'patienthood',

Another event which occurred in 1962 was the start of the Danish 'high risk for schizophrenia' study. While this was not the first study of this kind (for example, Fish 1957), it was the first sizeable study and one which has been used either as a model or as a source of controversy since it was initiated. In particular Mednick and McNeil (1968) put forward a rationale for high-risk research which has been generally accepted as an important basis for the technique. They pointed out that the behaviour of the adult patient as seen in hospital was the result of the interaction of the 'primary disease process' and the subsequent events happening to the person in becoming a patient. They suggested that 'the behavior of these individuals may be markedly altered in response to correlates of the illness, such as educational, economic and social failure, pre-hospital, and post-hospital drug regimes, bachelorhood, long-term institutionalization, chronic illness and sheer misery' (p.681).

These two events therefore provide an indication of the background against which the present change of emphasis in research on schizophrenia has taken place. In the present chapter the emphasis is on longitudinal research. The logic of this approach is, of course, that there is something to observe in the pre-morbid state which is a precursor of the morbid state. A 'diathesis' point of view suggests that there are factors which predispose the individual to develop a disorder (the 'schizotaxia' of the Meehl (1962) approach) a 'trait' characteristic of the person, most likely biological, if not definitely genetic. This 'diathesis' should be set against the environmental or 'stress' factors leading to the disorder; the 'life events' which may be identifiable as the immediate precursors of the contact with psychiatric services. However schizophrenia is *par excellence* a disorder: in which a 'stress–diathesis' approach should be taken rather than a 'stress vs diathesis' stance. The literature gives no support for a wholly biological or a wholly environmental point of view. The proportion of 'nature' and the proportion of 'nurture' involved, however, vary from case to case. In some instances the disorder will develop insidiously with a long history of developing abnormality of behaviour and no particular identifiable precipitant. In other instances, however, it may be possible to point clearly to an event in the person's life after which behaviour became noticeably abnormal.

Longitudinal research proceeds, therefore, on the assumption that it will be possible to identify both relatively permanent features of the individual, 'markers' for subsequent disorder, and those critical features of the environment which may act as precipitants or triggers for the onset of the disorder.

Longitudinal research is basically of two kinds: 'prospective' or 'follow forward' and 'retrospective' or 'follow backward'. Each form has its own advantages and disadvantages.

The starting-point for prospective research is the person in the pre-morbid state with the intention to follow up that person over the years as the disorder develops. The starting-point for the retrospective study is the patient, with the intention that relevant points about his or her development may be discovered from the use of records. Note that the term 'records' has been used as it may be taken as axiomatic that anamnestic data are virtually useless for this purpose (for example, Burton 1970; Yarrow et al. 1970). Even over a period of 3 years, Robbins (1963) has shown that mothers are extremely inaccurate in recollection of the details of their children's development.

Prospective research normally starts in childhood, bearing in mind that the period of risk for schizophrenia is usually considered to be between the ages of 15 and 55 years. It should be noted, parenthetically, that it is possible to conduct prospective research from an adult starting-point. Thus, for instance, it is to be considered that subjects with schizotypic characteristics have an elevated risk for schizophrenia. The early work of Hoch and his colleagues (1959, 1962), for example, showed that subjects diagnosed as exhibiting 'pseudoneurotic schizophrenia', who would now probably receive the DSM-III diagnosis of 'schizotypal personality disorder', had a 20 per cent morbid risk of becoming schizophrenic compared with a 1 per cent risk in the general population. The childhood start is more usual, however. The feature of high-risk research, which gives it its name, is that it takes account of the baseline estimate for the development of schizophrenia in the general population.

Pearson and Kley (1957) were the first to emphasize the need to take base rates into account in the study of the development of comparatively rare disorders. They proposed that the fact that abnormality of behaviour is known to 'run in families' may be used to produce economies of design in longitudinal studies.

Clearly it is inefficient to attempt to study the development of schizophrenia starting from a general population sample. Starting from such a sample in childhood and waiting, say, 20 years for the development of the disorder would result in less than 1 per cent of the original sample becoming schizophrenic. Most prospective studies have therefore taken into account the data on the risk for schizophrenia in subjects who have a parent who is schizophrenic. In these subjects the lifetime morbid risk is raised from 1 per cent to about 14 per cent, and the research then becomes a feasible possibility. Normally it is the mother who is the index case in this research as it is easier to identify her than it is the father. This may however have some, at present unknown, influence on these studies, as recent research has shown that the nature of schizophrenia in female patients tends to have different characteristics from those which are exhibited in the male (Lewine 1981). A further possible bias in using the presence of familial factors to elevate the level of risk in an experimental group is that those who eventually develop schizophrenia but do not have a sick parent are not investigated. Data are available (Rosenthal 1974) which suggest that only between 5 and 10 per cent of schizophrenics have a schizophrenic parent.

Other methods may be used in an attempt to mitigate the bias introduced by using familial risk as the selection factor. All, however, have their own intrinsic difficulties. Asarnow et al. (1983), for instance, used a group of unemployed unskilled workers in a study on perceptual anomalies in schizotypics because of the finding (for example, Goldberg and Morrison 1963) of a greater number of schizophrenics in social class V (which is, of course, defined on the basis of occupational criteria). Venables (1978) used measures of electrodermal activity as a means of selecting a risk population in a high-risk study in Mauritius, partly because the use of familial criteria was unavailable without a population survey (there was only one 200-bed mental hospital for a population of 900,000) and partly to avoid the bias referred to above. Selection was based on the patterns of electrodermal hypo- and hyper-responsivity which have been found in other high-risk studies (Mednick and Schulsinger 1968) and in adult patients (for example, Gruzelier and Venables 1972).

One of the advantages of the prospective paradigm over the

retrospective is that the data which are collected in the pre-morbid state are gathered with the specific end of the study in mind, whereas in the retrospective study, almost by definition, the data have been gathered for other purposes. However, in a long prospective study, the data collection is designed on the basis of the then current hypotheses about schizophrenia which may with hindsight, decades later, be seen to be erroneous.

A more subtle source of error, pointed out by Mednick (1978), is that which arises when the experimental high-risk group and the control group are not representative, on a particular characteristic, of the distribution of that characteristic in the general population. Thus, if having a schizophrenic parent results in the experimental group having many broken homes and there is therefore an attempt to match this feature in the control group, it is likely that neither group will be representative of the general population on this characteristic. Finally, the greatest practical difficulty in carrying out prospective longitudinal studies is the maintenance of the coherence of the group carrying out the study and the difficulty in obtaining continued support.

Such difficulties do not occur, or occur less with retrospective research. Starting from a population of current patients and working back means that results are obtained from the time of completion of the search of relevant records. The difficulties in finding the relevant records should not of course be minimized. However, the particular difficulty with retrospective studies is centred around the word 'relevant'. The data which are used are, in general, collected for some other purpose, may not be collected in a standard form, and may have elements randomly or, worse, systematically missing. A study such as that of Watt (1978) and colleagues which started from a total school population of both sexes and made use of school records did not introduce such errors. Although these were available in a more standard form than might be seen in some instances, they nevertheless required considerable coding and manipulation before their use. On the other hand the study by Roff and Knight (1978, 1980) was inevitably biased in its sampling by being started from a group of male ex-service schizophrenics who also had child-guidance records. Thus, these two studies exemplify a trade-off between the validity and extensiveness of the records available and the representativeness of the sample.

188

The conclusion to be drawn is that neither prospective nor retrospective studies are free from difficulties; nevertheless they both represent significant improvements over purely cross-sectional studies of the patient in his or her morbid state. Advances in the study of schizophrenia are likely to be made with the help of converging approaches, supporting the findings of one type of paradigm with those from the others. An examination of some of the findings from the two major longitudinal techniques, prospective and retrospective, will be made in order to see to what extent they are mutually supportive and make significant advances. Bearing in mind the growth in the numbers of studies in this area (for example, Watt et al. 1984; Goldstein and Tuma 1987), the material reviewed must necessarily be selective. The principle of selection, however, will be to examine those studies whose findings exemplify particularly the *interaction* of factors which appear to underlie the development of schizophrenia.

There are some research designs which have a longitudinal element but which will not be discussed here. Adoption studies necessarily have a longitudinal element, in so far as they start from the point of adoption and follow the subject until he or she becomes abnormal or not (for example, the paradigm classically introduced by Heston 1966). Alternatively the Kety et al. (1968) model starts with the patient drawn from a sample of adoptees and pursues a retrospective course to look at the degree of abnormality among relatives of the patient. While these studies provide valuable data which may be used alongside the studies discussed here, they are perhaps not truly longitudinal in so far as no developmental data are usually collected.

Before proceeding to discuss particular studies, it is worthwhile introducing the topic of path analysis, as this is a statistical method used in this area of research and is particularly appropriate when it is necessary to examine the interaction between variables or sets of variables. One of the difficulties of this approach is that it assumes that the variables it relates are error-free. As this assumption is, in practice, not attainable, a much-used procedure (LISREL) uses the concept of 'latent variables'. These are variables which are not themselves the result of direct measurement but are the result of the combination of a group of indicator variables. The use of several indicator variables means that the latent variable is less biased than the indicators which comprise it, and for the purposes of the procedure are thought of as error-free. The latent variable may be compared to a single factor resulting from a factor analysis. Most importantly, path analysis should be considered as a hypothetico-deductive procedure in so far as it is necessary at the outset to specify the model that the investigator has in mind and wishes to test. This model is specified by a path diagram in which the hypothesized relations between variables are stated. The path-analysis procedure (for example, the computer program LISREL – see Joreskog 1981) then enables the existence of the hypothesized relations to be tested. In testing the relationship between a pair of (latent) variables, the relations between other variables are held constant, so that there is an analogy in this instance with partial correlation. Path analysis provides a particularly strong and conservative means of testing relationships between variables, so that capitalization on chance findings from attempted interpretations of large matrices of correlations is avoided.

RETROSPECTIVE RESEARCH

The study of Roff and Knight (1978, 1980, 1981) provides a useful starting-point for a review of retrospective studies. The 1981 paper provides details of the process of selection which was necessary to obtain an eventual sample having complete data. This selection process is one of the inevitable difficulties of a retrospective study that attempts to obtain full data from early developmental periods. As such the eventual sample must be a biased one, but as suggested earlier, if the results from such a study mesh with those from studies employing different designs, then the findings of the biased sample should not be thought of as being invalid. On the contrary, we should perhaps see them as providing a 'constructive' replication (Lykken 1968).

The starting-point of sample selection for this study was a compilation of 10,000 cases that had attended child-guidance clinics (Roff 1970). These subjects had eventually become members of the US armed forces. Post-service information on a subsample of these suggested that they might have a diagnosis of schizophrenia. This subsample of ninety-five was further reduced to an eventual working sample of forty-five because they met the

DSM-II criteria for schizophrenia (not the more stringent DSM-III criteria), and adequate information was available on them from three record sources. These were: child-guidance clinics, military service, and the Veterans Administration hospital in which they were patients. All the subjects were male. The average age at child-guidance-clinic attendance was 10·9 years and the average age at eventual follow-up was 43·7 years. Thus, the span of the longitudinal study was over 30 years and at least part of the aim of the study was to see how far associations could be made between variables over that period. Data were available in the child-guidance-clinic records which were concerned with the family circumstances of each subject at the time of his initial contact.

Roff and Knight (1981) present a path analysis (see above) of the data including the family state existing at the time of the child-guidance visit, the data gathered at that visit, the data from the 'young adult' period (that is, when the subject was in the services), and the 'middle adult' period (the time when the subject was a patient). There was only a weak direct effect on eventual outcome of family status, measured by a global rating of family disturbance by trained observers. Otherwise the major effect that this variable exercised was in two directions. First, the adverse effect of family disturbance was manifest on the variable 'poor social competence/affect' measured in young adulthood. This latter variable was measured by ratings of flatness or inappropriateness of affect, social adjustment, and work performance. Second, there was a significant path relating family disturbance to asocial behaviour in the childhood period, and this asociality measured in the child-guidance clinic was also related to poor affect/social competence in young adulthood and also directly to poor schizophrenic outcome. The highest predictor of poor schizophrenic outcome was poor affect/social competence in young adulthood. Three other variables were measured at the time of the child-guidance contact. A pair of these, labelled after the clusters outlined in the literature on ratings of childhood behaviour (for example, Achenbach and Edelbrock 1978), were 'externalizing' and 'internalizing'. The former was defined by items dealing with agression, acting out, and conduct problems in school or at home, the latter by ratings of anxiety, fears, phobias, somatic complaints, and feelings of inferiority. The third of the childhood variables was IQ. The path analysis showed that poor

191

affect/social competence and poor schizophrenic outcome were related to low IQ. On the other hand, poor affect/social competence and poor outcome were also related to low 'externalizing'. In other words, good outcome was shown in those with above-average levels of aggression or acting out. No relationship was shown with any variable at any stage of the study by 'internalizing'. Thus, the possible expectation that it is the shy, worried, fearful child who develops schizophrenia is not supported by these data. Another analysis of the same data (Roff and Knight 1980) shows that if the data on aggressiveness and IQ are dichotomized, then those with low aggressiveness and low IQ show a 92 per cent unfavourable outcome compared with around 30 per cent in the other three groups. (It must be remembered that all the subjects from this sample were child-guidance contacts and thus the high level of poor outcome from even the high-IQ, high-aggression subgroups is not unexpected.)

The finding of low IQ as a predictor of poor schizophrenic outcome is in accord with other findings in the literature (see the review by Aylward et al. 1984). One particularly relevant and classic report is that by Offord (1974). In this he presents data from fifty-one male and sixty-five female schizophrenics, for whom there were male and female sibling and unrelated controls. IQ data were available from school records and the criterion for schizophrenia was that diagnosis had to be made before the age of 45. The results showed that the mean pre-schizophrenic IQ of the male subjects was significantly lower than that of any of their controls, while that of the females did not differ from control values. This finding should be seen in relation to the Roff and Knight study where the sample was all male.

A study which has relevance in this context is that of Rieder et al. (1977). Sixty children of schizophrenic parents were studied. Of these parents, forty-five were designated as 'continuous' with diagnoses of chronic, chronic schizo-affective, and borderline, fifteen were diagnosed as 'acute'. (This categorization is the same as that employed by Kety et al. (1968) in the Danish adoption study which provided evidence for the grouping of the three subgroups as continuous and for the acute group to be considered separately.) Rieder et al. (1977) showed that, at age 7, the offspring of the 'continuous' schizophrenics had a lower IQ than that of matched controls and *that this deficit could be attributed entirely to the male offspring'* (p. 789, emphasis added). Furthermore the IQ of the 'continuous' schizophrenics was found to have a lower correlation with socio-economic status than that of controls but was related to the presence of certain perinatal events. Thus, the findings of Roff and Knight reviewed above (which suggest that low IQ is a factor leading to predisposition to schizophrenia) are in line with other material in the literature. The data also suggest that this diathesis is applicable only to male subjects and may be the result of perinatal trauma rather than the level of intelligence having a familial determination.

The study by Watt and colleagues (for example, Watt 1978) adopts a different approach from that of Roff and Knight. The starting-point in this instance was a computer list of every psychiatric patient between 15 and 34 years-old in Massachusetts. The number of first admissions with functional disorder was 15,811. This list was checked against the files of a large public high school in the suburbs of Boston. In this way ninety patients, of whom twenty-three were schizophrenics, who had not moved from the area, were identified. A further sample of sixteen was found, the members of which had migrated from the area. Thus, in contrast to the Roff and Knight study the sample, in so far as it is drawn from a large public school, rather than those who had attended child-guidance clinics, should be more generally representative of the population. Controls were drawn from the school files and were matched for age, sex, race, and social class. The first point to be noted is that Watt reports that average intelligence measured at school did not differ significantly between patients and their siblings or controls. However, as the report on intelligence is not broken down by sex, it is possible that any difference between the pre-morbid intelligence of male schizophrenics and controls may not have been evident when the total group was examined.

The notable methodological feature of this study is the use of teachers' records to provide details of early behaviour. The method used an analysis of the ad lib comments written annually by the child's class teacher. Initially, *a priori* clusters of behaviour were used to classify the comments. Later work (Lewine et al. 1978) used factor-analytically defined groupings of items. In the case of the *a priori* clusters the data were analysed by adding together all the comments in each scoring category for every child's total record and dividing that sum by the number of years for which the comments were written. This yielded a ratio score indicating the number of comments per year for each category. Finally, the ratio score for the negative comments in the cluster were subtracted from the ratio score of the positive comments to yield a difference score. It was this score which was used in most of the subsequent analyses. This method has been described in some detail in so far as it makes evident the steps which have to be gone through to make usable data which have not been specifically gathered for the purpose of the investigation. How far the eventual data are to be considered 'strong' must be a matter for conjecture. However, as stated above, if they provide material which in general supplements a picture which is derived using an alternative method then they are of supportive value.

The strength of the data from this study is that it presents material from both sexes and divides the school period into two parts which enables the influence of factors early in the child's development to be separated from those closer to adolescence. Watt (1978) summarizes the findings of an earlier analysis on an initial sample as follows: 'Pre-schizophrenic boys became more irritable, aggressive, negativistic and defiant of authority, but not more introverted. Though less definite, comparisons among the girls showed strong trends towards increasing shyness and introversion in those destined to become schizophrenic.'

An analysis of the complete sample, and employing the revised coding categories of 'conscientiousness', 'emotional stability', 'extraversion', 'assertiveness', and 'agreeableness' provides a picture capable of a slightly different interpretation. Before the age of 11 no differences on these variables are shown between pre-schizophrenics and controls amongst the boys, although differences are shown amongst the girls. The young pre-schizophrenic girls are less emotionally stable, more introverted, and less assertive. After age 12, both boys and girls are rated as less emotionally stable; the girls continue to be more introverted while there is no difference among the boys on this variable. Among the older boys, the controls are rated as more agreeable than the pre-schizophrenics. Although not significantly so, both boys and girls who are to become schizophrenic are less assertive than controls.

In comparing these results to those of Roff and Knight, the

first thing to notice is the differences introduced by the inclusion of females. In the Roff and Knight data using males only there was no contribution to eventual outcome from the variable 'internalization'. This is replicated in the boys in the Watt study; however, among the girls the pre-schizophrenics were more introverted. In the earlier analysis of the Watt material the pre-schizophrenic boys were said to be more irritable and aggressive: this was in opposition to the Roff and Knight data where the pre-schizophrenics, particularly those with poor outcome, were rated as less aggressive. The re-analysis of the Watt data suggests that what was rated previously as aggressiveness was better labelled as disagreeableness, and when assertiveness rather than aggression was rated then the pre-schizophrenics were if anything less assertive, which perhaps fits more closely with the Roff and Knight data. The other point to be particularly noted is that abnormal behaviour does not seem to be an early characteristic of pre-schizophrenic boys, whereas abnormalities, if they are to become apparent, are seen earlier in girls.

These two examples of retrospective studies provide some material against which results from prospective studies may be examined.

PROSPECTIVE RESEARCH

From the wide range of prospective studies which are being carried out, two will be discussed in detail. The first is the 'Copenhagen High-risk Project' initiated in 1962 by Mednick and Schulsinger: a recent summary is provided by Mednick et al. (1987). The second is the New York High-risk Project started by Erlenmeyer-Kimling and the subject of a recent report (Erlenmeyer-Kimling and Cornblatt 1987).

The reason for concentrating on these is that the former is a pioneering study whose subjects are now sufficiently old to be well into the risk period for schizophrenia, and the second, in its methodology, paralleled some of the features of the Copenhagen study so that the rather different results reported from the two somewhat different social settings are of interest.

The Danish study was started there, in part because of the existence of population and psychiatric registers which make the process of follow-up particularly easy and enable patient identification to be facilitated and also because the population is relatively homogeneous and stable. The effect of the latter factor is that biological and genetic factors probably become more apparent when the variance which can be attributed to environmental factors is minimized. This should be noted when comparing the Danish study with the New York study, where the population is socially more heterogeneous.

The risk sample for the study consisted of 207 children of severely ill schizophrenic mothers. The control sample was made up of 104 children in whose families there was no evidence of mental illness in the previous two generations. Because of the severity of illness of the mothers, many of the children in the sample came from broken homes and some were in institutions. An attempt was made to match this non-intactness of families in the control group. In consequence it was later found that the control group contained an unusually large number of children with criminal parents. This is consequently a factor which needs to be taken into account when comparing groups on, for instance, electrodermal activity where opposite deviations from normal might be expected. The members of the sample had a mean age of 15·1 years at the time of the start of the study and were thus on the brink of the breakdown period, although none were reported as being abnormal at the time of the initial contact. A follow-up at the end of 10 years (Schulsinger 1976) showed that fifteen of the high-risk and one of the control subjects had been diagnosed as suffering from schizophrenia. Fifty-five high-risk and four low-risk subjects were classified as suffering from borderline states (probably now to be thought of as DSM-III 'schizotypal personality disorder'). The diagnoses referred to above are consensus diagnoses where three diagnostic systems produce the same result. This result, showing 7·2 per cent schizophrenics at age 25 in offspring of schizophrenic mothers, is comparable to the results from another study from Denmark by Reisby (1967) which reported a figure of 8 per cent. The result is also comparable to that of Heston (1966) in which it was shown that 10·6 per cent of children of schizophrenic mothers, who had been separated shortly after birth, had been diagnosed as schizophrenic by the age of 36.

The results are thus comparable with those from studies whose structure is aimed at exposing genetic factors. The material from the Danish study does however enable the role of environmental factors to be made explicit when operating on a risk group. Walker et al. (1981) carried out a path analysis on data from the study which was made up of figures for maternal and paternal absence (in terms of the age at which the parent was separated from the child), the age at which this resulted in institutionalization (if it did so), and the schizophrenic symptoms exhibited at age 25 (from the study by H. Schulsinger referred to above). These symptoms were grouped into five clusters: 'anti-social and social impairment', 'paranoia and autism', 'borderline features, hallucinations, and delusions', 'hebephrenic traits', and 'thought disorder'. The path analysis was carried out separately for males and females. One of the straightforward findings was that, as would be expected, maternal absence tended to result in the institutionalization of the child. While there was some effect of father's absence on institutionalization it was very much weaker and only shown in male offspring. The indirect effect of maternal absence via institutionalization was a positive one on schizophrenic symptoms with the exception of the second 'paranoid autistic' cluster. Thus, the Roff and Knight (1981) finding that adverse family circumstances have an influence on the development of schizophrenia is in line with this finding. However, the Danish material enables another question to be answered. Looking only at the indirect effect of maternal absence, it might be said that separation from the mother had an adverse effect; but when we look at the *direct* effect, the path analysis shows paths with negative coefficients relating maternal absence to schizophrenic symptoms. Thus, not being in contact with a schizophrenic mother has beneficial effects and the adverse effects of absence are shown because it may result in institutionalization. All that has just been said refers only to male offspring. The only direct effect of maternal absence on females is a positive one on antisocial behaviour and social impairment. The same effect is paralleled in males by a direct positive effect of paternal absence on antisocial behaviour in male offspring. It should be emphasized that the results which have been described are taken from an analysis of the data from the high-risk sample and therefore are to be seen as an example of environment/ diathesis interaction. In particular it should be noted that the effects are sex-specific. This may be due to the factors which have been discussed in relation to the retrospective studies described earlier; but on the other hand, it could merely reflect a statistical restriction brought about by insufficient females having become schizophrenic by age 25. The data reviewed by Lewine (1981) and Al-Issa (1985) suggest that the peak age of onset of schizophrenia in women is, on the whole, some 7–10 years later than in men, in whom the modal age is around 25 years.

One of the issues raised earlier was that of the possible effect of perinatal complications on the development of schizophrenia. This arose particularly from the work of Rieder et al. (1977) which indicated that reduced levels of intelligence on pre-schizophrenic males might be due to perinatal insult. The first report from the Danish study on this topic was that of Mednick (1970), in which he showed that if the high-risk group were divided up into those who had become psychiatrically ill (the 'sick' group) and those who remained well (the 'well' group), then 70 per cent of the 'sick' group had suffered one or more serious pregnancy or birth complications, while only 15 per cent of the 'well' group had had similar complications. These figures should be compared with those from the control group, in which 33 per cent had perinatal birth complications but remained psychiatrically well. In this paper, Mednick raised the possibility that the mediating mechanism in the production of schizophrenia was hippocampal dysfunction brought about by perinatal anoxia. A further clue that this might be the case was provided in data from Bagshaw et al. (1965) which showed that monkeys with hippocampal lesions tended to be electrodermally hyper-responsive, a pattern of response shown by a proportion of adult schizophrenics and reported as being characteristic of the 'sick' group in the Danish study. The case for thinking that hippocampal dysfunction might be involved in the development of schizophrenia has been reviewed by Venables (1973, 1987).

An early application of path analysis to the Danish data by Mednick et al. (1978) showed that in males, but not in females, there was not a direct path from perinatal birth complications to the presence of schizophrenia, but rather an indirect path where the birth complications appeared to be related to abnormalities of autonomic system function which, in turn, were related to the presence of schizophrenia. Again, it should be pointed out that the sex difference shown in this analysis may be due to a lack of sufficient breakdowns among the female members of the sample to enable significant relations to appear.

A further analysis of the data, subsequent to the clinical assessment at age 25, is provided by Parnas et al. (1982). In this report, the scoring of perinatal complications is tackled in a more extensive fashion, but more particularly, the availability of data on the existence of borderline schizophrenia provides additional insights. In summary, the data, which are all from the high-risk group, show a perinatal birth complication (PBC) score of 3·17 for the members of the sample who have developed schizophrenia, and 0·76 for those diagnosed as borderline schizophrenic. Those with no mental illness had a mean PBC score of 1·92. Thus, it would appear that, taking the score of 1·92 as a base-rate figure for this population, if the subject has a score markedly higher than this he or she is likely to develop schizophrenia. However, with the same diathesis but with a particularly benign, low level of PBCs, only borderline schizophrenia is manifest. These data seem to be a very close confirmation, but at a very early period of development, of the model put forward by Meehl (1962) outlined earlier. The schizotaxic (genetic) predisposition to schizophrenia resulted in schizophrenia under adverse conditions but only schizotypy under benign conditions.

A similar association was shown in a study of cerebral ventricular size in a subsample of the subjects. Following the first report of evidence of enlarged ventricular size in some schizophrenic patients (Johnstone et al. 1976), there have been numerous reports which confirm this finding. Increased ventricular size, while reported regularly, is, however, seen in only a subgroup of patients. Computerized axial tomography scanning was carried out on a subsample of thirty-six of the members of the Danish high-risk group (Schulsinger et al. 1984). Those who carried the diagnosis of schizophrenia had a ventricular: brain ratio (VBR) of 9·76 compared to 7·48 for those with no mental illness. In contrast the VBR of the subjects with borderline diagnosis was 5·41. While the total score of perinatal complications was not significantly related to VBR, weight at birth was, and length at birth nearly so. The pattern of results is similar to that reported by Parnas et al. (1982), with the borderline or schizotypal subjects showing evidence of less adverse development than schizophrenics and with the normal subjects having an intermediate score.

The New York High-risk study (for example, Erlenmeyer-Kimling et al. 1984) has some parallels to the Danish project but also some important differences. The project was initiated in 1971 using children from the New York metropolitan area as subjects. The initial sample (A) has been followed continuously since 1971–2. More recently a further sample (B) has been drawn so that the findings obtained on the first sample may be replicated. Both samples contain children of schizophrenic fathers as well as mothers and exceptionally also have extremely high-risk subsamples – namely, children of two schizophrenic parents. More experimental data have been collected on these subjects than were collected on the Danish subjects. Both projects obtained psychophysiological data consisting of electrodermal measures and EEG and Evoked Potential indices (obtained at a later stage in the Danish study). Both projects incorporated a neurological examination but the New York study obtained more neuropsychological data. In particular the latter project made use of the wealth of data that had then appeared, showing that schizophrenic patients were considerably impaired on tests of attention, and incorporated a variety of attention tests.

Considerable emphasis was given to early reports from the Danish study concerning patterns of abnormal electrodermal responding, both in the high-risk group as a whole and subsequently the 'sick' subgroup from amongst the high-risk group. The observation (Mednick 1967) that the high-risk group exhibited a hyper-responsive pattern of electrodermal activity was surprising in so far as only a limited number of that group would be expected, eventually, to become abnormal. What, however, had in a sense become a yardstick for later studies was this report of hyper-responsivity, and in particular the finding of a faster skin conductance response-recovery time in the high-risk group. This latter aspect was important because Mednick (1974) had incorporated speed of response recovery into a theory of the development of schizophrenia. The later finding from the New York study (for example, Erlenmeyer-Kimling and Cornblatt 1987) of no relationship between electrodermal response pattern and risk status was thus of considerable importance.

Several explanations for this discrepancy are possible, and are in themselves to be seen as of theoretical importance. Thus, rather than invalidating either of the two studies, or both, the discrepancy may, in fact, add something to our knowledge of the area. The first possibility is that age may be a relevant variable. The New York children were first tested at the ages of 7 to 12, whereas the Danish subjects had a mean age of 15 years. (Unpublished data from the present author's laboratory suggests that this explanation is unlikely.) A second possibility is raised by Mednick(1978). In this report he shows that the findings of electrodermal hyper-responsivity in the high-risk group are restricted to the offspring from non-intact homes. In the New York study the sample was drawn from children from intact homes and this may provide a reason for the discrepant finding. This is clearly of importance in its own right in so far as it appears to indicate an interaction between genetic risk and environmental experience that is exhibited in activity of the autonomic nervous system. A third possibility is that neither study appears to have taken into account the now extensive findings of two classes of abnormal electrodermal responsivity among adult schizophrenics. Gruzelier and Venables (1972) showed that, among a heterogeneous population of schizophrenic patients in hospital, there were some 50 per cent who could be classed as non-responders, showing no electrodermal activity to orienting stimuli, while on the other hand a large proportion of the remainder showed electrodermal hyper-responsivity. While the finding of hyper-responsivity has not been replicated in a majority of studies of severely ill schizophrenics, it has been shown to be a characteristic of freshly admitted patients exhibiting largely 'positive' symptoms (Frith et al. 1979; Zahn et al. 1981). The finding of non-responsivity has however been shown to be universal (Ohman 1981; Bernstein et al. 1982). Data are available which indicate that aspects of electrodermal activity have a heritable component (Bell et al. 1977; Kotchubei 1987). Bearing this in mind, it is possible that, depending on the diagnosis of the parents, which in part is reflected in the type of electrodermal activity which they exhibit, the electrodermal activity of the subjects of these projects will be heterogeneous.

There is a further possibility, enabling explanation of the discrepant results, that requires the introduction of another high-risk project of a somewhat different pattern. In 1972 a study was commenced on the island of Mauritius which, instead of using familial indicators of risk as had been the case in Copenhagen and

New York, made use of patterns of electrodermal activity as risk factors. The rationale for this was based on the studies which have been described which suggest that indicators (or, to use the current term, 'markers') of schizophrenia may be electrodermal hyper-responsivity or non-responsivity. The project started with the screening of 1,800 3-year-old children using measures of electrodermal response to standard stimulus tones, and the later selection of 200 of these for further study based on their electrodermal hyper-responsivity or non-responsivity. A control group was drawn from the modal part of the distribution of electrodermal activity (Venables 1978). Thus, some of the disadvantages of basing a risk sample on the children of schizophrenic parents were obviated, although, of course, other problems were introduced. Not the least of these is the questionable legitimacy of using age 3 electrodermal activity as a predictor when the patterns of development of the electrodermal system are inadequately understood. Between 1979 and 1981, when the children had a mean age of 10·5 years, amongst other measures, data were collected on smooth-pursuit eye movement. This measure is probably considered to be one of the strongest of the genetic markers for schizophrenia (Iacono 1985; Siever and Coursey 1985). Thus, if there were no indication that the original selection on the basis of electrodermal activity at age 3 produced groups with differences in smooth-pursuit eye-movement indices, it could be thought that the original selection process was probably erroneous. The preliminary analyses of the data indicated that the original selection had not produced groups of subjects with differences in smooth-pursuit eye-movement indices. However, bearing in mind the work which suggests a mediating role for intelligence in the development of schizophrenia, it was decided to divide the risk and control groups on the basis of IQ scores. Other material had also been published in the mean time which supported this idea. Kimmel and Deboskey (1978) had reported that gifted children had patterns of electrodermal activity which were comparable to those of the hyper-responsive group in the Mauritius study. It was thus likely that this latter group contained two subgroups of subjects: highly intelligent children who might be thought of as gifted, and pre-schizophrenic children characterized by below-average intelligence. When the groups were divided on the basis of IQ scores it was found that the low-IQ hyper-responsive group exhibited abnormal smooth-pursuit eye movements, while the high-IQ hyper-responsive group did not. Neither high- nor low-IQ control subjects showed abnormal smooth-pursuit eye movements (Venables 1987).

Thus, there is a fourth possibility introduced by this material to explain the difference between the Danish and New York studies with respect to patterns of electrodermal activity. Neither study examines the role of IQ as a moderating variable in this particular context. However, in an analysis of the school behaviour of the New York subjects Watt et al. (1982: 171) reported that 'it was tentatively concluded that disharmony, emotional instability and *low intelligence* are the early markers for vulnerability to schizophrenia most worthy of attention' (emphasis added).

Thus, the prospective New York study suggests a role for low intelligence as a mediating variable for the development of schizophrenia as also indicated by data from the Mauritius study. It also provides data which support other aspects of the retrospective material which has been reviewed.

CONCLUSION

This brief review has been able to do no more than to outline some of the benefits and also some of the difficulties of longitudinal research into the development of schizophrenia. It has pointed out the need to take into account a variety of important variables such as conditions at birth, parental absence, early institutionalization, pre-morbid intelligence, sex differences, differences in subdiagnoses, and in particular the *interaction* between these variables. There is no sense in which longitudinal work suggests that the concept of schizophrenia is not of value as a focus for the understanding of the development of 'madness' in a group of people with a particular range or cluster of symptoms. To move away from this *unifying* concept would be to set back work in this area to at least the middle of the nineteenth century. To state that schizophrenia is an appropriate unifying concept is not the same as to suggest that it is a *unitary* concept. There is too much literature available which points to possible heterogeneity. Furthermore, this is by no means to say that we should be immobilized in the amber of Kraepelian doctrine, but rather that to deny the usefulness of the concept of schizophrenia as an anchor from which developments can take place is a foolish step. Longitudinal studies lead us to recognize the essentially dimensional nature of disorder with severe schizophrenia at one end of that dimension and somewhere along that dimension the milder madnesses of belief in horoscopes and magical intervention before reaching the sanity of the less interesting members of the population. The other aspect that is urged upon workers in the field is the recognition of the multivariate nature of the disorder, exemplified by the present spate of research on 'positive vs negative' schizophrenia (Andreasen and Olsen 1982) or Type I vs Type II schizophrenia (Crow 1980). Longitudinal research can, at least, help towards the elucidation of the precursors of patienthood and the continuity or otherwise of the different symptomatologies of what we usefully encapsulate under the rubric of 'schizophrenia'.

REFERENCES

Achenbach, T.M. and Edelbrock, C.S. (1978) 'The classification of child psychopathology: a review and an analysis of empirical efforts', *Psychological Bulletin* 85: 1275–301.

Al-Issa, I. (1985) 'Sex differences in the aetiology of schizophrenia', *International Review of Applied Psychology* 34: 315–33.

Andreasen, N.C. and Olsen, S. (1982) 'Negative v positive schizophrenia', *Archives of General Psychiatry* 39: 789–94.

Asarnow, R.F., Nuechterlein, K.H., and Marder, S.R. (1983) 'Span of apprehension performance, neuropsychological functioning, and indices of psychosis proneness', *Journal of Nervous and Mental Disease* 171: 662–9.

Aylward, E., Walker, E., and Bettes, B. (1984) 'Intelligence in schizophrenia: meta-analysis of the research', *Schizophrenia Bulletin* 10: 430–59.

Bagshaw, M.H., Kimble, D.P., and Pribram, K.H. (1965) 'The GSR of monkeys during orienting and habituation and after ablation of the amygdala, hippocampus and inferotemporal cortex', *Neuropsychologia* 3: 111–19.

Bell, B., Mednick, S.A., Gottesman, I.I., and Sergeant, J. (1977) 'Electrodermal parameters in male twins', in S.A. Mednick and K.O. Christiansen (eds) *Biosocial Bases of Criminal Behavior*, New York: Gardner Press, pp. 217–28.

Bernstein, A.S., Frith, C.D., Gruzelier, J.H., Patterson, T., Straube, E., Venables, P.H., and Zahn, T.P. (1982) 'An analysis of skin conductance orienting response in samples of American, British and German schizophrenics', *Biological Psychology* 14: 155–211.

Burton, R.V. (1970) 'Validity of retrospective reports assessed by the multi-track multi-method analysis', *Developmental Psychology Monographs* 3: 1–15.

Crow, T.J. (1980) 'Molecular pathology of schizophrenia: more than one disease process?', *British Medical Journal* 280: 66–8.

Erlenmeyer-Kimling, L. and Cornblatt, B. (1987) 'The New York High-risk Project: a follow up report', *Schizophrenia Bulletin* 13: 451–62.

Erlenmeyer-Kimling, L., Marcuse, Y., Cornblatt, B., Friedman, D., Rainer, J.D., and Rutschmann, J. (1984) 'The New York High-risk Project', in N.F. Watt, E.J. Anthony, L.C. Wynne, and J.E. Rolfe (eds) *Children at Risk for Schizophrenia*, Cambridge, Cambridge University Press, pp. 169–89.

Fish, B. (1957) 'The detection of schizophrenia in infancy', *Journal of Nervous and Mental Disease* 125: 1–24.

Frith, C.D., Stevens M., Johnstone, E.C., and Crow, T.J. (1979) 'Skin conductance responsivity during acute episodes of schizophrenia as a predictor of symptomatic improvement', *Psychological Medicine* 9: 101–6.

Goldberg, E.M. and Morrison, S.L. (1963) 'Schizophrenia and social class', *British Journal of Psychiatry* 109: 785–802.

Goldstein, M.J. and Tuma, A.H. (1987) 'High-risk research', *Schizophrenia Bulletin* 13: 369–71.

Gruzelier, J.H. and Venables, P.H. (1972) 'Skin conductance orienting activity in a heterogeneous sample of schizophrenics', *Journal of Nervous and Mental Disease* 155: 277–87.

Heston, L.L. (1966) 'Psychiatric disorders in foster home reared children of schizophrenic mothers', *British Journal of Psychiatry* 112: 819–25.

Hoch, P.H. and Cattell, J.P. (1959) 'The diagnosis of pseudoneurotic schizophrenia', *Psychiatric Quarterly* 33: 17–34.

— Strahl, M.O., and Pennes, H.H. (1962) 'The course and outcome of pseudoneurotic schizophrenia', *American Journal of Psychiatry* 11: 106–15.

Iacono, W.G. (1985) 'Psychophysiological markers of psychopathology: a review', *Canadian Psychology* 26: 96–112.

Johnstone, E.C., Frith, C.D., Crow, T.J., Husband, E.J., and Kreel, L. (1976) 'Cerebral ventricular size and cognitive impairment in chronic schizophrenia', *Lancet* 2: 924–6.

Joreskog, K.G. (1981) Statistical models for longitudinal studies', in F. Schulsinger, S.A. Mednick, and J. Knop (eds) *Longitudinal Research*, Boston: Martinus Nijhoff, pp. 118–24.

Kety, S.S., Rosenthal, D., Wender, P.H., and Schulsinger, F. (1968) 'The types and prevalence of mental illness in the biological and adoptive families of adopted schizophrenics', in D. Rosenthal and S.S. Kety (eds) *The Transmission of Schizophrenia*, Oxford: Pergamon Press, pp. 345–62.

Kimmel, H.D. and Deboskey, D. (1978) 'Habituation and conditioning of the orienting reflex in intellectually gifted and average children', *Physiological Psychology* 6: 377–80.

Kotchubei, B.I. (1987) 'Human orienting reaction: The role of genetic and environmental factors in the variability of evoked potentials and autonomic components', *Activitas Nervosa Superior* 29: 103–8.

Lewine, R.R.J. (1981) 'Sex differences in schizophrenia: timing or sub-types?', *Psychological Bulletin* 90: 432–44.

— Watt, N.F., Prentky, R.A., and Fryer, J.H. (1978) 'Childhood behaviour in schizophrenia, personality disorder, depression and neurosis', *British Journal of Psychiatry* 132: 347–57.

Lykken, D.T. (1968) 'Statistical significance in psychological research', *Psychological Bulletin* 70: 151–9.

Mednick, S.A. (1967) 'The children of schizophrenics: serious difficulties in current research methodologies which suggest the use of the "high-risk group" method', in J. Romano (ed.) *The Origins of Schizophrenia*, Amsterdam: Excerpta Medica, pp. 179–200.

— (1970) 'Breakdown in individuals at high risk for schizophrenia: possible predispositional perinatal factors', *Mental Hygiene* 54: 50–63.

— (1974) 'Electrodermal recovery and psychopathology', in S.A. Mednick, F. Schulsinger, J. Higgins, and B. Bell (eds) *Genetics, Environment and Psychopathology*, Amsterdam: Elsevier/North Holland, pp. 135–46.

— (1978) 'Berkson's fallacy and high-risk research', in L.C. Wynne, R.L. Cromwell, and S. Matthysse (eds) *The Nature of Schizophrenia*, New York: John Wiley, pp. 442–52.

— and McNeil, T.F. (1968) 'Current methodology in research on the etiology of schizophrenia. Serious difficulties which suggest the use of the high-risk group method', *Psychological Bulletin* 70: 681–93.

Mednick, S.A., and Schulsinger, F. (1968) 'Some premorbid characteristics related to breakdown in children with schizophrenic mothers', in D. Rosenthal and S.S. Kety (eds) *The Transmission of Schizophrenia*, Oxford: Pergamon Press, pp. 267–91.

Mednick, S.A., Parnas, J., and Schulsinger, F. (1987) 'The Copenhagen High-risk Project 1962–1986', *Schizophrenia Bulletin* 13: 485–95.

Mednick, S.A., Schulsinger, F., Teasdale, T.W., Schulsinger, H., Venables, P.H., and Rock, D.R. (1978) 'Schizophrenia in high-risk children: sex differences in pre-disposing factors', in G. Serban (ed.) *Cognitive Defects in the Development of Mental Illness*, New York: Brunner/Mazel, pp. 169–97.

Meehl, P.E. (1962) 'Schizotaxia, schizotypy and schizophrenia', *American Psychologist* 17: 827–38.

Offord, D.R. (1974) 'School performance of adult schizophrenics, their siblings and age mates', *British Journal of Psychiatry* 125: 12–19.

Ohman, A. (1981) 'Electrodermal activity and vulnerability to schizophrenia: a review', *Biological Psychology* 12: 87–145.

Parnas, J., Schulsinger, F., Teasdale, T.W., Schulsinger, H., Feldman, P.M., and Mednick, S.A. (1982) 'Perinatal complications and clinical outcome within the schizophrenic spectrum', *British Journal of Psychiatry* 140: 416–20.

Pearson, J.S. and Kley, I.B. (1957) 'On the application of genetic expectancies as age-specific base rates in the study of human behaviour disorders', *Psychological Bulletin* 54: 406–20.

Reisby, N. (1967) 'Psychoses in children of schizophrenic mothers', *Acta Psychiatrica Scandinavica* 53: 371–86.

Rieder, R.O., Broman, S.H., and Rosenthal, D. (1977) 'The offspring of schizophrenics. II: Perinatal factors and IQ', *Archives of General Psychiatry* 34: 789–99.

Robbins, L.C. (1963) 'The accuracy of parental recall of aspects of child development and of child rearing practices', *Journal of Abnormal and Social Psychology* 66: 261–70.

Roff, J.D. and Knight, R. (1978) 'Young adult schizophrenics: prediction

of outcome and antecedent childhood factors', *Journal of Consulting and Clinical Psychology* 46: 947–52.
— (1980) 'Pre-schizophrenics: low IQ and aggressive symptoms as predictors of adult outcome and marital status', *Journal of Nervous and Mental Disease* 168: 129–32.
— (1981) 'Family characteristics, childhood symptoms, and adult outcome in schizophrenia', *Journal of Abnormal Psychology* 90: 510–20.
Roff, M. (1970) 'Some life history factors in relation to various types of adult maladjusment', in M. Roff and D.F. Ricks (eds) *Life History Research in Psychopathology (Vol. 1.)*, Minneapolis: University of Minnesota Press, pp. 213–58.
Rosenthal, D. (1974) 'Issues in high-risk studies of schizophrenia', in D.F. Ricks, A. Thomas, and M. Roff (eds) *Life History Research in Psychopathology (Vol. 3)*, Minneapolis: University of Minnesota Press, pp. 25–41.
Schulsinger, F., Parnas, J., Petersen, E.T., Schulsinger, H., Teasdale, T., Mednick, S.A., Moller, L., and Silverton, L. (1984) 'Cerebral ventricular size in the offspring of schizophrenic mothers', *Archives of General Psychiatry* 41: 602–6.
Schulsinger, H. (1976) 'A ten year follow up of children of schizophrenic mothers: clinical assessment', *Acta Psychiatrica Scandinavica* 53: 371–86.
Siever, L.J. and Coursey, R.D. (1985) 'Biological markers for schizophrenia and the biological high risk approach', *Journal of Nervous and Mental Disease* 173: 4–16.
Venables, P.H. (1973) 'Input regulation and psychopathology', in M., Hammer, K. Salzinger, and S. Sutton (eds) *Psychopathology*, John Wiley: New York, pp. 261–84.
— (1978) 'Psychophysiology and psychometrics', *Psychophysiology*, 15: 302–15.
— (1987) 'Cognitive and attentional disorders in the development of schizophrenia', in H. Hafner, W.F. Gattaz, and W. Janzarik (eds) *Search for the Causes of Schizophrenia*, Berlin: Springer-Verlag, pp. 203–13.
Walker, E.F., Cudeck, R., Mednick, S.A., and Schulsinger, F. (1981) 'Effects of parental absence and institutionalisation on the development of clinical symptoms in high risk children', *Acta Psychiatrica Scandinavica* 63: 95–109.
Watt, N.F. (1978) 'Patterns of childhood social development in adult schizophrenics', *Archives of General Psychiatry* 35: 160–5.
— Grubb, T.W., and Erlenmeyer-Kimling, L. (1982) 'Social, emotional, and intellectual behaviour at school among children at high risk for schizophrenia', *Journal of Consulting and Clinical Psychology* 50: 171–81.
— Anthony, E.J., Wynne, L.C., and Rolf, J.E. (1984) *Children at Risk for Schizophrenia: A Longitudinal Perspective*, Cambridge: Cambridge University Press.
Yarrow, M.D., Campbell, J.D., and Burton, R.V. (1970) 'Recollections of childhood: a study of the retrospective method', *Monographs of the Society for Research in Child Development* 35: 1–81.
Zahn, T.P., Carpenter, W.T., and McGlashan, T.H. (1981) 'Autonomic nervous system activity in acute schizophrenia. I. Method and comparison with normal controls', *Archives of General Psychiatry* 38: 251–8.

Part Three

FROM THEORY TO THERAPY

Chapter Eight

COMPETING HISTORIES OF MADNESS

Some implications for modern psychiatry

DAVID PILGRIM

'Insanity is purely a disease of the brain. The physician is now the responsible guardian of the lunatic and must ever remain so.' (From an editorial in the *Journal of Mental Science*, 1858.)

This pronouncement, from the forerunner of the *British Journal of Psychiatry*, was made in the same year that the General Medical Bill passed through Parliament. The Bill succeeded after sixteen failed drafted attempts and innumerable internecine disputes within the nascent profession of medicine (Parry and Parry 1976). Thus, the middle of the nineteenth century was a crucial period in the history of medicine. It was a time when the medical profession eventually gained a mandate from the State to define and manage certain forms of deviance as illness.

This Victorian phase of early medical professionalization set the stage for later constructions of mental distress, or emotional deviance, which were eventually formalized, as far as the psychiatric branch of medicine is concerned, in the nosology of Kraepelin (the inventor of 'dementia praecox' in 1896, relabelled 'schizophrenia' by Bleuler later). In this period, as now, the power to label and control illness was inextricably bound up with professional politics. In the light of what is known about this period, this chapter will explore ways in which histories of madness can illuminate the status of schizophrenia within our contemporary debates about mental health. Three main questions will be examined.

First, given that schizophrenia is an extremely weak concept in terms of its logical coherence (Bannister 1968; Bentall et al 1988), does history tell us anything about its retention by clinicians and researchers? Second, following from this first question, has history anything to tell us about the continued acceptance of such a weak concept by the general public, along with their tolerance of the extensive iatrogenic consequences of leaving the treatment of 'schizophrenics' to biologically oriented psychiatrists? Third, does history tell us anything about why psychiatric labelling has led to more frequent charges of invalidation and stigmatization (Szasz 1964; Laing 1967) than has been the case in physical medicine, even though both mental and physical illness can be unified conceptually as forms of deviance (Sedgwick 1982; Pilgrim 1984)?

These three questions will be reconsidered in the concluding section of this chapter. In order to build up a rationale for the answers which will be offered, some exploration will be made of the competing claims that have been made about the history of psychiatry.

VARIETIES OF HISTORY

An advantage of any historical perspective is that it has the potential of showing our present assumptions in relative terms. However, this historical relativism is double-edged. Self-congratulatory versions of history compare modern progress and enlightenment in a field with the ignorance of the past. In total contrast, the past may be invoked to uncover the historical roots of present misconceptions and inadequacies. In one version of history, the past comforts the present; in the other, the past is found guilty for its legacy. It is likely that there are political motives on both sides for pursuing one, rather than the other, broad reading of the history of the psychiatric treatment of madness. Thus, an important distinction can be made between 'public relations' versions of psychiatric history (to use Sedgwick's term) and 'revisionist' versions (Cohen and Scull 1983). It should also be noted that a style of historical account has emerged recently, which might be dubbed 'post-revisionist', exemplified in the work edited by Bynum et al. (1985). This places a greater emphasis on specific empirical projects rather than grand theorizing. No attempt will be made within the limits of this chapter to describe the detailed content of these competing historiographies (the interested reader will need to consult the original texts quoted and Boyle's examination of the history of the schizophrenia concept in Chapter 1 of this volume). What will be attempted instead is a description of the impact of these competing views of history on the professions, the public, and mental-health policies. The turbulence caused by these competing claims undoubtedly reflects the importance of schizophrenia as a political issue for the conservative majority within the psychiatric profession and for politicians concerned with social policy, as well as for their radical critics. This concern about schizophrenia arises from the tension between viewing it as a socio-political problem on one hand or as a technical medical problem on the other.

Traditional histories

Whilst psychiatry has had its critics since its early days, the dominant view that psychiatry had of its own development by the turn of this century has been summarized by Doerner (1981) as follows:

> Around 1900, psychiatry looked on itself with uncritical matter-of-factness as natural-scientific enlightenment, as a fight against demonologic and other social superstitions and for the rights of the mentally ill, a fight that was waged now against, now in league with the state authorities, and especially against religious attitudes and institutions.
>
> (ibid.: 292)

This type of account, according to Doerner, continued throughout the twentieth century and dominated social histories until the 1960s. This pattern changed with the appearance of *Madness and Civilisation* by Foucault (1965) and *Three Hundred Years of Psychiatry* by Hunter and MacAlpine (1963). These works are mentioned in particular because they represented a departure from a dominant trend of psychiatric historiography. In the 1980s 'revisionist' accounts have gained such a reputation, and have so competed for pride of place in the intellectual culture critical of professional psychiatry, that it could be overlooked that the 'public relations' version of history dominated the field until 30 years ago.

This point is important because the dominance of the traditional account of psychiatric history reached hegemonic proportions in the first half of this century. Thus, it is likely during this period that the great majority of lay people and those being socialized afresh in the mental-health professions took for granted that psychiatry, like the rest of medicine, represented one of the key triumphs of modernity: the blending of science and humanitarianism for the amelioration of human distress; a blend which becomes more refined and effective with the passing of time. Thus, Scull (1983a) notes that scientific humanism in psychiatric practice, in combination with increasing government inspection, are components in an equation constructed by a variety of writers, before 1961, who argued for the unambiguously progressive nature of Victorian psychiatry (for example, Roberts 1960).

Thus, traditionalism within psychiatric historiography itself can be divided into two phases: pre- and post-1960. However, the emergence of critical historiographies in the 1960s did not halt the pattern set in motion by these earlier studies. (An excellent example of traditional thinking after the 1960s is that of Jones (1972), who produced a prestigious apologia for modern psychiatry.) Moreover, the existence of a new counter-current of revisionist accounts mattered little to conservative psychiatrists if the new discourse did not impinge, to any significant extent, on neophyte mental-health professionals or the general public. In basic psychiatric textbooks widely used after 1960, there is little indication that the traditional account was seriously threatened (for example, Slater and Roth 1969).

Critical histories

Alternative accounts to the public-relations exercises, noted above, are not a monolithic body of knowledge. They contradict one another at points (sometimes in relation to unresolvable ideological issues) which makes terms like 'antipsychiatric' or even 'revisionist' as dubious in their coherence as some of the psychiatric concepts being brought into question. It is probably more accurate simply to record that a variety of forces emerged during the 1960s and 1970s, throughout Europe and in the USA, which opposed traditional psychiatric theory and practice. These forces of refusal or opposition had, as one component, versions of psychiatric history which challenged the dominant view sketched above. Sometimes this historical dimension was little more than a retrospective gibe at heroes of the past, as in Laing's ridiculing of Kraepelin's behaviour when examining a patient (Laing 1959).

The work of the US psychoanalyst Szasz entailed some attempt to explore systematically the medicalization of madness. The two noteworthy social historical accounts given by non-clinicians which have had a profound academic impact are those of Foucault (1965) and Scull (1979). These three key writers in the field of critical historiography share a concern to debunk the conservative consensus which flattered medicine, but their methods of doing so are quite discrepant.

Szasz's (1971) main concern has been to extend his insistence that minds can be sick only in a metaphorical sense (like economies) in order to show how the notion of mental illness has acted as a smokescreen in modern times, hiding subjugation and ill-treatment of non-conformists by the State. Thus, *The Myth of Mental Illness* is not merely a neat (if rather boringly repeated) logical argument for the benefit of his fellow psychiatrists. Szasz is also keen to emphasize that the concept of mental illness has served as a rationalization for forms of social control dressed up in the guise of medical treatment. Szasz proceeds to quote several examples of how the 'treatment' of 'illnesses' like 'schizophrenia' has entailed unwarranted loss of liberty for 'sufferers'. Within this coercive tradition, existing up to and including the present day, uncooperative bodies have been incarcerated, drugged, and given shock treatment in the name of medical benevolence. Thus, the main reason for considering history for Szasz is largely about proving a moral point. This point enables him to extend his outrage about present psychiatric practices back into an era when such events began to be rationalized by the medical profession. He is careful to emphasize that he has no objection in principle to people with emotional difficulties ('problems in living') contracting with anybody (including medical practitioners) to seek comfort or help with problem resolution. His objections only centre on the mystification of language (calling people ill when they are not) and on the hypocrisy of psychiatric practice (claiming to care for people when coercive interventions and loss of liberty are actually what is happening). Arguably, the use of the term 'mental illness' in itself is not necessarily offensive (what after all is in a name?) and Szasz's preoccupation with this issue can be better described as moralistic, rather than moral.

The second problem Szasz highlights is the issue of mystified coercive social control and the emergence during the last century of psychiatrists who were prepared to play out that role. The radical individualism of Szasz makes him focus on the issue of personal liberty. Consequently, his analysis of suprapersonal forces (the realm of sociology) is thin. What is left is a strong message that the State in all conditions is a threat to liberty. This (contestable) amalgam critique of the State is not helpful in providing a social explanation of the forms of modern psychiatric discourse and practice.

The lengthy deliberations of Foucault on the complexities of historical suprapersonal forces and processes starkly contrasts with the work of Szasz. The impact of Foucault on our contemporary understanding of social policy and professionalism has been enormous and has spawned a school of academics who have tried to emulate their master by extending his ideas, and at times imitating his cryptic style, when analysing psychiatric practices, since and including the last century (for example, Castel et al. 1979; Castel 1983; Miller and Rose 1986). Foucault, within a larger project about medical discourses, began to establish a central thesis that knowledge and power are inextricably linked. He also claims that between the middle of the seventeenth century and the beginning of the nineteenth, the conditions were established under which professional psychiatry became possible. The two most salient aspects of these conditions were the segregation of the mad and the breakdown of the dialogue between rationality and irrationality after the Renaissance. Probably the most important and controversial implication of this early Foucauldian reasoning was that our modern understanding of madness was *constituted* by the social policy of segregation (i.e. segregation shaped or constructed the form of madness rather than it simply being a response to a pre-existing problem).

This period for Foucault marked a time when not only economic but *moral* factors informed the project to put irrationality out of sight. This emphasis on the ethical thrust of the segregative answer to madness contrasts with Scull's work. Foucault inverts the conclusion drawn by conservative historians about historically significant events, such as Pinel's unchaining of the Bicêtre residents at the end of the eighteenth century. Whereas conservative historians celebrate this period as the moment of the birth of humanitarian attitudes towards the mad, Foucault maintains that it marked the triumph of rationality over 'frenzied unreason', so that the latter became invalid. Once this reframing was complete, social reformers could advocate a liberal attitude towards the mad, who were now cast in the role of outsiders or strangers. In other words the mad had to lose their full rights of personhood if they were to be considered for re-entry into ordinary civil society. For Foucault, then, madness, during the seventeenth century was 'sequestered and, in the fortress of confinement, bound to reason, to the rules of morality and to their monotonous nights' (p. 64).

Scull (1979) places more emphasis than Foucault on the *economic* necessity of segregation. He starts his period of analysis in the nineteenth century, pointing out that, until then, the majority of the mad roamed free in society. For Scull, the State-asylum system emerged primarily (along with other institutions like the workhouse) to control the nuisance created by the poor who were unemployed or unemployable. The control of the pauper lunatic then became a central political project for the newly established capitalist state, with segregation being the dominant solution for social-policy makers, until it was brought into question in the 1930 Mental Treatment Act (Ramon 1985; Busfield 1986).

The medical profession (via acts of Parliament related to its control of the asylums and the legitimacy of its monopolization of the management of illness in all its forms) was invested with powers by the State to have ultimate authority over the mad. The interplay between economic necessity and professional power is the main relationship that Scull seeks to detail in his work. According to this perspective, present-day medical authority over the mad is predicated on this Victorian period of medical profession-alization, when biological reductionism and the territorial base of the asylum ensured the dominance of medical practitioners in the domain of emotional deviance. Then, as now, there was no evidence that biology could explain madness. Such a claim was vital, though, if medical authority was to have any credibility.

Reactions to criticism

Since the 1960s, the disparate criticisms made of conservative accounts of psychiatry, past and present, have triggered important professional and academic responses. On one side there has been a series of sympathetic critiques (for example, Baruch and

DAVID PILGRIM

Treacher 1978; Ingleby 1981, 1983a; Sedgwick 1982; Ramon 1985; Miller and Rose 1986). These authors incorporated, with varying degrees of enthusiasm, the main concerns of Foucault or Scull, extending them here or criticizing them there. Thus, a set of derivative works appeared in the 1970s and 1980s. On the other side there has been a set of professional psychiatric responses. These have varied from outraged condemnation (for example, Hamilton 1973; Roth 1973) to calmer but equally reactionary critiques (for example, Clare 1976; Wing 1978). The first group of defences of psychiatry were a response to the first wave of critical histories, whereas the latter reacted also to the later derivations. Hamilton (ironically in his Presidential Address to the British *Psychological* Society) dismissed critics of psychiatry in the following way:

> This is what comes of the abandonment of science. It can only end in one way, the way that of the other antiscientific movements have ended. It will end in the gun and the gas chamber, not the revolution but the putsch, not the people but the colonels. These movements are *le trahison des clercs* – the treason of the intellectuals.
>
> (Hamilton 1973: 188)

As a further example of the tone of contempt with which critiques of psychiatry are dealt with by these spokespeople for the profession, here are the opening comments of Roth's 1972 Presidential Address to the Royal College of Psychiatrists:

> The anti-medical critique of psychiatry represents one approach within a wider movement which has assumed international proportions and adopts a critical or derogatory stance towards psychiatry's methods, aims and social role; it is anti-medical, anti-therapeutic, anti-institutional and anti-scientific, either by expressed aims or implicitly through the dogmatic, hortatory, diffuse and inconsistent character of its utterances.
>
> (Roth 1973: 373)

The rest of the address is taken up with re-asserting the scientific status of psychiatric custom and practice, and with arguing that the critics' comments are extreme and absurd. The address finishes with the following cool sociological opinion:

218

The self-righteous conviction, aggressive and denunciatory tone and the extravagant language used by some critical colleagues represent a new phenomenon on the social scene. Constructive endeavour to resolve the manifold problems of contemporary psychiatry requires attitudes of a different kind.

(ibid.: 378)

The colourful language and indignant protests of Hamilton and Roth mean that their work, though implicitly prestigious because of their status in the profession of psychiatry, is largely of interest to sociologists of the professions studying rhetorics of justification; they have little of substance to contribute to the issues raised by critics. In other words the *form* of their response is of academic interest but the content is not. This cannot be said of Clare and Wing. Whilst Clare and Wing are described above as reactionary, it should be noted that largely they abandoned a frontal attack of the Hamilton–Roth type. Instead, they opted for a selective incorporation of ideas from the opposition. Consequently, Clare and Wing championed continued medical dominance by a subtle process of reformism.

Wing, within the first three pages of his *Reasoning About Madness,* as well as sneering at the irrationality of critics of the Kraepelinian view of schizophrenia ('nihilist, anarchist, extreme left-wing, extreme right-wing but all are agreed on the necessity for violent change' – p. 2), also appears to credit Foucault with some insight about the nature of madness. This credit is soon removed, though, when he notes that Kraepelin's formulation of mental illness was more precise and liberating than Foucault's vague notion of madness. Even more menacing consequences are conjured up for the reader, unwise enough to take the Foucauldian version of history seriously, which Wing warns would be 'at best romantic and impractical and at worst...barbarous and inhuman' (p. 4). Above all, Wing is concerned to project an image of (reformed) Kraepelinian psychiatry as representing the voice of moderation still struggling to offer the correct blend of humanitarianism and science (in contrast to the shrill voice of political extremism). He opines, for instance, that: 'Much of the criticism of psychiatry so evident during the past decade has been a reaction to a medical tendency, accurately recognised but over-generalised by the critics, to go too far' (p. 43). Note here the deference to substantive criticism in principle but the objection (yet again) to the extremism of the critics.

The main reform on offer by Wing is not that of abandoning diagnosis but of making it more efficient. For him, schizophrenia is not the incoherent concept its critics claim but instead is scientifically valid, provided that it is described more accurately than has been the case in the past. What Wing does by this logic (in combination with developing the technology to defend it–the Present State Examination, Wing et al. 1967 and Wing et al. 1974) is to make a plea that schizophrenia is a technical description. If schizophrenia is a technical description it is under the jurisdiction of medicine. If people are simply mad (i.e. aspects of their conduct are unintelligible to the lay person – Coulter 1973), then anybody could speak with as much authority as anyone else about it. By continuing to assert that schizophrenia is essentially a *technical-medical* matter, Wing implicitly argues that only psychiatrists can be permitted to have (i.e. retain) a mandate to manage people so labelled.

Thus, *Reasoning About Madness* is a vitally important book because it represents one of the best examples (to be studied by future historians) of psychiatrists re-asserting their authority in the field of mental health and excluding competing bids for legitimacy, be they from critical fellow professionals, or from the radical consumer lobby within that large population labelled as mentally ill. One of the key indicators that the book is first and foremost an attempt to re-assert this authority, after its foundations had been shaken by a critical European and Anglo-American intelligentsia, is the focus on schizophrenia. In the light of increasingly plausible psychological and social explanations being offered for depression and the anxiety-based problems, schizophrenics represented the irreducible core population which psychiatrists depend on for their general mandate to manage emotional deviance on behalf of the State. It was there-fore vital that in the aftermath of the 1960s, some version of the 1858 claim, cited at the beginning of this chapter, was re-asserted by a doyen of the profession. Wing provided this re-assertion.

It should be emphasized that Wing's claim for continued medical authority is not only based on making psychiatric diagnosis more scientific, but also upon the acceptance of the psychological and social factors (both causal and consequential) implicated in 'mental illness'. Thus, the credibility of Wing's case is strengthened by shoring up his rhetoric of moderation with a form of generous eclectic thinking (in line with the British cultural tradition of incorporating new ideas and practices in order to obstruct more radical shifts of thought or practice).

This type of liberal–humanitarian–eclectic psychiatry, fit for the second half of the twentieth century, is also advocated by Clare in *Psychiatry in Dissent*. The emphasis in this book is on rejecting a crude catch-all bio-determinism, into which so much of modern psychiatry has degenerated, and replacing it with a new eclecticism, which incorporates psychological and social reasoning when diagnosing and caring for 'mentally ill' people. (Contemporary psychiatry is now eclectic, although the strong skew towards biological interventions remains apparent: Pilgrim 1986; Richards 1986.) The acceptance of the dangers of biological reductionism by Clare is a basis, then, for claiming a continued mandate to have ultimate authority over emotional deviance. This sleight of hand, whereby progressive reforms were being advocated for reactionary ends, was neatly revealed by Baruch and Treacher (1978) shortly after the appearance of Clare's book. Baruch and Treacher seek to expose the rhetoric of psychiatry in the 1970s which asserts the type of 'portmanteau' model offered by Clare, uncovering the strong biological, historically sedimented undertow to the new eclecticism when rhetoric is compared to practice. Without alluding to the specific critique that Baruch and Treacher made of his work, Clare reacted in the following way when reviewing their book *Psychiatry Observed*:

Doubts at the outset are strengthened by the knowledge that the observers in question are a research sociologist and a clinical psychologist. After all, a number of sociologists have done much to disparage effectively the notion of 'scientific' impartiality while endorsing the role of participant-observer.... As far as clinical psychology is concerned, it is in the midst of clarifying the precise terms and conditions of its takeover bid for those assets of Psychiatry Limited which it believes more properly belong to it....It is worth noting that one of the authors of this dismal book (AT) is described as a lecturer in mental health at one of the country's most reputable medical schools. One shudders at the possible effect he is likely to have

with such efforts as he makes to introduce some sociological
concepts into medical training given that his own
understanding of medicine is so rudimentary and inadequate.

(Clare 1979: 387–9).

Clare's evaluation is not supported by Treacher's later reputation.
(He went on to co-edit a prestigious text in the sociology of
medical knowledge – Wright and Treacher 1982.) At the same
time that these acrimonious academic debates were occurring
(shielded for structural reasons from the general public), policy
shifts of great importance were occurring in the mental-health
field. In particular, the crisis of the welfare state in a period of
capitalist recession during the 1970s ensured that the segregation
of psychiatric patients could not remain a viable policy for the
social control of the mad (Offe 1984; Busfield 1986). Whether the
rhetoric of community care enshrined in official government
reports since the 1930 Mental Treatment Act (for example, DHSS
1975) will produce real benefits to patients is being tested by this
most recent phase of de-carceration.

IMPLICATIONS

An attempt has been made to highlight some of the professional
and political processes surrounding the historiography of
psychiatry and madness. A few additional and summary points can
now be made, which will lead into a discussion of contemporary
mental-health debates. Following Horwitz (1983) it seems fair to
say that madness is acknowledged to have existed in all past and
present societies but the particular way it is understood, both in
terms of the causes implicated (exogenous versus endogenous)
and the words used to describe it, vary over time and place. Some
people for varying amounts of time act and communicate in ways
which their fellow citizens find unintelligible. Although some
progress has been made in accounting for *some* aspects of mad
behaviour in *some* people, medical research has yielded no
convincing evidence that 'schizophrenia' is a superior notion to
that of the lay concept of 'madness'.

A second point raised by Horwitz is that societies vary in the
way in which they respond to madness. This emphasis was also
made by Sedgwick (1982) when noting that, whilst the medical

framing of madness as mental illness is associated with a particular historical and cultural context, there has been a trans-historical tension between hard and soft ways of responding to insanity. Since ancient Greece, mad people have been counselled and tolerated on one side or segregated and their bodies interfered with on the other. In the light of these cross-cultural and trans-historical points, the medical profession, especially when represented by liberal eclectics like Wing, have done no great service to those they have the mandate to manage when they have attempted to refute the claims made by critical social historians.

For their part, clinical psychologists have, by and large, in their shorter (i.e. post-war) history done little to challenge the view that madness is essentially a medical problem (Bannister 1983). Clinical psychologists have taken little interest in the mad, compared with less disturbed clinical populations, and the empirical psychological research that has been done into madness has been parasitical upon the psychiatric *a priori* concept of schizophrenia. (Where this is not the case, systematic psychological theorizing about madness has still often been heavily biologically orientated, evading sociological and anthropological models of deviance.)

This poor showing by psychologists in relation to the study of madness is for two main reasons. First, those seeking to stabilize the profession of clinical psychology have sought to make a bid for legitimacy to manage the 'neurotic' population, leaving madness to the medical profession (Eysenck 1975). Second, most of the research money available to psychologists interested in madness has been supplied by the drug companies or, when State-funded, has been regulated by committees dominated by psychiatrists. Both the drug companies and psychiatrists have a vested interest in further legitimizing traditional concepts of mental illness, by investing money in research projects formulated to investigate these and not other concepts. As schizophrenia is the bedrock condition which justifies the existence of psychiatry, the role of research-as-legitimizer-of-the-status-quo is of central professional importance.

Another implication of the discourse on madness being left today in the expert hands of psychiatrists is the tendency to individualize what are social processes. Thus, for instance, in the never-ending debate about more precise descriptions of schizophrenia and the endless search for the cause of this disease, the most important dimensions of the lives of mad people are underscrutinized. Most psychiatric patients in the community are poor, unemployed or unemployable, homeless or living in poor accommodation, exploited by government-funded landlords, and often sad, lonely, and frightened. Given the justifiable critiques concerning degradation in the State-asylum system, some commentators hold the pessimistic view that patients are effectively trapped between the devil and the deep blue sea (for example, Horwitz 1983; Scull 1983b).

Whether the heated debates concerning the feasibility of properly funded community care will culminate in a more humane deal for the mad depends not on a set of heroic medical and scientific investigations about the nature of 'schizophrenia' but instead on the victory of one set of political processes over another. A reliance on the medical profession to solve the puzzle of 'schizophrenia' will divert attention from the need to address the following social policy requirements: a widespread educational programme concerning the tolerance of deviance (in this case of the 'mentally ill'); a massive increase in housing stock so that decent accommodation is available to the poorest and most disabled members of the community; a democratization of the mental-health services to break down medical dominance and to make decisions about patients a matter of negotiation with them not about them; a greater availability of non-coercive, non-invasive methods of helping patients (less drugs and electroconvulsive therapy (ECT) and more voluntary psychological interventions); a massive reduction in unemployment to give less-able citizens the right of access to jobs; and the availability of settings tailored to a variety of needs (day centres for ordinary human contact and residential settings for those in acute turmoil and distress).

The above is a political shopping list, in whole or in part endorsed by Warner (1985) in his thoughtful analysis of processes affecting recovery from madness. In Britain in the early 1990s the shopper has a nearly empty pocket and the shelves are nearly bare, as far as services for the poor are concerned (Walker and Walker 1987). This gloomy picture can only be rectified by a new alliance of progressive forces preparing a programme for a less socially divided time. A model in Italy is available which, though not directly transferable, offers lessons from successes and mistakes for Britain (Rogers and Pilgrim 1986).

As yet, there is little evidence that this type of progressive alliance is forming. The sectional interests of (a weakened) trade-union movement in the mental-health field in Britain have not encouraged its formation. Likewise, the consumer lobby in Britain is split three ways. On one wing is the National Schizophrenia Fellowship (NSF), which enshrines in its title and philosophy a conservative disease model (and consequently has a close relationship with the medical profession); on the other wing is the Campaign Against Psychiatric Oppression (CAPO); and in the middle, occupying the largest ground, is the National Association for Mental Health (MIND).

These consumer groups do share certain demands with regard to better funding of community resources. However, there is a massive ideological gap outside of this area of agreement. The NSF has either not heard, or refuses to accept, critical accounts of psychiatry. It shares certain pro-medical aims such as the need for compulsory treatment in the community and publicizes – and thereby legitimizes – the disease status of schizophrenia. CAPO seeks to outlaw all coercive interventions and ECT whether or not compulsorily administered. Moreover, it espouses a militantly antipsychiatric philosophy. MIND is internally divided in several ways. The national organization, based in London, is split off from, and feeds poorly into, its local affiliated associations. Within national MIND several lobbies jostle for position (variously emphasizing legal advocacy for individuals, advice-giving about treatment, normalization, education, and policy development), so no coherent overall philosophy is evident. Moreover, whilst MIND has certain traditional lobbying links with the State, it has no formal policy-making powers. Even these links have an inhibiting implication, given that the Department of Health provides funding for MIND which is sufficiently large that the latter could not survive if it were withdrawn. This threat of withdrawal of funds reduces the power of MIND to develop policies in a free, critical manner: a point that civil servants at the department enjoy emphasizing when MIND challenges government policy on mental-health matters too strongly. Thus, the national consumer lobby, in its widest sense, is divided and weakened by its enmeshment with the medical profession and a conservative State apparatus. A more hopeful reading of the British mental-health scene relates to local initiatives, which could act as models for practice elsewhere. These include the efforts on the part of Good Practices in Mental Health to encourage a process of client empowerment, the therapeutic residences of the Philadelphia and Arbours Associations in London (which grew out of Laingian initiatives in the 1960s), and experiments in patient democracy, such as the Nottingham Patient Council.

The resolution of these debates in favour, ultimately, of the mentally distressed (whatever their psychiatric label) depends on programmatic changes concerning mental health, which will not be facilitated by the acceptance of the historically based mandate of medical practitioners to be trusted as benevolent scientists. This type of dependency has always obscured or mystified the social and political dimensions of madness and its treatment.

Two examples of this claim are worth noting briefly here. The first relates to the suppression, in the majority of histories of psychiatry, of knowledge of the pro-active role of the psychiatric profession in killing a quarter of a million patients for eugenic reasons in Nazi Germany (Wertham 1966, cited in Hill 1983). (One bizarre twist to this macabre tale was that Jewish patients were excluded from the programme on the grounds that they did not deserve the 'treatment'.) The second, less dramatic, but equally important, example relates to the myth that major tranquillizers were the reason why doors could be opened and patients could readily leave psychiatric hospitals during the 1950s. With the exception of a few honest academic psychiatrists (for example, Lader 1979) the majority of the profession silently collude with this inaccurate assumption. (Numbers were dropping in the inpatient population *before* the introduction of major tranquillizers – Scull 1977.)

The biological slant to research and the treatment of madness has meant that psychotherapeutic interventions have remained relatively neglected. When systematic attempts have been made to study psychotherapeutic efficacy with those labelled as schizophrenic, the outcome is very encouraging and is certainly far removed from the therapeutic pessimism of the 'maintenance-dose-of-phenothiazines' philosophy generally associated with the dominant chemotherapeutic tradition (Alenen et al. 1986). What does remain controversial is whether one form of psychological treatment intervention is superior to another (Karon 1984).

From the main studies available, individual analytically orientated therapy seems to be effective (Karon and VandenBos 1981) although this interpretation of outcome has been criticized for failing to control for random medication effects (Stanton et al. 1984). The continued use of medication with patients studied in the US literature seems to confound the ability of investigators to make clear-cut statements about the amount of variance in the improved subjects which is attributable to the impact of psychotherapy (cf. the Scandinavian study of Alenen et al. 1986). As Karon (1984) notes, there is inertia in the system of US research, characterized by a fearfulness to experiment with drug-free subjects. This, Karon suggests, is a result of psychiatrists being influenced by their inherited, professional conventional wisdom and by drug-company advertising campaigns. Moreover, the high drop-out rates in research studies which continue to use medication with their psychotherapy subjects (which undermine the ability of researchers to interpret their data) may be a result of many patients finding the iatrogenic effects of drugs aversive. Thus, medication may be interfering with better designed research into psychotherapy in two ways: data interpretation is clouded and patients may weaken the sample size by avoiding the concurrent drug regime.

When these studies are set against other research in which the effectiveness of neuroleptic medication and the long-term recovery of those labelled as schizophrenic are assessed, a further complication arises. This relates not to whether *psychotherapy* remains a dubious treatment of choice for mad patients, but whether there are rational and ethical grounds for *medication* being used with this group. Long-term follow ups of 'schizophrenic' (medicated) subjects indicate that good social opportunities and support seem to predict good outcome (Strauss and Carpenter 1977; Bleuler 1978; Ciompi 1984; Warner 1985). Moreover, estimates of the effectiveness of major tranquillizers cast a serious doubt on the ethical appropriateness of their continued use. With estimates of the effectiveness of medication as low as 20 per cent for patients diagnosed as schizophrenic (Crow et al. 1986), alongside the high probability of reported iatrogenic tardive dyskinesia (an irreversible disorder of motor control which is a frequently observed side-effect of neuroleptic medication), it seems that the majority of patients are being exposed to a damaging and ineffective intervention. Thus, the need for a psychological approach to the amelioration of the distress entailed in the experience of madness is made compelling by the consequences of traditional chemical approaches. They have had a massive iatrogenic impact. Hill (1983) estimates that around half of the world's 150 million recipients of major tranquillizers suffer from some degree of tardive dyskinesia.

Some reviewers of the evidence on drug-induced brain damage claim that the emphasis on tardive dyskinesia is too limited. Breggin (1983), for instance, in an extensive review of the topic, draws attention to the types of higher brain function which are impaired by neuroleptic medication leading to symptoms of brain damage in addition to tardive dyskinesia. If this scale of iatrogenic brain damage existed in a non-psychiatric population, the drug involved would probably be banned, or its use strictly controlled. The overriding need to control the mad, along with their lack of power of protest about their treatment, can be the only explanation why this prevalence of medically induced brain damage is considered acceptable by professionals and their employers.

In a recent US review of the literature on tardive dyskinesia, Brown and Funk (1986) provide a detailed analysis of this state of affairs. They argue that the powerlessness of psychotic patients allows a doctor-centred set of practices to be maintained in psychiatry. Studies which in contrast record patient accounts of their treatment (for example, Estroff 1981) indicate that patients are mainly interested in the disabling impact of drugs on their daily living in contrast to their treating psychiatrists, who focus on symptom reduction. Moreover, the need to retain a biological rationale within psychiatry has distorted the awareness of its practitioners about the disadvantages of their chemotherapeutic zeal, such that many are ignorant about toxicity and lack caution in their prescribing practices (Waldron 1977). A naïve reliance on drug-company-supplied information about medication amplifies these practices (Cooperstock 1974). Recently, professional anxieties about iatrogenic tardive dyskinesia have prompted some academic psychiatrists to caution their British colleagues to use only low-maintenance doses of phenothiazines (Manchada and Hirsch 1986), but there is no evidence at present that clinicians are heeding these warnings. Indeed, public alarm about the use of phenothiazines, expressed at length in the correspondence columns of the *Guardian* (in the summer of 1987) merely led to a set of defensive justifications for existing diagnostic and treatment practices from psychiatrists (Pilgrim 1987). It seems that the conclusions drawn by Brown and Funk about the reluctance of psychiatrists to admit the extent of iatrogenic damage linked to psychotropic medication are as true in Britain as on the other side of the Atlantic.

CONCLUSIONS

Returning now to the three questions posed at the outset, the following conclusions can be drawn. First, with regard to the continuing survival of the schizophrenia concept, it is clear that the power of psychiatrists to assert the legitimacy of the concept is at the centre of this paradox. From the middle of the nineteenth century, psychiatrists have claimed a special knowledge about madness without providing, to this day, a single shred of evidence to support the assertion that 'insanity is purely a disease of the brain'. Concepts clearly do not survive only because of their logical coherence or empirical validation. In the case of the schizophrenia concept, crude professional assertion assures its viability.

Moving to the second question regarding the public acceptance of current psychiatric practice, the public seems to continue to accept this albeit illogical position. There are three possible explanations for this, which are not mutually exclusive. The first is presented by Ingleby (1983b) and relates to the transference reactions ordinary people typically have towards medical authority. Our socialization into accepting the authority of medical experts means that they are often trusted by members of the public in a childlike way. The second possible explanation concerns the role of psychiatrists as agents of social control. Given that mad people generally are not popular as a result of their demeanor, most people are happy to hand over the responsibility for removing the perceived source of a social crisis to a medical expert. This is true whether the crisis is in the family (Scott 1973) or in public (Rogers 1988). Lay people identify madness prior to psychiatrists intervening (Coulter 1973). What they do not want is the responsibility of managing the consequences of madness.

Once they hand over this responsibility to a medical expert, they are probably little concerned about how the latter prefers to construe the problem in hand. Technicalizing madness as 'schizophrenia' suits psychiatrists and solves the social nuisance created by 'schizophrenics' in the domestic or public arena.

The third possibility is that lay people are badly informed about the problematic status of psychiatric knowledge. With popular misconceptions such as the idea that schizophrenia refers to a split personality being widespread (and reinforced by tabloid newspaper definitions), it may simply be that most people are ill-informed about mental-health matters, so they cannot offer a critical opinion about psychiatric knowledge. (When a systematic campaign is launched to inform the public it tends to be that of the disease model of the NSF or a more elaborate psychiatric conventional wisdom offered by drug-company-sponsored paperbacks – Seeman et al. 1982.)

Moving to the third question posed at the beginning of this chapter, it seems that history does tell us something about why psychiatric labelling has provoked more concern than other types of medical diagnosis. Psychiatry commonly entails the management of people, often for lengthy periods of time. Their fate is largely in the hands of psychiatrists but the psychiatrists' diagnoses push the person further and further into the 'stranger' role described by Foucault. They are cast from the role of ordinary citizenship and lose all of the rights and obligations normally attached to that status.

Psychiatric patients *are*, then, different from other types of medically managed populations (as are other 'chronic' analogues such as the incurably disabled, the mentally handicapped, and the frail elderly). The chronic management of those who are invalidated already because of their lack or loss of reason means that civil rights, which are normally taken for granted, are retained precariously by them, or are irredeemably lost. In these circumstances, special concern should be directed towards these people and their plight. Stigmatizing labels like 'schizophrenia' are not helpful; rather, they compound these problems of citizenship. For historical reasons outlined in this chapter, the medical profession has its own interests to consider, as well as those of its patients, when deciding whether or not to retain or abandon the concept of schizophrenia.

REFERENCES

Alenen, Y.O., Rakkolainen, V., Laakso, J., Rasimus, R., and Kaljonen, A. (1986) *Towards a Need-specific Treatment of Schizophrenic Psychosis*, New York: Springer-Verlag.

Bannister, D. (1968) 'The logical requirements for research into schizophrenia', *British Journal of Psychiatry* 14: 181–8.

— (1983) 'The internal politics of psychotherapy', in D. Pilgrim (ed.) *Psychology and Psychotherapy*, London: Routledge & Kegan Paul.

Baruch, G. and Treacher, A. (1978) *Psychiatry Observed*, London: Routledge & Kegan Paul.

Bentall, R., Jackson, H., and Pilgrim, D. (1988) 'Abandoning the concept of "schizophrenia": some implications of validity arguments for psychological research into psychotic phenomena', *British Journal of Clinical Psychology* 27: 303–24.

Bleuler, M. (1978) 'The long-term course of schizophrenic psychoses', in L.C. Wynne et al. (eds) *The Nature of Schizophrenia*, New York: Wiley.

Breggin, P.R. (1983) *Psychiatric Drugs: Hazards to the Brain*, New York: Springer.

Brown, P. and Funk, S.C. (1986) 'Tardive dyskinesia: barriers to the professional recognition of iatrogenic disease', *Journal of Health and Social Behaviour* 27: 116–32.

Busfield, J. (1986) *Managing Madness*, London: Hutchinson.

Bynum, W.F., Porter, R., and Shepherd, M. (eds) (1985) *The Anatomy of Madness*, London: Tavistock.

Castel, F., Castel, R., and Lovell, A. (1979) *The Psychiatric Society*, New York: Columbia University Press.

Castel, R. (1983) 'Moral treatment: mental therapy and social control in the nineteenth century', in S. Cohen and A. Scull (eds) *Social Control and the State*, Oxford: Blackwell.

Ciompi, L. (1984) 'Is there really a schizophrenia? The long term course of psychotic phenomena', *British Journal of Psychiatry* 145: 636–40.

Clare, A. (1976) *Psychiatry in Dissent*, London: Tavistock.

— (1979) 'Review of *Psychiatry Observed* by Baruch and Treacher', *Psychological Medicine* 9: 387–9.

Cohen, S. and Scull, A. (eds) (1983) *Social Control and the State*, Oxford: Blackwell.

Cooperstock, R. (1974) 'Some factors involved in the increased prescribing of psychotropic drugs', in R. Cooperstock (ed.) *Social Aspects of the Medical Use of Psychotropic Drugs*, Toronto: Addiction Research Foundation.

Coulter, J. (1973) *Approaches to Insanity*, New York: Wiley.

Crow, T.J., MacMillan, J.F., Johnson, A.L., and Johnston, E.C. (1986) 'The Northwick Park study of first episodes of schizophrenia: II: A controlled trial of prophylactic neuroleptic medication', *British Journal of Psychiatry* 148: 120–7.

Department of Health and Social Security (1975) *Better Services for the Mentally Ill*, London: HMSO.

Doerner, K. (1981) *Madmen and the Bourgeoisie*, Oxford: Basil Blackwell.

Estroff, S.E. (1981) *Making It Crazy: An Ethnography of Psychiatric Clients in an American Community*, Berkeley University of California Press.

Eysenck, H.J. (1975) *The Future of Psychiatry*, London: Methuen.

Foucault, M. (1965) *Madness and Civilisation*, New York: Pantheon.

Hamilton, M. (1973) 'Psychology in society: end or ends?', *Bulletin of the British Psychological Society* 26: 185–9.

Hill, D. (1983) *The Politics of Schizophrenia*, London: University Press of America.

Horwitz, A. (1983) *The Social Control of Mental Illness*, New York: Academic Press.

Hunter, R.A. and MacAlpine, I. (1965) *Three Hundred Years of Psychiatry*, Oxford: Oxford University Press.

Ingleby, D. (ed.) (1981) *Critical Psychiatry*, Harmondsworth: Penguin.

— (1983a) 'Mental health and social order', in S. Cohen and A. Scull (eds) *Social Control and the State*, Oxford: Blackwell.

— (1983b) 'Professionals as socialisers: the psy complex', Paper presented to the 1983 British Sociological Association Conference (Medical Section).

Jones, K. (1972) *A History of the Mental Health Services*, London: Routledge & Kegan Paul.

— (1984) 'The fear of reducing medication and where have all the patients gone?', *Schizophrenia Bulletin* 10 (4): 613–17.

Karon, B.P. and VandenBos, G.R. (1981) *Psychotherapy of Schizophrenia: The Treatment of Choice*, New York: Jason Aronson.

Lader, M. (1979) 'Drug research and mental health service', in M. Meacher (ed.) *New Methods of Mental Health Care*, London: Pergamon.

Laing, R.D. (1959) *The Divided Self*, London: Tavistock.

— (1967) *The Politics of Experience*, Harmondsworth: Penguin.

Manchada, R. and Hirsch, S.R. (1986) 'Low dose maintenence medication for schizophrenia, *British Medical Journal* 293 (6546): 515.

Miller, P. and Rose, N. (1986) *The Power of Psychiatry*, London: Polity Press.

Offe, C. (1984) *Contradictions of the Welfare State*, London: Hutchinson.

Parry, N. and Parry, J. (1976) *The Rise of the Medical Profession*, London: Croom Helm.

Pilgrim, D. (1984) 'Some implications for psychology of formulating all illness as deviance', *British Journal of Medical Psychology* 57: 227–23.

— (1986) 'NHS psychotherapy: personal accounts' unpublished Ph.D. thesis, Nottingham University.

— (1987) 'The representation of mental health issues in the media', Paper presented at the London Conference of the British Psychological Society.

Ramon, S. (1985) *Psychiatry in Britain*, London: Croom Helm.

Richards, B. (1986) 'Psychological practice and social democracy', *Free Associations* 5: 105–36.

Roberts, D. (1960) *Victorian Origins of the British Welfare State*, New Haven: Yale University Press.

Rogers, A. (1989) 'Psychiatric referrals from the police' or medical

dominance?', unpublished Ph.D. thesis, Nottingham University.
— and Pilgrim, D. (1986) 'Mental health reforms: some contrasts between Britain and Italy', *Free Associations* 6: 65–79.
Roth, M. (1973) 'Psychiatry and its critics', *British Journal of Psychiatry* 122: 374.
Scott, R.D. (1973) 'The treatment barrier', *British Journal Medical Psychology* 46: 46–50.
Scull, A. (1977) *Decarceration*, New Jersey: Prentice Hall.
— (1979) *Museums of Madness*, London: Allen Lane.
— (1983a) 'Humanitarianism or control? Some observations on the historiography of Anglo-American psychiatry', in S. Cohen and A. Scull (eds) *Social Control and the State*, Oxford: Blackwell.
— (1983b) 'The asylum as community or the community as asylum?: paradoxes and contradictions of mental health care', in P. Bean (ed.) *Mental Illness: Changes and Trends*, London: Wiley.
Sedgwick, P. (1982) *PsychoPolitics*, London: Pluto Press.
Seeman, M.V., Littman, S.K., Plummer, E., Thornton, J.F., and Jeffries, J.J. (1982) *Living and Working with Schizophrenia*, Milton Keynes: Janssen Pharmaceutical Ltd/Open University Press.
Slater, E. and Roth, M. (1969) *Clinical Psychiatry*, London: Balliere, Tindall & Cassell.
Stanton, A.H., Gunderson, J.G., Knapp, P.H., Frank, A.F., Vannicelli, M.L., Schnitzer, R., and Rosenthal, R. (1984) 'Effects of psychotherapy in schizophrenia', *Schizophrenia Bulletin* 10: 520–63.
Strauss, J.S. and Carpenter, W.T. (1977) 'Prediction of outcome in schizophrenia: III. Five year outcome and its predictors', *Archives of General Psychiatry* 34: 159–63.
Szasz, T. (1964) *The Myth of Mental Illness*, New York: Harper & Row.
— (1971) *The Manufacture of Madness*, London: Routledge & Kegan Paul.
Waldron, I. (1977) 'Increased prescribing of valium, librium and other drugs', *International Journal of Health Services* 7: 37–61.
Walker, A. and Walker, C. (eds) (1987) *The Growing Divide*, London: Child Poverty Action Group.
Warner, R. (1985) *Recovery from Schizophrenia: Psychiatry and Political Economy*, London: Routledge & Kegan Paul.
Wing, J.K. (1978) *Reasoning About Madness*, Oxford: Oxford University Press.
— Cooper, J.E., and Sartorius, N. (1974) *Description and Classification of Psychiatric Symptoms*, London: Cambridge University Press.
— Birley, J.L.T., Cooper, J.E., Graham, P., and Isaacs, A.D. (1967) 'Reliability of a procedure for measuring "Present Psychiatric State"', *British Journal of Psychiatry* 113: 499–515.
Wright, P. and Treacher, A. (eds) (1982) *The Problem of Medical Knowledge*, Edinburgh: Edinburgh University Press.

Chapter Nine

BEHAVIOURAL AND
TIVE TREATMENT OF
HOTIC SYMPTOMS

PETER D. SLADE

Over the years, much has been written about the biology of schizophrenia (its genetics, biochemistry, pharmacology, and so on), but somewhat less has been written about its epidemiology and social aspects of the disorder; a lot has been written about the psychological deficits (although unfortunately most of this is disorganized and probably inconsequential), but very little has been said about psychological interventions for specific kinds of functional disturbances seen in patients classified as schizophrenic. This chapter is an attempt to review the latter and to generate some ideas about useful, non-physical treatments which may be worth exploring further with such patients.

TOWARDS A PSYCHIATRIC – PSYCHOLOGICAL
CLASSIFICATION OF SCHIZOPHRENIC SYMPTOMS

From the very introduction of the schizophrenia concept the need was evident to recognize 'differing clinical pictures'. Thus, Kraepelin (1896) found it useful to subdivide dementia praecox into four main types: simple, hebephrenic, catatonic, and paranoid. Subsequent workers, however, tended to prefer dichotomous classifications such as acute vs chronic, good premorbid vs poor premorbid, process vs reactive, and paranoid vs non-paranoid. For many years attempts were made to explain the heterogeneity found among groups of diagnosed schizophrenic patients by subdividing them in terms of these dichotomies (for example, Rausch 1952; Becker 1956; Shakow 1962; Phillips et al. 1966).

The problematic nature of these dichotomies was amply demonstrated by an early review of the literature on the 'problem of attention in schizophrenia' (Silverman 1964). Silverman concluded that 'acute-process' patients were similar to 'chronic-reactive' patients in manifesting size overestimation and minimal scanning, while 'acute-reactive' patients showed the opposite pattern of characeristics: that is, there appeared to be an inter-action between the acute-chronic and process-reactive distinctions, whereby process and reactive patients differed in one direction during the acute phase but exhibited a complete turnaround when they became chronic. The meaning of such an interaction is very difficult to fathom.

The above kind of sub-classification problem was largely instrumental in Richard Cooper and the present author (Slade and Cooper 1979) questioning the existence of a single disease-entity of schizophrenia. In that paper we demonstrated that the correlations observed in one major study (Trouton and Maxwell 1956) could have been the result of patient selection procedures operating on randomly distributed schizophrenic symptoms. We also suggested an alternative and weaker form of the random-symptom model of schizophrenia, namely one in which some symptoms of schizophrenia may be correlated while others may be independent. Such a model might involve two or three separate and independent sets of schizophrenic symptoms. Recent psychiatric ideas and data have indeed moved in this direction (see Chapter 2 by Bentall in this volume for a detailed discussion of this issue).

Crow (1980), for example, argued for the distinction between 'positive' symptoms of schizophrenia (hallucinations, delusions, and thought disorder) and 'negative' symptoms (flattening of affect, poverty of speech, loss of drive, and so on). This distinction has been taken up by Andreasen (1985), who has produced operational definitions and measures of the two classes of symptoms. However, this two-category solution has not been without its critics (for example, Lewine 1985), and indeed a fairly recent well-conducted, factor-analytic study (Liddle 1987) suggested that schizophrenic symptoms fall into three distinct groups: (a) positive symptoms (hallucinations and delusions); (b) negative symptoms – Type 1 (poverty of speech, poverty of affect, and so on); and (c) negative symptoms – Type 2 (speech disorganization, incongruity of affect, and so on). This grouping of symptoms seems to make psychological sense and, probably for the very first time in this area, it is possible to envisage a psychological classification (i.e. one based on the nature of psychological dysfunction) mapping on to a psychiatric classification (i.e. one based on clinical phenomenology). On the basis of these kinds of considerations, a speculative psychiatric–psychological classification of schizophrenic symptoms can be proposed (see Table 9.1).

Table 9.1 A speculative psychiatric–psychological classification of schizophrenic symptoms based on the study of Liddle (1987)

Psychiatric		Psychological
(A) Symptom category	*(B) Specific symptoms*	*(C) Nature of psychological dysfunction*
1. Positive	Hallucinations and delusions	Difficulty in controlling and/or understanding internally generated private experiences
2. Negative – Type 1	Poverty of speech, lack of affect, etc.	Difficulty in initiating responses (i.e. starter-motor problem)
3. Negative – Type 2	Speech disorganization, incongruity of affect, etc.	Difficulty in regulating responses, once initiated (i.e. timing problem)

In Table 9.1 three sets of schizophrenic symptoms emerging from the study of Liddle (1987) are separated out psychiatrically and, for each of them, a possible underlying psychological dysfunction is specified. Thus, the common theme underlying 'positive' symptoms (hallucinations and delusions) seems to be a difficulty in controlling and/or understanding internally generated private experiences. By contrast, the common theme underlying 'type 1 – negative' symptoms seems to be that of a difficulty in initiating responses, while the commonality underlying 'type 2 – negative' symptoms can be seen as a difficulty in regulating behaviour on a continuing basis. Such a psychiatric–psychological framework could prove useful in the future in helping to generate new psychological treatments for schizophrenic symptoms. For the present, I shall concentrate on describing the range of psychological interventions which have been attempted to date. These can be divided into treatments directed primarily at 'positive' symptoms of hallucinations and delusions and other more general interventions which have been directed at the range of 'negative' symptoms.

PSYCHOLOGICAL TREATMENTS FOR HALLUCINATIONS

Recently, the editor of this volume and myself (Slade and Bentall 1988) have reviewed the general scientific and medical literature on the subject of hallucinations. One of the chapters in the book is devoted entirely to the treatment of hallucinations, concentrating particularly on the various psychological methods that have been tried as these are less well known than their physical counterparts. In this section I shall limit myself to a brief description of the eight psychological (mainly cognitive or

Table 9.2 Summary table of psychological treatments for schizophrenic hallucinations

Type of treatment intervention	No. of studies	Type of study i.e. single case, group, etc.	Overall evaluation
1. Operant procedures	6	1 laboratory 5 single case	Good results apart from the laboratory study
2. Systematic desensitization	6	6 single case	Generally a reduction in hallucination frequency obtained
3. Thought-stopping	3	2 single case 1 controlled trial	Good results overall
4. Counter stimulation (distraction)	7	4 single case 3 small-group laboratory	Immediate effects good but no longer-term generalization
5. Self-monitoring	4	3 single case 1 small group	good results especially with concurrent self-monitoring
6. Aversion therapy	7	5 single case 1 small group 1 controlled trial	Good results but non-specific
7. Ear-plug therapy	4	3 single case 1 small group	Good results with differing ears
8. First-person singular	2	2 small group	Mixed results

behavioural) treatments which have been used in an attempt to modify hallucinatory experiences and to a consideration of the three major processes we think may underlie their effects. The eight treatment strategies are listed in Table 9.2, together with the number and type of studies that have used them and an overall evaluation of the results achieved.

Operant procedures

The first reported attempt to bring hallucinations under operant control was described by Lindsley (1959, 1963). He used what amounted to a human Skinner box: a small 6-foot-square laboratory containing a chair and, on one wall, a small plunger and delivery tray. He then attempted differentially to reinforce either non-symptomatic behaviour or hallucinatory activity (defined in terms of vocalization rate). His work, which involved the study of eighty psychotic patients for a total of more than 30,000 hours, unfortunately led him to the conclusion that 'vocal psychotic symptoms appear to be under some form of strong control that resists direct differential positive reinforcement.' (Lindsley 1959: 269)

By contrast with these laboratory studies, clinical applications of operant procedures have proved to be much more effective. Nydegger (1972), for example, successfully treated a 20-year-old male paranoid schizophrenic patient whose symptoms included auditory and visual hallucinations, delusions, and social withdrawal. The intervention used by Nydegger involved instructing the patient to refer to his 'voices' as 'thoughts' and then reinforcing him by social approval when he did so. The patient was also given a combination of assertion training and systematic desensitization to deal with his problems in interpersonal situations. Finally, his delusional speech was treated in a direct manner by verbal conditioning. The patient showed immediate relief from his symptoms, which was maintained at follow-up two-and-a-half years later.

Systematic desensitization

The use of systematic desensitization has been reported in a number of single-case studies of hallucinating patients, the primary aim being to reduce specific stresses which appear to be

238

associated with the occurrence of hallucinations. Two such studies have been reported by the present writer. In the first (Slade 1972) an imaginal desensitization programme was directed at sources of stress associated with the family. Reported reductions in tension and other mood states were found to be associated with a reduced frequency of auditory hallucination. In a second case-report (Slade 1973) another male hallucinating patient was found to respond to an *in vivo* desensitization programme directed at his interpersonal and social-skills problems. Once again, improvement in the stress problem was associated with a reduction in hallucination frequency.

Thought-stopping

The 'thought-stopping' procedure described by Rimm and Masters (1974) involves four stages. In the first stage, the therapist instructs the patient to raise his or her index finger every time he or she experiences an unwanted thought (or hallucination). The therapist then shouts 'STOP IT' repeatedly, in a loud voice, until the patient reports that the thought (hallucination) has ceased. In the second stage the patient is instructed to shout 'STOP IT' until this occurs, and then in the third the patient is instructed to whisper 'stop it' until the end-result is achieved. Finally, in the fourth stage, the patient is instructed to make the terminating stimulus covert by simply thinking 'stop it' until the unwanted thoughts (or hallucinations) cease.

This procedure has been used successfully in two single-case studies (Samaan 1975: Johnson et al. 1983). It has also been used in a controlled trial by Lamontagne et al. (1983) in which chlorpromazine alone was compared with chlorpromazine plus four sessions of thought-stopping. Twenty patients with DSM–III diagnoses of paranoid schizophrenia were randomly assigned to one or other treatment group. The daily frequencies of paranoid thoughts and hallucinations were carefully monitored and represented the target behaviours. The main finding was that the group receiving thought-stopping in addition to chlorpromazine improved more, on most measures, although only the difference in paranoid thoughts was statistically significant. The authors suggested that even better results with 'thought-stopping' might have been achieved with less chronic patients.

Counter-stimulation (distraction)

The application of counter-stimulation or distraction procedures to the treatment of hallucinations has been reported by seven sets of investigators, including two experimental studies reported by the present author (Slade 1974; Margo et al. 1981). The general finding has been that counter-stimulation methods are very effective, in the short term, in blocking hallucinations, but that the effects have not as yet been shown to generalize.

One clinical study which illustrates the transient nature of distraction procedures is that of Feder (1982). He reported the case of a patient with a 3-year history of intermittent 'voices'. The patient was advised to purchase and wear a pair of stereo headphones with an AM–FM radio. The patient reported a complete cessation of his voices at work while he wore the headphones but a continuation of his voices at other times when not wearing the headphones.

Self-monitoring

Self-monitoring in this context refers to the patient keeping an ongoing record of the occurrence and duration of his or her voices. Four studies of this procedure have been reported to date, all of which have found positive results. However, it would appear that it is only concurrent (and not retrospective) self-monitoring which has an impact. A study which demonstrated the necessity for concurrent self-monitoring was carried out by Reybee and Kinch (1973). They attempted to treat two male, chronic schizophrenic patients who had persistent auditory hallucinations as their major complaint. The therapist initially asked these patients to rate the frequency of their voices 'retrospectively' at various times throughout the day. This had no effect on hallucination frequency. Then they applied a 'concomitant' self-monitoring procedure in which the patients sat in front of an event-recorder and signalled the start, length, and termination of their 'voices' by pressing a button. This latter procedure produced a marked reduction in hallucination frequency in both patients.

Aversion and punishment techniques

A number of investigators have used an aversive procedure with hallucinating patients, in some cases utilizing electric shock as the aversive stimulus (for example, Bucher and Fabricatore 1970; Alford and Turner 1976), in others using aversive white noise (for example, Watts and Clements 1971). A good example of the former is the study by Turner et al. (1977), who employed a repeated-measures reversal-design with a female hallucinating patient, in which three interventions were systematically compared (social disruption, stimulus interference, and electrical-aversion therapy). As the patient only showed a transitory response to the social disruption and stimulus-interference conditions, the authors concluded that only the aversive procedure had an enduring effect.

A rather different result had previously been obtained in a controlled trial by Weingaertner (1971), who wanted to establish whether punishment is specifically effective in the suppression of auditory hallucinations. He assigned patients randomly to one of three groups: (a) a shock group, (b) a pseudoshock group, and (c) a no-treatment control group. The first two groups were given shock boxes and told to press the button when they heard their 'voices'. For the first group button-pressing caused a shock to be delivered, while for the pseudo-shock group the circuit had been disconnected, resulting in no shock. All three groups improved in terms of reported frequency of hallucination, but there were no significant differences between the three groups. The author concluded, as a consequence, that the primary agent of change was a 'placebo' effect.

The present writer has experimented, together with colleagues (Fonagy and Slade 1982; Slade et al. 1986), with the effect of white-noise treatment for hallucinating patients. The results have been promising, with a negative reinforcement condition proving to be maximally efficacious: that is, the initiation of 80+ decibels of white noise at the reported onset of a hallucination and the termination of the white noise consequent on reported offset. However, I have come to the conclusion that the therapeutic effects of aversion therapy (both electrical and white noise) are achieved not so much through aversive conditioning but rather as a result of a precise signalling effect (cf. self-monitoring). I shall return to this point later.

Ear-plug therapy

The use of unilateral ear-plugs to control auditory hallucinations was first suggested by Paul Green (1978) on the basis of his theory that there is defective interhemispheric transfer of information in schizophrenic patients. He suggested that the effect could be corrected if an ear-plug was inserted into the *left* ear (see Slade and Bentall (1988) for a discussion and critique of the neuropsychological rationale for this treatment). Since Green's suggestion, there have been four reports from investigators who have tried the 'ear-plug' procedure, all of which have described dramatic therapeutic results (James 1983; Done et al. 1986; Birchwood 1987; Morley 1987). However, the best results have sometimes been achieved when the patient has worn the ear-plug in the right rather than the left ear and sometimes when it has been switched from one ear to the other. The 'ear-plug' intervention therefore seems to be a useful one although the theory behind it seems to be in some doubt.

First-person-singular therapy

The explicit rationale for this type of treatment was described by Robert Greene (1978). His basic premiss was that, 'a key factor in auditory hallucinations is the message of maximum external control and minimum personal responsibility.' (p. 167) He therefore proposed that hallucinating patients should be told that their voices are internally generated and should be instructed to take responsibility for them. Greene reported the successful use of this therapeutic strategy with two female patients, both of whom were relieved of their voices once they had accepted full responsibility for them. Fowler (1986) also reported a dramatic reduction in hallucinations in one out of five patients treated by a similar approach.

Underlying processes

In this section it has been shown that eight different intervention strategies have produced beneficial results with hallucinating patients. This raises the obvious question of how these different, and sometimes seemingly incompatible treatments, produce their observed effects. One possibility is that they all operate at a different point on the hallucinatory mechanism. Alternatively there is the possibility that they all share a common factor, such as a placebo effect (i.e. they all generate positive expectations of change). There are, however, several studies which show that a placebo effect could not be the sole explanation for all observed effects (for example, Alford and Turner 1976; Turner et al. 1977; Fonagy and Slade 1982).

In our recent review of the literature (Slade and Bentall 1988) we came to the conclusion that the eight treatment strategies may be reducible to three change processes, namely: (a) focusing, (b) anxiety reduction, and (c) distraction. The crucial feature of 'focusing', we suggested, is the concurrent self-monitoring of hallucinatory experiences which is ensured either through the use of an event-recorder or through the requirement on the part of the patient to make a contingent response. We suggest that the commonality among five out of the eight treatment strategies was this requirement to focus on or attend to ongoing private experience of a hallucinatory nature. The five strategies included in this group are self-monitoring, aversion therapy, thought-stopping, ear-plug therapy, and first-person-singular therapy.

The second process of anxiety reduction is represented in the literature so far by only one treatment strategy, namely systematic desensitization. However, it seems clear that the mechanism of action of desensitization is different to that involved in the focusing procedures.

Finally, distraction procedures seem to represent a third and different process. They seem to have either a marked but transitory effect (i.e. counter-stimulation methods) or in some cases a marked and long-term effect when they involve the reinforcement of behaviour incompatible with hallucinatory activity (i.e. operant procedures).

THE PSYCHOLOGICAL TREATMENT OF DELUSIONS

By comparison with hallucinations, delusions have attracted very few attempts at psychological as opposed to physical interventions. Such interventions as have been tried fall into two main categories: operant methods and cognitive–behavioural methods.

Operant methods

Following on from some uncontrolled case reports, Ayllon and Haughton (1964) described what is now regarded a classic study in this area. They reported that the effect of attention, approval, and concrete reinforcers, when made contingent on delusional talk, was to increase its frequency of occurrence in a severely deluded patient. However, when the social and other reinforcers were made contingent on non-delusional talk, the frequency of occurrence of delusional talk decreased.

In a larger-scale study, Wincze et al. (1972) reported on the value of token reinforcement as opposed to direct instructions with ten paranoid-schizophrenic patients. They found that contingent-token reinforcement had a superior effect in that it reduced delusional verbal behaviour in seven, as opposed to four, of the patients. In a further study by Liberman et al. (1973), four patients with paranoid and grandiose delusions were exposed to social-reinforcement contingencies in a multiple-baseline design. The particular contingencies were found to produce the desired effect, although the degree of generalization was limited.

Thus, reinforcing deluded patients for rational speech seems to be effective, at least in the short term.

Cognitive–behavioural methods

The first explicit cognitive approach to the treatment of delusions was described by Watts et al. (1973), who called their procedure 'belief modification'. The hallmark of this procedure is the avoidance of a confrontational stance and the sensitive questioning of the evidence underlying the patient's abnormal beliefs. The authors reported on the use of this method with three individual clients, all of whom exhibited a decrease in delusional belief and a corresponding increase in positive areas of functioning. Milton et al. (1978) reported a further study of belief modification, this time comparing it with a 'confrontation' approach. Following the random allocation of sixteen deluded patients to the two groups they concluded that, while both interventions had a short-term effect, only the belief-modification procedure gave rise to a longer-term result.

Not dissimilar from the above approach is the 'reattribution therapy' described by Johnson et al. (1977). They successfully treated a male patient who developed a delusional belief on the basis of his unexplained nocturnal emissions by leading him to reattribute his experiences to his own sexual arousal rather than to the occult 'warm forms' he believed were sexually molesting him.

244

Finally, Hartman and Cashman (1983) reported on the treatment of three delusional patients (two male and one female) using a combination of psychopharmacological and cognitive–behavioural procedures. The greater impact achieved by the psychological methods led the authors to conclude: 'These results indicate that cognitive therapy is of apparent clinical value for interpersonally-medicated dysfunctional thought and perceptual experiences.' (ibid.: 59)

PSYCHOLOGICAL TREATMENTS FOR NEGATIVE SYMPTOMS

As suggested in the introduction to this chapter, negative symptoms of schizophrenia can be viewed psychologically as involving a problem either in initiating responses or in regulating behaviour once initiated. Although not specifically developed to deal with either an initiation or a behaviour-regulation problem, five general strategies have been described in the literature which have been directed primarily at negative symptoms of schizophrenia (Slade and Bentall 1989).

The token economy

The value of behaviour modification in the training of psychotic patients was extensively explored in the late 1950s and early 1960s, particularly in North America (for example, Ullmann and Krasner 1965). This approach used the principles of operant conditioning which were applied both to individual patients and also to whole wards of patients. The latter group application came to be known as the 'token economy' approach (Ayllon and Azrin 1968). The basic idea of the token economy is to motivate patients to behave appropriately and constructively by giving them tokens whenever they behave in an acceptable manner. These tokens can later be exchanged for a number of different reinforcers, which might range from access to cigarettes, drinks, and watching television to permission to sleep in a pleasant single room.

Token-economy regimes were introduced into large psychiatric hospitals in the US in the 1960s with fairly dramatic results. In the early 1970s they began to be used in the United Kingdom and produced good but perhaps less dramatic results with long-stay, chronic, institutionalized patients. The major impact of token regimes appears to be on negative symptoms. However, the efficaciousness of the regimes does not seem to be dependent on the token contingency but on changes in the way that staff interact with patients (Baker et al. 1977). It is important to note that, like other behaviour-modification programmes, token systems work best when patients are explicitly instructed about the contingencies at the outset, and the failure to do this has been cited as a reason why token systems sometimes fail to be effective (Kazdin 1977).

Token-economy programmes are still thought to be useful, particularly within the context of attempting to transfer long-stay patients from institutions into the community. They do, however, raise a number of problems which include the following: (a) the need to select a relatively homogeneous group of patients; (b) the need to select, train, and keep high-calibre nursing staff; (c) the need for a favourable staff–patient ratio; (d) the need to have the overwhelming support and commitment of all hospital staff and all the relevant professional groups; and (e) the need for every staff member to subscribe to a common set of objectives. A further problem posed by token systems concerns their ethical acceptability, as some token regimes require patients to 'earn' reinforcers which are usually regarded as theirs by right (Karasu 1981).

Social-skills training

The major problem underlying most of the negative symptoms is a lack of social skills. Thus, in the Scale for the Assessment of Negative Symptoms (Andreasen 1982) three out of the five types of negative symptoms considered concern behaviours which are social in nature (i.e. affective flattening, anhedonia-asociality, and attention). It is not surprising, therefore, that social-skills training has been seen as a useful approach with psychotic patients. Unfortunately, such studies that have been undertaken and reported have usually demonstrated only short-term benefits from training, although it is interesting to note that a large study of family interventions with schizophrenics (Hogarty et al. 1986 – see Chapter 10 by Tarrier in this volume) demonstrated that patients receiving a combination of social-skills training and family therapy were least likely to relapse over a 2-year period. Questions remain concerning the durability and generalization of the improvements achieved (Curran and Monti 1982).

Life-skills training

The training approach to the problems of long-term patients, particularly those presenting with negative symptoms, has been extended to encompass not only social but also other skills which are necessary for daily living. An example of a life-skills training approach for chronic schizophrenic patients was described by Murray Brown (1982). The programme was carried out in a day-patient unit and lasted for 7 weeks on a 5-days a week basis. The seven training modules focused on (a) interpersonal-skills training; (b) nutrition and meal planning (two modules); (c) health and hygiene; (d) managing money; (e) prevocational issues; and (f) the use of community resources and social networks. The major feature of this programme was the emphasis on teaching or training as opposed to treatment. Thus, for example, instead of simply telling patients to take their medication, psychiatrists gave lectures and seminars to groups of patients about the value, and possible side-effects of their drugs.

The initial outcome of this programme was favourable (Brown 1982) but the longer-term effects of life-skills training are unknown. However, the conceptual framework of the life-skills approach provides an innovative model of treatment which holds considerable promise for the future.

Self-instructional training

Cognitive–behavioural interventions have already been discussed with respect to the treatment of delusions. The distinctive feature of this approach is that, unlike earlier behavioural approaches which were narrowly tied to animal research, cognitive–behavioural techniques take into account the patient's capacity to plan and regulate his or her own behaviour (Lowe and Higson 1981). It might therefore be thought that such approaches hold particular promise for patients suffering from negative symptoms who find it difficult to initiate and control their own actions.

Perhaps the simplest cognitive–behavioural treatment is self-instructional training, which involves teaching patients to plan and control their own behaviour, first by instructing themselves out aloud and then by instructing themselves covertly (i.e. silently).

Meichenbaum and Cameron (1973) first used self-instructional training to improve the performance of schizophrenics on various cognitive tasks and to reduce psychotic speech. However, subsequent studies have called into question the extent to which the gains achieved following self-instructional training generalize. Bentall et al. (1987), in a series of three experiments, confirmed that this method could be used to bring about improvements in the cognitive performance of patients suffering predominantly from negative symptoms but little improvement was observed on generalization tasks, even when attempts were made to teach problem-solving self-instructions that might maximize generalization. The difficulties observed with respect to generalization suggest that the efficaciousness of self-instruction and other similar cognitive–behavioural techniques might be enchanced if they could be tailored to the specific cognitive deficits of particular patients. Self-instructional training, as it has so far been applied, assumes a simple lack of self-directed 'inner' speech. This may be an oversimplified view of the cognitive deficits involved in negative symptoms.

Problem-solving approaches

Given that patients exhibiting negative symptoms tend to have difficulty in both initiating reponses (for example, poverty of speech, lack of affect) and in organizing their behaviour (for example, speech disorganization, incongruity of affect), it is of some importance that Liddle's (1987) recent study of psychotic symptoms demonstrated separate factors corresponding to these two types of deficits. Both of these types of problems are important in the area of interpersonal relationships.

Recent approaches to the social difficulties of long-stay patients, particularly those exhibiting negative symptoms, have adopted a 'problem-solving' approach (for example, Wallace and Boone 1983; Hansen et al. 1985). These approaches have been influenced both by the growing interest in cognitive approaches to psychopathology alluded to above and by the observation that effective interpersonal problem-solving is related to the number of close friendships and the degree of family support available to discharged patients (Mitchell 1982).

Hansen et al. (1985) reported a study carried out with seven chronic psychiatric patients (six with a diagnosis of schizophrenia) who were trained in a procedure for solving interpersonal problems. The procedure involved five steps: (a) problem identification; (b) goal definition; (c) solution generation; (d) evaluation of alternatives; and (e) selection of the best solution. Hansen et al. found that this approach produced positive effects which generalized to non-training problems. The benefits of training were found to persist at 1 and 4-month follow-ups.

SUMMARY AND CONCLUSIONS

This chapter has reviewed some of the most important psychological interventions which have been tried with schizophrenic symptoms. For the sake of clarity these have been separated out into two main classes, namely those directed primarily at 'positive' symptoms and those directed primarily at 'negative' symptoms.

In the introduction it was suggested that psychiatric classification was now moving towards the recognition of three sets of schizophrenic symptoms, namely: a group of 'positive' symptoms (hallucinations and delusions) and two sets of 'negative' symptoms (i.e. 'poverty' symptoms and 'disorga- nization' symptoms). It was further suggested that these three sets of symptoms can be readily understood in terms of aspects of psychological dysfunction (see Table 9.1). It seems likely that in the future, psychologists will wish to develop and apply psychological interventions which are specifically suited to these three types of dysfunction. The limited research carried out to date, reviewed in this chapter, certainly suggests that the potential benefits of cognitive and behavioural strategies for schizophrenic patients have only just begun to be explored. It is to be hoped that future research will further develop these techniques and that they will become widely used in practice.

REFERENCES

Alford, G.S. and Turner, S.M. (1976) 'Stimulus interference and conditioned inhibition of auditory hallucinations', *Journal of Behaviour Therapy and Experimental Psychiatry* 7: 155–60.

Andreasen, N.C. (1982) 'Negative symptoms in schizophrenia', *Archives of General Psychiatry* 39: 784–8.

— (1985) 'Positive versus negative schizophrenia: a critical evaluation', *Schizophrenia Bulletin* 11: 380–9.

PETER D. SLADE

Ayllon, T. and Azrin, N.H. (1968) *The Token Economy*, New York: Appleton-Century-Crofts.

Ayllon, T. and Haughton, E. (1964) 'Modification of symptomatic behaviour of mental patients', *Behaviour Research and Therapy* 2: 87–9.

Baker, R., Hall, J.N., Hutchinson, K., and Bridge, G. (1977) 'Symptom changes in chronic schizophrenic patients on a token economy: a controlled experiment', *British Journal of Psychiatry* 131: 381–93.

Becker, W.C. (1956) 'A genetic approach to the interpretation and evaluation of the process–reactive distinction in schizophrenia', *Journal Abnormal and Social Psychology* 47: 489–96.

Bentall, R.P., Higson, P.J., and Lowe, C.F. (1987) 'Teaching self-instructions to chronic schizophrenic patients: efficacy and generalisation', *Behavioural Psychotherapy* 15: 58–76.

Birchwood, M. (1987) 'Control of auditory hallucinations through occlusion of monaural auditory input', *British Journal of Psychiatry* 149: 104–7.

Brown, M. (1982) 'Maintenance and generalisation issues in skills training with chronic schizophrenics', in J.P. Curraan and P.M. Monti (eds) *Social Skills Training: A Practical Handbook for Assessment and Treatment*, London: Guildford Press.

Bucher, B. and Fabricatore, J. (1970) 'Use of patient-administered shock to suppress hallucinations', *Behaviour Therapy* 1: 382–5.

Crow, T.J. (1980) 'Molecular pathology of schizophrenia: more than one disease process?', *British Medical Journal* 280: 1–9.

Curran, J.P. and Monti, P.M. (eds.) (1982) *Social Skills Training: A Practical Handbook for Assessment and Treatment*, New York: Guildford Press.

Done, D.J., Frith, C.D., and Owens, D.C. (1986) 'Reducing persistent auditory hallucinations by wearing an ear-plug', *British Journal of Clinical Psychology* 25: 151–2.

Feder, R. (1982) 'Auditory hallucinations treated by radio headphones', *American Journal of Psychiatry* 139: 1188–90.

Fonagy, P. and Slade, P.D. (1986) Unpublished study.

Fowler, D. (1986) 'A cognitive approach to hallucinations: implications for theory and therapy', Unpublished M.Sc. thesis, University of Leeds.

Green, P. (1978) 'Defective interhemispheric transfer in schizophrenia', *Journal of Abnormal Psychology* 87: 472–80.

Greene, R. (1978) 'Auditory hallucination reduction: first-person singular therapy, *Journal of Contemporary Psychotherapy* 9: 167–70.

Hansen, D.J., Lawrence, J.S.S., and Christoff, K.A. (1985) 'Effects of interpersonal problem-solving training with chronic aftercare patients on problem-solving component skills and effectiveness of solutions', *Journal of Consulting and Clinical Psychology* 53: 167–74.

Hartman, L.M. and Cashman, F.E. (1983) 'Cognitive–behavioural and psychopharmacological treatment of delusional symptoms: a preliminary report', *Behavioural Psychotherapy* 11: 50–61.

Hogarty, G.E., Anderson, C.M., Reiss, D.J., Kornblith, S.J., Greenwald, P., Javan, C.D., Manonia, M.J., and the EPICS Research Group (1986) 'Family psychoeducation, social skills training and maintenance

250

chemotherapy in the aftercare of schizophrenic patients', *Archives of General Psychiatry* 43: 633–42.

James, D.A.E. (1983) 'The experimental treatment of two cases of auditory hallucinations', *British Journal of Psychiatry* 143: 515–16.

Johnson, C.H., Gilmore, J.D., and Shenoy, R.S. (1983) 'Thought-stopping and anger induction in the treatment of hallucinations and obsessional ruminations', *Psychotherapy: Theory, Research, Practice* 20: 445–8.

Johnson, W.G., Ross, J.M., and Mastria, M.A. (1977) 'Delusional behaviour: an attributional analysis of development and modification', *Journal of Abnormal Psychology* 86: 421–6.

Karasu, T. (1981) 'Ethical aspects of psychotherapy', in S. Bloch and P. Chodoff (eds) *Psychiatric Ethics*, Oxford: Oxford University Press.

Kazdin, A.E. (1977) *The Token Economy: A Review and Evaluation*, New York: Plenum Press.

Kraepelin E, (1896) *Psychiatrie*, Leipzig: Barth.

Lamontagne, Y., Audet, N., and Elie, R. (1983) 'Thought-stopping for delusions and hallucinations: a pilot study', *Behavioural Psychotherapy* 11: 177–84.

Lewine, R.R.J. (ed.) (1985) 'Negative symptoms in schizophrenia', *Schizophrenia Bulletin* 11: 361–486.

Liberman, R.P., Teigen, J., Patterson, R., and Baker, V. (1973) 'Reducing delusional speech in chronic, paranoid schizophrenics, *Journal of Applied Behaviour Analysis* 6: 57–64.

Liddle, P.F. (1987) 'The symptoms of chronic schizophrenia: a re-examination of the positive–negative dichotomy', *British Journal of Psychiatry* 151: 145–51.

Lindsley, O.R. (1959) 'Reduction in rate of vocal psychotic symptoms by differential positive reinforcement', *Journal of the Experimental Analysis of Behaviour* 2: 269.

— (1963) 'Direct measurement and functional definition of vocal hallu-cination symptoms', *Journal of Nervous and Mental Disease* 136: 293–7.

Lowe, C.F. and Higson, P.J. (1981) 'Self-instructional training and cognitive–behaviour modification', in G. Davey (ed.) *Aspects of Conditioning Theory*, London: Methuen.

Margo, A., Hemsley, D.R., and Slade, P.D. (1981) 'The effects of varying auditory input on schizophrenic hallucinations', *British Journal of Psychiatry* 139: 122–7.

Meichenbaum, D.M. and Cameron, R. (1973) 'Training schizophrenics to talk to themselves: a means of developing attentional control', *Behaviour Therapy* 4: 515–34.

Milton, F., Patwa, V.K., and Hafner, R.J. (1978) 'Confrontation versus belief modification in persistently deluded patients', *British Journal of Medical Psychology* 51: 127–30.

Mitchell, R.E. (1982) 'Social networks and psychiatric clients: the personal and environmental context', *American Journal of Community Psychology* 10: 387–401.

Morley, S. (1987) 'Modification of auditory hallucinations: experimental studies of headphones and earplugs', *Behavioural Psychotherapy* 15: 252–71.

Nydegger, R.V. (1972) 'The elimination of hallucinatory and delusional behaviour by verbal conditioning and assertive training: a case study', *Journal of Behaviour Therapy and Experimental Psychiatry* 3: 225–7.

Phillips, L., Broverman, I.K., and Zigler, E. (1966) 'Social competence and psychiatric diagnosis', *Journal of Abnormal Psychology* 71: 209–14.

Rausch, H.L. (1952) 'Perceptual constancy in schizophrenia', *Archives of General Psychiatry* 6: 1–17.

Reybee, J. and Kinch, B. (1973) 'Treatment of auditory hallucinations using focussing', unpublished study.

Rimm, D. and Masters, J. (1974) *Behaviour Therapy: Techniques and Empirical Findings*, New York: Academic Press.

Samaan, M. (1975) 'Thought-stopping and flooding in a case of hallucinations, obsessions, and homicidal–suicidal behaviour', *Journal of Behaviour Therapy and Experimental Psychiatry* 6: 65–7.

Shakow, D. (1962) 'Segmental set', *Archives of General Psychiatry* 6: 1–17.

Silverman, J. (1964) 'The problem of attention in research and theory in schizophrenia', *Psychological Review* 71: 352–78.

Slade, P.D. (1972) 'The effects of desensitization on auditory hallucinations', *Behaviour, Research and Therapy* 10: 85–91.

— (1973) 'The psychological investigation and treatment of auditory hallucinations: a second case report', *British Journal of Social and Clinical Psychology* 13: 73–9.

— (1974) 'The external control of auditory hallucinations: an information theory analysis', *British Journal of Social and Clinical Psychology* 15: 415–23.

— and Bentall, R.P. (1988) *Sensory Deception: A Scientific Analysis of Hallucinations*, London: Croom Helm.

— (1989) 'Psychological treatments for negative symptoms', *British Journal of Psychiatry Supplement*, in press.

Slade P.D. and Cooper, R. (1979) 'Some conceptual difficulties with the term "schizophrenia": an alternative model', *British Journal of Social and Clinical Psychology* 18: 309–17.

Slade, P.D., Judkins, M., Clark, P., and Fonagy, P. (1986) Unpublished study.

Trouton, D.S. and Maxwell, A.E. (1956) 'The relation between neurosis and psychosis: an analysis of symptoms and past history of 819 psychotics and neurotics', *Journal of Mental Science* 102: 1–21.

Turner, S.M., Hersen, M., and Bellack, A.S. (1977) 'Effects of social disruption, stimulus interference and aversive conditioning on auditory hallucinations', *Behaviour Modification* 1: 249–58.

Ullmann, L.P. and Krasner, L. (1965) *Case Studies in Behaviour Modification*, New York: Holt, Rinehart and Winston.

Wallace, C.J. and Boone, S.E. (1983) 'Cognitive factors in the social skills of schizophrenic patients: implications for treatment', in W.D. Spaulding and J.K. Cole (eds) *Nebraska Symposium on Motivation: Theories of Schizophrenia and Psychoses*, Lincoln: University of Nebraska Press.

Watts, F.N. and Clements, J. (1971) The modification of schizophrenic hallucinations and associated delusions: a case report. Unpublished paper.

Watts, F.N., Powell, E.G., and Austin, S.V. (1973) 'The modification of abnormal belief's, *British Journal of Medical Psychology*, 46: 359–63.

Weingaertner, A.H. (1971) 'Self-administered aversive stimulation with hallucinating hospitalised schizophrenics', *Journal of Consulting and Clinical Psychology* 36: 422–9.

Wincze, J.P., Leitenberg, H., and Agras, W.S. (1972) 'The effects of token reinforcement on the delusional verbal behaviour of chronic paranoid schizophrenics', *Journal of Applied Behaviour Analysis* 247–62.

Chapter Ten

THE FAMILY MANAGEMENT OF SCHIZOPHRENIA

NICHOLAS TARRIER

INTRODUCTION

The purpose of this chapter is to describe a biopsychosocial model of the disorders known as schizophrenia and to show that, although there may be a biological basis for these phenomena, psychological interventions can be very successful at preventing relapse and increasing the level of functioning of patients. A further aim of the chapter is to emphasize that these methods are particularly important for psychologists working in community care.

MODELS OF SCHIZOPHRENIA AND CONCEPTUAL ISSUES

Implicit in an attempt to treat, modify, or manage a disorder, disease, dysfunction, or undesirable state is a conceptualization of the factors that are responsible for the origin and maintenance of that phenomenon. Since Kraepelin's first description of dementia praecox as a disease (see Chapter 1 by Boyle in this volume), a purely biological explanation of schizophrenia has been dominant in clinical psychiatry, and especially in European psychiatry. In discussing this issue Neale and Oltmanns (1980:7), conclude that 'the disease model has...been shown to be largely inappropriate for medical disorders', and they further quote Meehl (1972: 194–5) who points out that, 'there is actually no clearly formulated disease-entity model, even in neurology or internal medicine'. Thus, the simple disease-model is an inadequate explanation in general medicine and psychiatry, and serves a function which is closer to attempting to maintain the psychiatrists' professional power base within the mental-health field rather than aiding scientific enquiry (Tarrier 1979). Medicine is primarily a practical endeavour and not a theoretical science. Neale and Oltmanns (1980: 16–20) attempt to resolve the problem of the nature of schizophrenia by rejecting the concepts of disease, syndrome (although they say 'the syndrome concept does...capture many of the factors of schizophrenia'), or label, and opt for thinking of schizophrenia as 'an open scientific construct' (see ibid. for an explanatory discussion). However, it is unclear how, if at all, this helps to advance our knowledge of the disorder or whether this formulation can generate any further predictions which could be tested. Contemporary models of mental-health problems have become multifaceted to fill the vacuum left by the inadequacies of unitary inter- or intrapersonal explanations. These attempt to explain phenomena at several different levels, including biological, psychological, and social factors (Turpin et al. 1988). An influential formulation of the biopsychosocial model is that put forward by Zubin and Spring (1977). They proposed a second-order vulnerability model of schizophrenia as a 'common denominator' of the biological and environmental models. They differentiate between *vulnerability* to schizophrenia, which is a relatively permanent and enduring trait, and *episodes* of schizophrenic illness when the symptoms recur, which are temporary states interspersed with periods of remission. Symptoms will occur when the level of environmental stress reaches a threshold for that individual's level of vulnerability. The importance of this model for any proposed intervention is the emphasis on the interaction between biological and environmental factors which result in the illness episodes. Nuechterlein and Dawson (1984) went on to develop this model into a schema which attempted to draw together diverse possible vulnerability and stress factors in order to explain a schizophrenic psychotic episode (see Figure 10.1.)

Their focus has been to examine contributory factors in the recurrence of schizophrenic symptoms or relapses rather than to explain solely the origins of schizophrenia. This has implications for clinical practice as the model and the empirical data can be used to formulate interventions to prevent relapse. If it is possible to identify the environmental factors implicated in schizophrenic relapse then it may be possible to modify or influence them so as

Figure 10.1 An interactive vulnerability/stress model for the development of schizophrenic psychotic episodes.

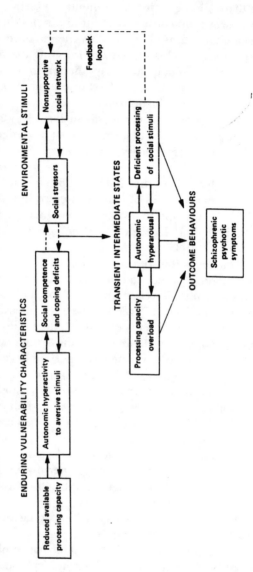

Source: Nuechterlein and Dawson 1984, reprinted with permission from *Schizophrenia Bulletin* 10: 300–12.

to prevent relapse. This has profound importance for clinical psychology, since this is the profession with both theoretical knowledge and practical expertise in the analysis and modification of environmental influences on behaviour. It is the purpose of this chapter to argue that the development of more sophisticated multifaceted models to explain schizophrenia has moved the focus of the management of the disorder away from the sole preserve of psychiatrists and medication, towards the psychologists and their ability to modify environmental factors. The demise of the biological disease model with the empirical demonstration of the importance of environmental factors in determining symptom relapse has created the theoretical conditions for this development. However, it would be wrong to represent this as a *fait accompli*; Nuechterlein and Dawson (ibid.: 300) rightly describe their formulation as 'a framework or schema for further developments rather than a formal hypothetico-deductive model'.

Biological factors and medication

Nor would it be correct to relegate the influence of biological factors and the use of medication to the trivial. Without doubt, neuroleptic drug treatment is effective in promoting symptom reduction and in exerting a prophylactic effect in preventing subsequent symptom exacerbation. Davis (1975) reviewed twenty-four controlled studies comparing antipsychotic medication and placebo, and all these studies demonstrated the superiority of medication over placebo. Computing the probability that these results would have been achieved by chance alone, Davis found it to be less than 10^{-84}. The capability of neuroleptics to reduce relapse would appear to be a result of the effectiveness with which they reduce the high levels of autonomic arousal found in acute and withdrawn patients (Ohman and Straube, in press). However, relapse rates, even on continuous prophylactic medication, are still high. Hogarty et al. (1974), for example, found 48 per cent of patients in their sample relapsed over 2 years, and deterioration of mental and social function may occur in the absence of acute relapse (Johnson 1976). Long-term neuroleptic treatment is frequently accompanied by bothersome and often persistent side-effects. These unpleasant effects include a variety of movement disorders, such as slowed and stiff motor behaviour, involuntary facial and gestural expressions, tremor resembling Parkinson's disease, restlessness, apathy, or drowsiness, which may persist irreversibly as in the case of tardive dyskinesia (Falloon et al. 1984). Further, a sizeable number of patients will discontinue their medication once their mental state is stable.

There is strong evidence that drug-discontinued patients have more relapses compared to controls who continue their medication (Johnson et al. 1983). However, there is also evidence that a number of such treatment drop-out patients will do well, and that others with an unfavourable course of the illness would probably not do substantially better on drugs (Gardos and Cole 1976). Because of the risks of long-term, continuous neuroleptic medication, some psychiatrists have looked for alternatives. Carpenter and Heinrichs (1983) have described the use of targeted medication, in which patients are followed drug-free until prodromal signs of impending relapse appear. Medication is then initiated to abort the impending episode and discontinued when the patient's clinical condition stabilizes. The pharma-cotherapeutic programme is integrated with a psychosocial treatment programme which resembles some of the family-intervention programmes which will be described below. Their preliminary results revealed no difference between targeted- and continuous-medication groups in terms of global outcome and clinical measures. Although the targeted-medication group needed more frequent hospital admissions, these were of shorter duration. A similar study of this approach also showed favourable results (Herz et al. 1982). The rationale behind these approaches is that many patients will discontinue medication of their own volition and instead of being rejected by the mental-health services as treatment drop-outs they should be monitored and allowed access to the services as required. In summary, although maintenance medication is effective in preventing relapse the disadvantages of long-term neuroleptic use has precipitated the investigation of alternatives to continuous neuroleptic medication in specified patient groups. Recent comments by Harding (1987) seem pertinent: 'In the USA it is generally thought that more medication equals better management' but frequently 'people recover from the psychosis but not the medication'.

ENVIRONMENTAL FACTORS

Over the last 15 to 20 years there has been great interest in examining the family atmosphere to which the patient returns after discharge from hospital. This interest has been motivated by Brown et al.'s (1958) finding that schizophrenic patients returning to live with their spouses and parents had higher re-admission rates than those returning to live alone or in lodgings. This finding was not true of patients who had been given diagnoses other than schizophrenia. Re-admission rates were particularly high when a schizophrenic patient returned to live with his or her mother, and both were unemployed and hence in high contact with each other. This might be thought a surprising result, since it would be expected intuitively that living with one's close family would be supportive, as was found to be the case for non-schizophrenic patients. Brown and his colleagues went on to investigate what aspects of the family atmosphere could be responsible for precipitating relapse. The development of the Expressed Emotion (EE) scale was the result of this and its origins have been insightfully documented by Brown (1985).

Expressed Emotion is made up of a number of dimensions: the frequency of critical comments, hostility (a 4-point scale), marked emotional overinvolvement (a 6-point scale), warmth (a 6-point scale), and the frequency of positive remarks. These dimensions are rated from an audio-taped interview (the Camberwell Family Interview, CFI) with the patient's relative (Leff and Vaughn 1985). From ratings on these dimensions it is possible to classify the relative as High or Low on EE. (The High-EE classification is made if there are six or more critical comments and/or one or more scored on hostility and/or three or more scored on emotional overinvolvement.) A number of studies have examined the predictive value of EE, and the consistent finding that there is strong association between relapse and living with a High-EE relative has emerged across different cultural settings. Thus, for example studies from the UK (Brown et al. 1972; Vaughn and Leff 1976; Tarrier, Barrowclough, Vaughn, and others 1988), the US (Vaughn et al. 1984; Moline et al. 1985), Denmark (Wig et al. 1987), India (Wig et al. 1987), and Poland (Rostworowska, et al. 1987) have all indicated a relationship between EE and relapse. These studies tend to show a three- to four-fold increase in relapse rates over a 9-month post-discharge period when the patients return to live with High-EE relatives. Two studies (Kottgen et al. 1984, MacMillan et al. 1986) failed to find any relationship between EE and relapse. However, the Hamburg study reported by Kottgen et al. (1984) has numerous methodological weaknesses (Vaughn 1986). The study reported by MacMillan et al. has a number of methodological differences compared to other studies, and examined first episodes only. Although they initially found that patients with a High-EE relative had higher relapse rates, this effect disappeared when the relatives' estimates of length of the illness before admission were considered. This latter factor and not EE status was found to be predictive of relapse. However, there appears to be some confounding between the two measures since the CFI includes questions about the length of the illness and the history of behavioural disturbance and symptomatology. None the less there is some evidence that Low-EE status is associated with first episodes (Barrowclough and Tarrier, unpublished data) suggesting that High EE may be, at least in part, a developmental phenomenon that evolves as relatives learn to cope with a patient's behavioural disturbance and symptoms.

The study of Vaughn and Leff (1976) also investigated two other factors in relation to relapse: the continuous use of neuroleptic medication over the 9-month period and the amount of face-to-face contact with the relative. It was found that these two factors were important if the patient lived with a High-EE relative. Low contact (less than 35 hours a week) with his or her relative and continuous neuroleptic medication had a protective and apparently additive effect. Patients who took medication and had low contact with their High-EE relatives had relapse rates similar to those who lived with Low-EE relatives (approximately 12-15 per cent). Those who did not take continuous medication (i.e. missed medications for at least a month) and had high contact with their relatives had very high relapse rates (92 per cent). Neither of these factors appeared to be important in patients living with a Low-EE relative. However, at a 2-year follow-up the prophylactic effect of maintenance medication was no longer evident for patients from High-EE homes but there was a significant protective effect of medication in patients from Low-EE homes. Leff and Vaughn (1981) discussed the significance of these results, first by considering whether the lack of a significant effect of medication at 9 months was potentially of great practical importance as it may have identified a population who did not need medication. As the 2-year data contradicted this, they therefore suggested that the interaction between EE and life events explains the results. They had found previously that patients living with Low-EE relatives had a higher rate of life events (which had been shown by Brown and Birley (1968) to be associated with relapse) compared to those living with High-EE relatives (Leff and Vaughn 1980). They thus concluded that prophylactic medication may serve to protect patients living with Low-EE relatives from the acutely stressing effect of a life event (Leff and Vaughn 1981).

The evidence from EE research has produced a new interest in the investigation of environmental factors in schizophrenia, the rationale being that living with a High-EE relative produces high levels of ambient stress and overstimulation which results in increased risk of relapse. Psychophysiological studies of patients' reaction to their relatives' EE status lends support for this explanation (Tarrier et al. 1979, 1988; Sturgeon et al. 1984; Tarrier and Barrowclough 1984, 1987). At a psychological level the vulnerability/stress model would predict that High-EE relatives behave in such a way as to overload the patient's limited capacity for information processing and response selection. MacCarthy et al. (1986) have produced some evidence to substantiate this, in that they have shown that some measures of unpredictability are associated with High-EE relatives who show a high frequency of critical comments. A lack of predictability in information input would be expected to require an increase in processing capacity.

Problematic areas

Before going on to describe interventions it is worth raising a number of important points. As with most areas of investigation, the issues are not as clear as they may at first appear to be. First, most studies evaluate outcome in terms of relapse. Although relapse may seem an easily identifiable discrete event, there is in fact a lack of clear definitions of relapse (Falloon 1984) and the measure is much more confused when assessing an exacerbation compared to a recurrence of symptoms. In some patients who experience continual psychotic symptoms, a clear clinical deterioration may not be detectable due to a lack of sensitivity of many assessment instruments at the extremes of their ranges. Further, relapse is frequently defined in terms of florid positive symptoms (i.e. the experiential symptoms such as hallucinations and delusions) with less attention to what are described as the negative symptoms (i.e. the behavioural deficits such as poverty of speech, flattening of affect, and social withdrawal).

Non-medical professionals have criticized, and quite rightly so, the excessive focus on relapse as an outcome criterion to the exclusion of perhaps more relevant outcome measures such as quality of life or social functioning. Although many studies do attempt multiple assessments, the main goal of many if not of all intervention studies is to prevent relapse, and it is quite possible that other goals (increasing the patient's overall level of functioning) may become subsidiary to, or even conflict with, relapse prevention. On the other hand, there is always a danger that prompting a patient to function at a higher level will risk overstimulation and relapse. This latter issue becomes more crucial if, as is sometimes claimed, an increased number of relapses leads to an overall irreversible deterioration in the patient's condition. These are at present unresolved dilemmas.

A further area of considerable interest is the nature of EE itself. How are measurements rated from a 90- to 120-minute audio-taped interview related to events that occur naturally in the home environment? Difficulties, both practical and methodological, of performing unobtrusive naturalistic observational studies of relative and patient behaviour in the home are immense and as of yet have not been overcome. However, investigations have been made into direct patient–relative interactions which have examined communication patterns. Thus, for example, the Affective Style (AS) coding system was developed as a measure of actual verbal behaviour and assesses several different kinds of affectively toned remarks made by a parent to a patient during actual face-to-face discussion. High-EE relatives have been found to exhibit more negatively charged emotional verbal behaviour than Low-EE relatives and the High-EE critical parents were characterized by their frequent usage of critical comments during interactions. High-EE overinvolved relatives were characterized by their use of intrusive and invasive statements (Miklowitz et al. 1986). Similarly, Hahlweg has used the Interaction Coding System (KPI) (Hahlweg and Conrad 1983) to categorize sequences of verbal and nonverbal interactions and he has found different patterns of interactions between patients and relatives, depending on the EE of the relative (Hahlweg et al. 1985). High-EE relatives and patients had interactions that were characterized by an accelerating cohesive sequence whereas Low-EE relatives and patients did not exhibit this reciprocated sequence of negative responses. These results, when taken into account with the previously mentioned findings of MacCarthy et al. (1986), would suggest that relatives rated differently on EE do behave differently, at least in these short experimental interactions.

FAMILY-INTERVENTION STUDIES

Studies not using Expressed Emotion as a measure of 'risk'.

Pittsburgh studies (Hogarty and colleagues)

Two large studies were carried out by Hogarty and his colleagues. The first was designed to evaluate the effects of maintenance neuroleptic treatment, sociotherapy, and the interactions between the two (Hogarty et al. 1973). The sociotherapy was poorly described but consisted of 'intensive individual social casework and vocational rehabilitation counselling'. The results are interesting, even though there is a problem in knowing exactly what the intervention involved. First, those patients receiving neuroleptics compared to placebo did better in terms of relapse rates. Second, the sociotherapy did not affect relapse rates. Third, patients who received medication plus sociotherapy did better in terms of adjustment than those receiving medication alone, whereas patients on placebo were better adjusted if they did not receive sociotherapy (Hogarty et al. 1974). Hogarty and his colleagues also found that sociotherapy was more successful with asymptomatic patients but was associated with a greater risk of relapse in patients who still experienced psychotic symptoms (Goldberg et al. 1977). The authors concluded that social intervention can have a detrimental effect with patients who are not 'protected' by prophylactic medication or who are still experiencing symptoms.

In a second study, Hogarty and his colleagues compared oral and parentally administered neuroleptics with the use of 'sociotherapy' (Hogarty et al. 1979). Again there is little description of the social intervention. The results indicate that there is no apparent significant advantage of this intervention in combination with medication compared to medication alone.

California study (Goldstein and colleagues).

A study by Goldstein and his colleagues (Goldstein et al. 1978) examined the effect of high- and low-dose phenothiazine medication and the use of social therapy. The social therapy was a brief (6-week) crisis-orientated family therapy. There were no significant main effects, but high-dose medication with social therapy patients had significantly less relapses than low-dose patients without sociotherapy.

Trier study (Ehlert and colleagues)

A recent study in Trier, West Germany, compared a group receiving a family-education programme, a group receiving problem-solving training, and a group receiving both family education and problem-solving training (Ehlert 1987). Both family education and problem solving were highly structured and consisted of five sessions each. Initially the investigators intended to use ratings of the relatives' EE; however, they found that it 'was not possible to transfer...expressed emotion to German relatives of schizophrenic patients', and they developed their own instrument to assess relatives' problem-solving abilities and verbal behaviour. The results indicated that there were no significant differences in relapse rates between the three groups. Not surprisingly, the groups who received the family education showed significantly increased knowledge about the illness and the group who received problem-solving training showed increases in problem-solving ability. There were also improvements in measures of family climate in all groups except in the group that received family education alone.

Uncontrolled studies and case reports

There have been a number of other reports of family interventions in the literature that have been either uncontrolled or case reports. Hudson (1975) described several case-studies in which she attempted to implement behavioural programmes in the homes of chronic schizophrenics and their families. Hudson's accounts are interesting, first because at that time the approach was innovative, and second, because she outlined the problems and obstacles of working with these families. Behavioural programmes were implemented in five families, of which two were successful, one was discontinued, and two resulted in hospitalization. Similarly, Cheek et al. (1971) attempted to teach families how to modify the maladaptive behaviours of schizophrenic patients living at home. The drop-out rate of families was high and there was a lack of systematic evaluation. The measures that were taken appeared to show little in the way of positive change.

Colorado study of family-crisis therapy (Langsley and colleagues)

Langsley and his colleagues (Langsley et al. 1963) have compared the use of family-crisis therapy to routine hospital treatment in a mixed group of psychiatric patients. Patients seeking psychiatric hospitalization were randomly assigned to either out-patient family treatment or to a hospital control-group. Family therapists utilized a directive, problem-solving approach in helping families to resolve crisis situations. Although the family intervention was very successful, the results were not reported for specific diagnostic groups, hence it is not possible to determine which patients responded to the family intervention.

Family Therapy (Palazzoli and others)

Within the family-therapy literature there have also been attempts to intervene with schizophrenics and their families. Probably the best known is the work of Palazzoli and her colleagues (Palazzoli et al. 1978). They devised a therapeutic intervention based on a systemic model of family therapy using four main therapeutic tools: the positive connotation of all behaviours of each family member, the prescribing of family rituals, lengthy intervals between sessions, and paradoxical reframing. The aim of their therapy was to 'understand the game inside the family which maintained the symptomatic behaviour. Once the game was understood, our objective was to devise an intervention which would prevent its continuation' (Palazzoli and Prata 1983: 237). Although it is possible to draw parallels between the explanations and interventions used by this group of systemic family therapists and the assessment by functional analysis used in behavioural interventions (for example, Falloon et al. 1982; Tarrier, Barrowclough, Vaughn, and others 1988), there do appear to be major differences. The former consider the schizophrenic symptoms to be purely a product of family interactions, whereas the latter regard the psychotic symptoms to be due to the schizophrenic illness, which gets better or worse depending on the amount of stress in the home environment. These levels of stress are determined, at least in part, by family interactions. A number of descriptive accounts of systemic family therapy have been published (for example, Jones 1987). However, there does not appear to have been any formal evaluation, which must weaken the claims for the efficacy of this approach.

Family-intervention studies based on expressed emotion

As was mentioned earlier, the consistent finding of an association between living with a High-EE relative and high relapse rates has given a tremendous impetus to family interventions. Falloon et al. (in press) have stated that

> in view of these findings [the association of EE and relapse] – and in accordance with the vulnerability-stress model – it seems mandatory to include the family into a comprehensive after-care treatment programme in order to prevent relapse by improving the ability of the family in managing environmental stress.

Despite the large methodological and practical difficulties involved in family-intervention trials, a number have been reported. These studies have a number of common characteristics: patients and relatives are recruited during a period when the patient is hospitalized for an acute admission; the intervention is aimed at High-EE relatives and attempts to change them to Low-EE; patients are maintained on neuroleptic medication; and outcome is usually assessed in terms of relapse rates. A number of reviews of these studies have been published (Barrowclough and Tarrier 1984; Leff 1985; Koenigsberg and Handley, 1986; Strachan 1986; Falloon et al. in press) but further description here is pertinent.

Camberwell study (Leff and colleagues)

Julian Leff and his colleagues (Leff et al. 1982) recruited twenty-four families who had a High-EE relative who was in frequent contact with the patient. Twelve patients were allocated to the family-intervention group while twelve patients received routine psychiatric after-care. Twenty-two patients received long-acting injections of neuroleptics while two patients were maintained on oral medication. The intervention consisted of three components: (1) education of the relatives, (2) relatives' groups, and (3) individual family therapy. At 9 months after discharge the family-intervention group had significantly fewer relapses (9 per cent) compared with the control group (50 per cent). Reductions in EE status were reported in six out of twelve families at 9 months, and contact between patient and relative was reduced below the critical 35 hours per week in five families. At least one of these goals (reducing either EE or contact) was achieved in 75 per cent of the experimental families. These improvements were maintained at 2-year follow-up, with a 33 per cent relapse rate in the experimental group compared with 75 per cent in the control group (Leff et al. 1985).

California study (Falloon and colleagues)

Ian Falloon and his colleagues (Falloon et al. 1982) recruited thirty-six patients and their mostly High-EE relatives ('most' of the relatives were rated as High-EE, the few others were regarded as high-risk due to high levels of tension in the family). Eighteen families were allocated to a behavioural family intervention and eighteen to a client-based individual supportive psychotherapy. The intervention again consisted of a number of components: (1) education of the family and patient about schizophrenia, (2) communication training (where necessary), and (3) problem-solving training. If there were deficits in those interpersonal-communication skills which were regarded as necessary for effective problem solving then several sessions focused on improving family communications. When families demonstrated competency in basic communication skills the family members were taught a six-step problem-solving method that involved: (1) agreeing on the exact nature of the problem, (2) generating a list of five or more alternative solutions, (3) discussing the merits of each solution, (4) choosing the best solution, (5) formulating a specific plan of implementation, and (6) a subsequent review of success and praise for people's efforts in implementing the solution (Falloon et al. 1984).

At 9 months after discharge the family-intervention group was significantly superior to the control group in terms of relapses (6 per cent compared with 44 per cent), the number of patients whose symptoms were in remission, number of hospital admissions, and the problem-solving ability of the families. After 2 years' improvements in the clinical condition (17 per cent relapses in the family-intervention group compared with 83 per cent in the control group) and social functioning of the treated patients had been maintained (Falloon et al. 1985). Falloon and his colleagues (Falloon et al. 1984) also looked at a number of other outcome measures. They found that the subjective overall burden of living with a schizophrenic family member assessed by the relatives showed a significant and linear decrease over 2 years whilst the control group did not change. Investigation was also made of family-communication and interaction patterns since the family intervention was principally aimed at altering these. No changes were evident in the control group but significant positive changes were found in the family intervention group in the short term (3 months) using the Affective Style coding system (Doane et al. 1985) and in the long term (2 years) using the KPI (Hahlweg et al. 1985). There had been no significant differences on these measures between the family intervention and control groups at pre-treatment.

Lastly and very importantly, Falloon and his colleagues examined the economic benefits and costs of family intervention. All the direct and indirect costs of community management delivered to patients and their families in terms of the action of health, welfare, and community agencies were recorded. The results after 1 year showed that the overall costs of the family approach were approximately 20 per cent less than those of the control condition (Falloon 1986).

Pittsburgh study (Hogarty and colleagues)

In another large and important study Hogarty and his colleagues (Hogarty et al. 1986) recruited 103 patients and their High-EE relatives and allocated them to one of four groups: (1) psychoeducational family treatment; (2) social-skills training; (3) a combination of psychoeducational family treatment and social-skills training; and (4) a control group receiving individual supportive psychotherapy. All patients received neuroleptic medication. The psychoeducational family intervention consisted of five phases: (1) connection, (2) survival-skills workshops, (3) re-entry and application within the community, (4) work/social adjustment, and (5) maintenance. Similarly the patient-orientated social-skills training consisted of five phases: (1) stabilization and assessment, (2) social performance within the family, (3) social perception within the family, (4) extra-familial relationships, and (5) maintenance. After one year all treatment groups were significantly superior to the control group (41 per cent relapsed), but the combined treatment (0 per cent relapsed) was significantly better than either family intervention (19 per cent) or social-skills training (20 per cent) separately.

Similar to the Camberwell and Salford studies, Hogarty et al. also reassessed the relatives' EE at follow-up. They found that there were no relapses in any household that changed from High to Low-EE and that only a combination of treatments (family intervention and social-skills training) sustained remission in households in which the relative(s) remained High-EE.

Hamburg study (Kottgen and colleagues).

The Hamburg study is unusual in that it did not find an association between EE and relapse (Dulz and Hand 1986) and the intervention did not produce a significant reduction in relapse rates (Kottgen et al. 1984). However, this study has been strongly criticized on methodological grounds (Vaughn 1986). Fifteen families with High-EE relatives were allocated to the experimental condition in which the relatives and patients were treated separately in groups using psychodynamic methods. The relapse rates in this group (36 per cent) did not significantly differ from the High-EE control (54 per cent) and Low-EE control (65 per cent) groups. It has been suggested that the results may have occurred because of the overstimulating nature of the psychodynamic group treatment (Strachan 1986). Other possible explanations are the failure to use the practical and problem-orientated treatment techniques employed by the other studies, and the failure to deal with the family unit itself in order to reduce stress.

Salford study (Tarrier and colleagues)

Tarrier and his colleagues (Tarrier, Barrowclough, Vaughn, and others 1988) identified patients who were at 'high risk' of relapse through living with a High-EE relative. They compared four groups: two different 9-month behavioural interventions with families, a short (two-session) educational programme, and a routine-treatment control group. Patients who were at 'low risk' due to living only with Low-EE relatives received either the short educational programme or routine treatment. The two behavioural interventions were identical in content, consisting of the two-session educational programme (Barrowclough et al. 1987), stress management for the relatives, and goal planning (Barrowclough and Tarrier 1987). The educational programme, which was received by both behavioural-intervention groups and the education-only groups, aimed to assess the knowledge about schizophrenia already held by each relative by means of a semi-structured interview and to provide information that would result in positive management strategies (see Barrowclough et al. 1987). The stress-management programme was designed to teach relatives to monitor sources of stress within the family setting and their reactions to it, and then to learn more appropriate methods of coping. During the goal-setting sessions the patient and relatives were taught to identify areas of change or need, to set goals to meet these needs, and to operationalize procedures for achieving these goals using a constructional approach as originally described by Goldiamond (1974).

Although the two behavioural interventions were of similar duration and content, they functioned at different levels (enactive and symbolic). Both interventions were didactic, in that families were taught skills with which to manage the problems presented by schizophrenia. The difference between the two groups was in how the skills were taught, either through symbolic representations such as discussion and instruction or through an enactive method which required role playing, guided practice, record keeping, and corroborated active participation in the programme.

After 9 months the two behavioural interventions had significantly lower relapse rates (12 per cent) than the High-EE routine treatment (53 per cent) and the education programme only (43 per cent) groups, although there appeared to be no significant differences between the symbolic and enactive interventions. Evidence available at the time of writing suggests that at 2 years these improvements have been maintained. The two behavioural interventions have 33 per cent relapses·compared to

66 per cent in the combined education only and routine-treatment groups (Tarrier et al. unpublished). Within the Low-EE groups there were no differences at 9 months between the routine treatment (20 per cent) and education programme only (22 per cent) groups. At 2 years these combined Low-EE groups have a relapse rate similar to the behavioural intervention groups (33 per cent). These results indicate that the short education programme had no significant effects on relapse rates, even though it was aimed at encouraging positive management and not acquisition of information *per se*. The High-EE routine-treatment group had a significantly higher relapse rate at 9 months than the Low-EE routine-treatment group, further supporting the association between High-EE and higher relapse rates.

An analysis of medication compliance and contact with psychiatric services did not explain the differing relapse rates. Tarrier and his colleagues carried out the assessment battery at index admission and at 4·5 months and 9 months after discharge. Within the High-EE groups there were significantly greater reductions in the relatives' EE levels from High to Low in the behavioural-intervention groups compared with the education and routine-treatment groups. In the Low-EE routine-treatment group a number of relatives changed from Low to High-EE over the 9 months. This latter result did not occur in the Low-EE education group, indicating that if Low-EE relatives do not receive any specialist intervention, there is a risk of them becoming critical, hostile, or over involved.

Conclusions based on intervention studies

The overwhelming evidence from the studies reviewed is that it is possible to reduce relapse rates through family intervention. These results are even more impressive in the light of the failure of individual psychotherapy to have any effect with schizophrenic patients (Klerman 1984). Klerman's conclusions are telling: 'The evidence does not justify any further research on the intensive individual psychotherapy of schizophrenia' (p. 611), and 'This failure of individual psychotherapy should be compared with reports of recent controlled trials, which indicate the efficiency of family therapy in reducing intra-familial expressed emotion (EE) against individual therapy.' (p.611)

271

The methodological strategy of identifying High-EE families as high-risk is useful, since a relapse base rate of approximately 50 per cent over 9–12 months has consistently been found in prospective studies of EE: a significant reduction below this rate therefore indicates the clinical usefulness of an intervention.

Since a number of interventions have been successful this raises the question of what aspects of the intervention are effective and which mechanisms explain their efficacy?

What aspects of the interventions are effective?

All successful intervention studies have included an educational component. Providing information to the relative about the illness, its ramifications, treatment, and how to manage the patient at home has been recognized by most workers as a necessary starting-point for changing family-environments. Tarrier and Barrowclough (1986) have reviewed studies that provide information to relatives about schizophrenia. They suggested that there are two models of information-giving. A deficit model implies that a lack of information results in detrimental behaviour and that providing that information will therefore eliminate this behaviour. In contrast, an interaction model suggests that people produce their own explanations of illness and that information provided by professionals will be assimilated, organized, and possibly rejected on the basis of the person's own perceptions and explanations. If this is true, the idea that High-EE behaviours are a product of a deficit of information is probably simplistic and the providing of information is unlikely to have a great effect on the relative's behaviour. In support of this latter formulation, Barrowclough et al. (1987) produced evidence to show that the more chronic the patients' illness, the more the relatives knew about schizophrenia but the less they were likely to learn on being given new information. This strongly suggests that the education of relatives is more likely to be productive the earlier it occurs. However, Tarrier and Barrowclough (1986) also postulated that the provision of information to relatives may have benefits that do not result directly from information acquisition. Certainly, providing information is a useful and convenient way of engaging the family in the intervention.

As the interventions are packages of techniques it is difficult to isolate specific therapeutic components as effective unless it can be demonstrated that the implementation of a particular technique is followed by a change in a relative's behaviour which in turn results in an improvement in the patient's condition. Such demonstrations have been attempted (Barrowclough and Tarrier 1987) but have proven very difficult to achieve. At the present time, therefore, it is impossible to identify 'active ingredients' of therapeutic packages. Another way of looking at the question is to examine the function and aims of the intervention. Here it is possible to be slightly more concrete and conclude that interventions which aim to reduce stresses in the family environment are effective.

Why are interventions effective?

The goal of interventions aimed at High-EE families is to reduce the EE status of the relatives from High to Low-EE, because High-EE relatives are associated with higher relapse rates. It is reasonable to assume that if an intervention successfully reduces relapse rates compared with a control group, and changes in relatives' EE levels are evident in the intervention group compared with the control group, then the intervention has been effective because of this EE change. An alternative explanation of the prospective EE studies is that EE is purely an epiphenomenon of the severity of illness. Poor-prognosis patients are more likely to relapse and are more likely to provoke adverse responses from relatives. However, this alternative explanation is greatly weakened by these intervention studies which have randomly allocated patients to treatment groups and which have then demonstrated reduced relapse rates in association with changes in EE. Evidence for changes in EE in successful intervention groups has been provided by three studies (Leff et al. 1982; Hogarty et al. 1986; Tarrier, Barrowclough, Vaughn, and others 1988). The Hogarty et al. (1986) study provided very impressive evidence for the mediating role of EE in that there were no relapses in any family where the relatives changed from High to Low EE. Tarrier, Barrowclough, Vaughn, and others (1988) also showed that group differences could not be explained by medication dosages or compliance or by contact with any of the other psychiatric services. Further evidence for the role of EE in relapse comes from psychophysiological studies. Tarrier (1987) found that patients whose relatives remained High EE over 9 months showed greater levels of arousal and reactivity than patients whose relatives changed from High to Low-EE. This is an important finding because it implies that the importance of EE lies in the effect that living with a High-EE relative has on the patient's arousal system. This finding fits in very well with the vulnerability/stress model (see Figure 10.1) presented at the beginning of this chapter.

A schizophrenic episode should be characterized by an increase in general arousal levels and a hyper-reactivity to social stressors (i.e. the presence of a High-EE relative). A gradual habituation of arousal should occur after the episode when the patient is in remission. This does occur over 9 months and generally, with the exception of those who have high contact with a High-EE relative, patients show a decrease in reactivity to their relatives (Tarrier 1989). Patients remaining in high contact with High-EE relatives demonstrate increased levels of arousal in their presence.

This evidence therefore seems to suggest that the mechanism of EE in relapse is in maintaining both high levels of tonic arousal and reactivity. Patients who return to live with Low-EE relatives or who have low contact with High-EE relatives are less likely to relapse because their arousal levels and reactivity will slowly habituate over time during remission.

One result that does not fit in directly with this formulation is the finding of Hogarty et al. (1986) that a patient-centred, disorder-relevant intervention (social-skills training) was as effective as a family-centred approach. This may appear to contradict the recent emphasis on the family environment, but this is not necessarily so. If, as proposed by the vulnerability/stress model, the basic schizophrenic disorder is a cognitive dysfunction that impairs the sufferer's ability to perceive and respond to complex environmental (especially social) stimuli, coupled with a dysfunction in the regulation of autonomic arousal, then the precipitation of symptoms will occur in any environment in which this impairment results in a system overload. The importance of the family is that it is the environment in which many patients find themselves after discharge, and the utility of EE is as a 'marker', albeit gross, of the stress within that environment. Hence patient-centred approaches will also be efficacious if they allow the patient to function more effectively in that environment. Social-skills training may allow the patient to process and respond to social stimuli more effectively, and hence reduce the amount of stress experienced. Further, improved social functioning may result in a feedback loop which improves the relatives' perception of the patient, decreases negative management-strategies, and reduces levels of ambient stress. The basic mechanisms of intervention must therefore be in the reduction in stress experienced by the patient in his or her environment, either through reduction of the stress caused by relatives or by improving the ability of the patient to process and to respond to social and environmental stimuli.

DIFFICULTIES IN SERVICE IMPLEMENTATION

To have an impact on the social problem of schizophrenia the research into psychosocial interventions must be translated into an intervention which becomes an integral part of community services. Some of the research teams have written about or indicated some of the difficulties in implementing these interventions in a research setting which may have relevance to a service setting. It seems worthwhile to take note of some of these problems at this point.

These difficulties can roughly be divided into two areas: first, difficulties encountered with this client group and their families, and second, difficulties encountered applying these interventions in a multidisciplinary and organizational context.

Difficulties with the client group

The nature and severity of the schizophrenic illness creates its own difficulties. The therapeutic interaction, even with very compliant families, can be frustrating due to slow progress and the difficulty of implementing change. Frequently, patients and especially their relatives are not used to the intensity of attention that is involved in the assessment and intervention procedures. The comment from relatives 'that at last something is being done and we are getting somewhere' is a common one but can signify an unrealistic expectation of a rapid improvement in the patient's condition.

In working with High-EE relatives there is an opportunity to model good coping skills and Low-EE type behaviour. However, there can be a tendency to become the 'High-EE-Psychologist' and react frantically to a crisis. Berkowitz and Leff (1984: 79) wrote how it is possible for the therapist to feel

> a sense of urgency in response to a call for help from a desperate relative who says 'Help me now, I can't stand it', and we rush about, to telephone the doctor in charge, alert the nurses, social workers, communicating as the relatives did, 'Help me now, I can't stand it.'

It is also common to become frustrated and annoyed at other professionals when action is not immediately taken, just as the relatives have done! The approach requires the teaching and modelling of appropriate coping strategies in difficult situations and the setting up of efficient liaison with the services so that effective action can be taken when needed.

There are also a small but not insignificant group of clients and families who are very difficult to engage in any type of therapy and who are generally very poor compliers. This group also has a very poor outcome (Tarrier, Barrowclough, Vaughn, and others 1988). Frequently this group is viewed in a very negative light by the service providers and members are labelled as problem families. The way to deliver a service to this group is really unknown and needs to be investigated further, but it is probable that the service users and service providers have very different perceptions and definitions of the client's needs and how these should be met. Although we know very little about how to manage these families, services should be accessible for their use.

A further problem that appears to make the therapeutic context more difficult is the poor economic and social situation in which the schizophrenic sufferers and their families frequently find themselves. The lack of economic and material resources both of the family and frequently of the neighbourhood in which they live often restricts the alternatives in terms of activities, employment, and interests that are available. Frequently we encounter a cycle of inactivity and deterioration of functioning starting with a lack of appropriate 'normal' and community resources with the consequence that the client's choices of activities are limited to attendance at the day hospital. Many clients prefer not to mix exclusively with other psychiatric patients and given the choice between the day hospital and staying at home they will gravitate to the latter, frequently staying in bed. This results in higher face-to-face contact with increasingly frustrated relatives.

Difficulties within organizations

One of the major difficulties in implementing psychosocial interventions with families is. that the innovative nature of the intervention results in the crossing of traditional professional boundaries. This can be seen as an encroachment of established roles and may lead to the development of potential conflicts. Again, Berkowitz and Leff (1984) have written about the conflicts between the research and clinical teams that took place during the Camberwell intervention (Leff et al. 1982), and it would seem probable that similar experiences affected other research projects. At a conference, Ehlert (1987) spoke about the difficulty in recruiting families for her intervention in Trier:

> The most important problem was the recruitment of families for intervention. It was impossible to co-operate with local psychiatric hospitals or with psychiatrists in private practice. The reasons for refusal were lack of interest, mistrust in behaviour therapy, unwillingness to work with a psychologist, and fear of loss of patients.

Certainly, professional conflicts, the difficulty in effecting organizational change, and the lack of training in and knowledge of behavioural principles and methods by professions other than psychologists can be a block to implementing services which provide effective family interventions. However, two factors should help psychologists to overcome these difficulties. First, the commitment to the empirical evaluation of intervention strategies *should* provide convincing evidence for the necessity of such strategies within a community-care programme. Second, a knowledge and use of behavioural assessment principles can be applied to the organization within which the psychologist works so as to effect the appropriate changes.

The need to incorporate new research-based interventions within an established delivery system is an important challenge and one which needs further detailed investigation.

CONCLUDING REMARKS

The vulnerability/stress model of schizophrenia provides an exciting development for clinical psychology. The adoption of a multifaceted model of schizophrenic episodes allows the identification and modification of detrimental environments. A number of studies have been carried out that have used the family environment as an example of this and have consistently and successfully reduced relapse rates. The use of relatives as the primary rehabilitative agents has resulted in benefits for the patient, the relatives, and for the mental health services embarking on a care-in-the-community programme. The challenge, for clinical psychology and the other helping professions, is to find ways of adopting and implementing this model within the context of community-care services.

REFERENCES

Barrowclough, C. and Tarrier, N. (1984) 'Psychosocial interventions with families and their effects on the course of schizophrenia: a review', *Psychological Medicine* 14: 629–42.
— (1987) 'A behavioural family intervention with a schizophrenic patient', *Behavioural Psychotherapy* 15: 252–71.
— Watts, S., Vaughn, C., Bamrah, J.S., and Freeman, H.L. (1987) 'Assessing the functional value of relatives' reported knowledge about schizophrenia: a preliminary report', *British Journal of Psychiatry* 151: 1–8.
Berkowitz, R. and Leff, J. (1984) 'Clinical teams reflect family dysfunction', *Journal of Family Therapy* 6: 79–89.
Brown, G. (1985) 'The discovery of expressed emotion', in J. Leff, and C. Vaughn, (eds) *Expressed Emotion in Families*, New York: Guilford Press.
— and Birley, J. (1968) 'Crises and life change and the onset of schizophrenia', *Journal of Health and Social Behaviour* 9: 203–14.
— and Wing, J.K. (1972) 'Influence of family life on the course of schizophrenia: a replication', *British Journal of Psychiatry* 121: 241–58.
Brown, G., Carstairs, G., and Topping, G. (1958) 'Post hospital adjustment of chronic mental patients', *Lancet* ii: 685–9.
Carpenter, W. and Heinrichs, D. (1983) 'Early intervention, time-limited, targeted pharmacotherapy of schizophrenia', *Schizophrenia Bulletin* 9: 533–42.
Cheek, F., Laucius, J., Mahncke, M., and Beck, R. (1971) 'A behaviour modification training programme for parents of convalescent schizophrenics', in R. Rubin, (ed.) *Advances in Behaviour Therapy*, New York: Academic Press.
Davis, J., (1975), 'Maintenance therapy in psychiatry: I. Schizophrenia', *American Journal of Psychiatry* 132: 1237–45.
Doane, J. Falloon, I., Goldstein, M., and Mintz, J. (1985) 'Parental affective style and the treatment of schizophrenia', *Archives of General Psychiatry* 42: 34–42.

Dulz, B. and Hand, I. (1986) 'Short term relapse in young schizophrenics', in M. Goldstein, I. Hand, and K. Hahlweg, (eds) *Treatment of Schizophrenia: Family Assessment and Intervention*, Berlin: Springer-Verlag.

Ehlert, U. (1987) 'Psychological intervention for the relatives of schizophrenic patients', Paper presented at the *17th European Association for Behaviour Therapy Congress*, Amsterdam, August.

Falloon, I.R.H. (1984) 'Relapse: a re-appraisal of assessment of outcome in schizophrenia', *Schizophrenia Bulletin* 10: 293–9.

— (1986) *Family Management of Schizophrenia, Clinical, Social, Family and Economic Benefits*, Baltimore: Johns Hopkins University Press.

— Boyd, J.L., and McGill, C.W. (1984) *Family Care of Schizophrenia: A Problem Solving Approach to the Treatment of Mental Illness*, New York, Guilford Press.

Falloon, I.R.H., Hahlweg, K., and Tarrier, N. (in press) 'Family intervention in the community management of schizophrenia', in E. Straube and K. Hahlweg, (eds) *Schizophrenia: Models, Vulnerability and Intervention*, Heidelberg: Springer.

Falloon, I.R.H., Boyd, J.L., McGill, C.W., Razani, J., Moss, H.B., and Gilderman, A.M. (1982) 'Family management in the prevention of exacerbations of schizophrenia', *New England Journal of Medicine* 306: 1437–40.

Falloon, I.R.H., Boyd, J.L., McGill, C.W., Williamson, M., Razani, U., Moss, H.B., Gilderman, A.M., and Simpson, G.M. (1985) 'Family management in the prevention of morbidity of schizophrenia: clinical outcome of a two year longitudinal study', *Archives of General Psychiatry* 42: 887–96.

Gardos, G. and Cole, J. (1976) 'Maintenance anti-psychotic therapy: is the cure worse than the disease?' *American Journal of Psychiatry* 133: 32–6.

Goldberg, S., Schooler, N., Hogarty, G., and Roper, M. (1977) 'Prediction of relapse in schizophrenic out-patients treated by drug and sociotherapy', *Archives of General Psychiatry* 34: 171–84.

Goldiamond, I. (1974) 'Towards a constructional approach to social problems: ethical and constitutional issues raised by applied behaviour analysis', *Behaviourism* 2: 1–84.

Goldstein, M., Rodnick, E., Evans, J., May, P., and Steinberg, M. (1978) 'Drug and family therapy in the after care of acute schizophrenia', *Archives of General Psychiatry* 35: 1169–77.

Hahlweg, K. and Conrad, M. (1983) 'Kategoriensystem zur Beobachtung Partnerschaftlicker Interaktion, KPI', Coding manual, Interaction Coding System; unpublished English version.

Hahlweg, K., Falloon, I.R.H., and Goldstein, M. (1985) 'Changes in schizophrenic families, communication patterns', Paper presented at 15th *European Association of Behaviour Therapy Congress*, Munich, August.

Harding, C. (1987) 'Long term course trajectories of DSM-III schizophrenic patients', Paper presented at 2nd International Symposium on Schizophrenia, Bern, September.

279

Herz, M.I., Szymanski, H.E., and Simon, J.C. (1982) 'Intermittent medication for stable schizophrenic out-patients: an alternative to maintenance medication', *American Journal of Psychiatry* 139: 918–22.

Hogarty, G., Goldberg, S., and Collaborative Study Group (1973) 'Drug and sociotherapy in the after care of schizophrenic patients', *Archives of General Psychiatry* 28: 54–64.

Hogarty, G., Goldberg, S., Schooler, N., and Collaborative Study Group (1974) 'Drug and sociotherapy in the after care of schizophrenic patients: III. Adjustment of non-relapsed patients', *Archives of General Psychiatry* 31: 609–18.

Hogarty, G., Schooler, N., Ullrich, R., Mussare, F., Ferro, P., and Herron, E. (1979) 'Fluphenazine and social therapy in the after care of schizophrenic patients', *Archives of General Psychiatry* 36: 1283–94.

Hogarty, G.E., Anderson, C.M., Reiss, D.J., Kornblith, S.J., Greenwald, P., Javan, C.D., Manonia, M.J., and the EPICS Research Group (1986) 'Family psychoeducation, social skills training, and maintenance chemotherapy in the aftercare treatment of schizophrenia', *Archives of General Psychiatry* 43: 633–42.

Hudson, B. (1975) 'A behaviour modification project with chronic schizophrenics in the community', *Behaviour Research and Therapy* 13: 339–41.

Johnson, D.A.W. (1976) 'The expectation of outcome for maintenance therapy in chronic schizophrenia', *British Journal of Psychiatry* 128: 246–50.

— Pasterski, G., Ludlow, J., Street, K., and Taylor, R. (1983) 'The discontinuance of maintenance neuroleptic therapy in chronic schizophrenic patients: drug and social consequences', *Acta Psychiatrica Scandinavica* 67: 339–52.

Jones, E. (1987) 'Brief systemic work in psychiatric settings where a family member has been diagnosed as schizophrenic', *Journal of Family Therapy* 9: 3–25.

Klerman, G. (1984) 'Ideology and science in the individual psychotherapy of schizophrenia', *Schizophrenia Bulletin* 10: 608–12.

Koenigsberg, H. and Handley, R. (1986) 'Expressed Emotion: from predictive index to clinical construct', *American Journal of Psychiatry* 43: 1361–73.

Kottgen, C., Sonnichsen, I., Mollenhauer, K., and Jurth, R. (1984) 'Group therapy with families of schizophrenic patients: results of the Hamburg Camberwell Family Interview Study III', *International Journal of Family Psychiatry* 5: 83–94.

Langsley, D., Pittmans, F., Machotka, P., and Flomenhaft, K. (1963) 'Family crisis therapy – results and implications', *Family Process* 7: 145–58.

Leff, J. (1985) 'Family treatment of schizophrenia', in K. Granvillie-Grossman (ed.) *Recent Advances in Clinical Psychiatry*, London: Churchill-Livingston.

— and Vaughn, C. (1980) 'The interaction of life events and relatives' expressed emotion in schizophrenia and depressive neurosis', *British Journal of Psychiatry* 136: 146–53.

— (1981) 'The role of maintenance therapy and relatives' expressed emotion in relapse in schizophrenia. A two year follow up', *British Journal of Psychiatry* 139: 102–4.

— (1985) *Expressed Emotion in Families*, New York: Guilford Press.

Leff, J., Kuipers, L., Berkowitz, R., and Sturgeon, D. (1985) 'A controlled trial of social intervention in families of schizophrenic patients: two year follow up', *British Journal of Psychiatry* 146: 594–600.

Leff, J., Kuipers, L., Berkowitz, R., Eberlein-Fries, R., and Sturgeon, D. (1982) 'A controlled trial of social intervention in families of schizophrenic patients', *British Journal of Psychiatry* 141: 121–134.

MacCarthy, B., Hemsley, D., Shrank-Fernandez, C., Kuipers, L., and Katz, R. (1986) 'Unpredictability as a correlate of expressed emotion in the relatives of schizophrenics', *British Journal of Psychiatry*, 148: 727–31.

MacMillan, J.F., Gold, A., Crow, T.J., Johnson, A.L., and Johnstone, E.C. (1986) 'The Northwick Park study of first episodes of schizophrenia: IV. Expressed emotion and relapse', *British Journal of Psychiatry* 148: 133–43.

Meehl, P. (1972) 'Specific genetic etiology, psychodynamics and therapeutic nihilism', *International Journal of Mental Health* 1: 10–27.

Miklowitz, D., Strachan, A., Goldstein, M., Doane, J., Snyder, K., Hogarty, G., and Falloon, I. (1986) 'Expressed emotion and communication deviance in the families of schizophrenics', *Journal of Abnormal Psychology* 95: 60–6.

Moline, R.E., Singh, S., Morris, A., and Meltzer, H.Y. (1985) 'Family expressed emotion and relapse in schizophrenia in 24 urban American patients', *American Journal of Psychiatry* 142: 1078–81.

Neale, J. and Oltmanns, T. (1980) *Schizophrenia*, New York: John Wiley.

Nuechterlein, K.H. and Dawson, M.E. (1984) 'A heuristic vulnerability-stress model of schizophrenic episodes', *Schizophrenia Bulletin* 10: 300–12.

Ohmann, A. and Straube, E. (in press) 'Autonomic activity and schizophrenia', in E. Straube and K. Hahlweg (eds) *Schizophrenia: Models, Vulnerability and Intervention*, Heidelberg: Springer.

Palazzoli, M.S. and Prata, G. (1983) 'A new method for therapy and research in the treatment of schizophrenic families', in H. Stierlin, L. Wynne, and M. Wirsching (eds) *Psychosocial Intervention in Schizophrenia*, Berlin: Springer-Verlag.

Palazzoli, M.S., Boscolo, L., Cecchin, G., and Prata, G. (1978) *Paradox and Counter-paradox*, New York: Aronson.

Rostworowska, M., Barbaro, B., and Cechnicki, A. (1987) 'The influence of expressed emotion on the course of schizophrenia: a Polish replication', Paper presented at the 17th European Association of Behaviour Therapy Congress, Amsterdam, August.

Strachan, A.M. (1986) 'Family intervention for the rehabilitation of schizophrenia', *Schizophrenia Bulletin* 12: 678–98.

Sturgeon, D., Turpin, G., Kuipers, L., Berkowitz, R., and Leff, J.P. (1984) 'Psychophysiological responses of schizophrenic patients to high and low expressed emotion relatives: a follow up study', *British Journal of Psychiatry* 145: 62–9.

Tarrier, N. (1979) 'The future of the medical model: a reply to Guze', *Journal of Nervous and Mental Disease* 167: 71–3.
— (1987) 'Electrodermal activity, expressed emotion and outcome in schizophrenia', Paper presented at the *2nd International Symposium on Schizophrenia*, Bern, September.
— (1989) 'Arousal levels and relatives' expressed emotion in remitted schizophrenic patients', *British Journal of Clinical Psychology* 28: 177–80.
— and Barrowclough, C. (1984) 'Psychophysiological assessment of expressed emotion in schizophrenia: a case example', *British Journal of Psychiatry* 145: 197–203.
— (1986) 'Providing information to relatives about schizophrenia: some comments', *British Journal of Psychiatry* 149: 458–63.
— (1987) 'A longitudinal psychophysiological assessment of a schizophrenic patient in relation to the expressed emotion of his relative', *Behavioural Psychotherapy* 15: 45–57.
— Porceddu, K., and Watts, S. (1988) 'The assessment of psychophysiological reactivity to the expressed emotion of the relatives of schizophrenic patients', *British Journal of Psychiatry* 152: 618–24.
Tarrier, N., Vaughn, C., Lader, M., and Leff, J.P. (1979) 'Bodily reactions to people and events in schizophrenia', *Archives of General Psychiatry* 36: 311–15.
Tarrier, N., Barrowclough, C., Vaughn, C., Bamrah, J., and Freeman, H.L. (unpublished) 2-year follow-up of a controlled trial of family intervention with schizophrenic patients (unpublished data).
Tarrier, N., Barrowclough, C., Vaughn, C., Bamrah, J.S., Porceddu, K., Watts, S., and Freeman, H.L. (1988). 'The community management of schizophrenia: a controlled trial of a behavioural intervention with families to reduce relapse', *British Journal of Psychiatry* 153: 532–42.
Turpin, G., Tarrier, N., and Sturgeon, D. (1988) 'Social psychophysiology and the study of biopsychosocial models of schizophrenia', In H. Wagner (ed.) *Social Psychophysiology: Perspectives on Theory and Clinical Applications*, Chichester: Wiley.
Vaughn, C. (1986) 'Comments on Dulz and Hand', in M. Goldstein, L. Hand, and K. Hahlweg (eds) *Treatment of Schizophrenia: Family Assessment and Intervention*, Berlin: Springer-Verlag.
— and Leff, J. (1976) 'Influence of family and social factors on the course of psychiatric illnesses' *British Journal of Psychiatry* 129: 125–37.
Vaughn, C.E., Snyder, K.S., Jones, S., Freeman, W.B., and Falloon, I.R.H. (1984) 'Family factors in schizophrenic relapse. Replication in California of British research on expressed emotion', *Archives of General Psychiatry* 41: 1169–77.
Wig, N., Menon, D., Bedi, H., Leff, J., Kuipers, L., Ghosh, A., Day, R., Korten, A., Ernberg, G., Sartorius, N., and Jablensky, A. (1987) 'Distribution of expressed emotion components among relatives of schizophrenic patients in Aarhus and Chandigarh', *British Journal of Psychiatry* 151: 160–5.
Zubin, J. and Spring, B. (1977) 'Vulnerability – a new view of schizophrenia', *Journal of Abnormal Psychology* 86: 103–26.

CONCLUDING REMARKS

Schizophrenia – a suitable case for treatment?
RICHARD P. BENTALL

'Schizophrenia' is a problem which has attracted an enormous amount of attention from researchers, clinicians, politicians, and lay people for good reasons: as indicated by various writers in the present volume, the social, economic, and personal costs associated with the diagnosis are almost incalculable. The study of schizophrenia attracts enormous funds and a large volume of publications on the topic continue to appear every year. Most of these publications take the concept of schizophrenia for granted. Sarbin and Mancuso (1980), for example, surveyed the *Journal of Abnormal and Social Psychology* (later the *Journal of Abnormal Psychology*) for the years 1959–78 and found that 374 papers totalling 2,472 pages or 15·3 per cent of the journal space used the presence or absence of a diagnosis of schizophrenia as an independent variable. The trend over that period was for the proportion of papers devoted to schizophrenia to increase.

The chapters in the present volume mark something of a departure from the usual way of thinking about schizophrenia. In this brief conclusion I will therefore attempt to pull together whatever lessons may be drawn from the chapters taken as a whole. It should perhaps be indicated at the outset that this exercise is entirely my own: given that there are some points of disagreement between the contributors it is unlikely that all will agree with the general conclusions that I will reach. None the less, I hope that this exercise may be forgiven on the grounds that it will raise issues which future writers on the topic may wish to consider. (For convenience I will sometimes use the word 'schizophrenia' in a minimal sense to indicate whatever forms of psychopathology are usually covered by the term and the word 'schizophrenic' to indicate anyone diagnosed as suffering from any of these forms of psychopathology.)

RICHARD P. BENTALL

THE VALUE OF THE SCHIZOPHRENIA CONCEPT

All of the authors in the present volume address themselves to the question of whether or not the concept of schizophrenia is useful for scientific or other purposes. All, with the possible exception of Venables (Chapter 7), are sceptical to some degree about its value, at least in its traditional form as a Kraepelinian category. It will be useful briefly to summarize the relevant arguments.

In my own chapter (Chapter 2) I have argued that the diagnosis fails to meet many of the criteria that would be necessary to assure us of its usefulness. Thus, there is a dearth of evidence that schizophrenia constitutes a reliably identifiable and valid syndrome distinct from other forms of madness. Moreover, the diagnosis has proved to be a poor predictor of outcome, response to treatment, or aetiology. Barham and Hayward (Chapter 3), dealing particularly with the outcome of schizophrenic breakdowns, have pointed out that this is enormously variable and appears to be largely a function of social variables. More than any of the other contributors in the book, Barham and Hayward note how an exclusively biological perspective on mental disorder leads us to forget that people suffering from such disorders remain people, pursuing their life projects, constantly grappling with the everyday problems that face them, and perpetually fighting for a role within a rejecting society.

Taking a different tack, Claridge (Chapter 6) outlines a substantial body of evidence that establishes, beyond any reasonable doubt, that the simple distinction between schizophrenia and normal traits is a false one, and that the tendency towards psychotic behaviour is distributed along a series of continua which connect madness with ordinary mental life. (An interesting feature of these discoveries is the finding that *more than one dimension* is needed to describe psychotic traits; in other words even a unidimensional model of schizophrenia is inadequate.) Putting these arguments together, it seems that a categorical approach to the description and under-standing of psychopathology – the assumption that forms of madness can be subdivided into discrete diagnostic groups (for example those found in DSM-III R or any other diagnostic manual) – must be rejected as scientifically and practically useless. This is a strong conclusion and it is therefore worth considering, for a moment, the opinion of the one apparently dissenting voice in the volume.

Venables (Chapter 7) is clearly uncomfortable about the idea of rejecting the concept of schizophrenia altogether. However, he also argues that psychopathologists should not be 'immobilized in the amber of Kraepelinian doctrine' and that longitudinal studies point to the essentially dimensional nature of the disorder, with severe schizophrenia at one end of that dimension, 'the milder madnesses of belief in horoscopes and magical intervention' somewhere in the middle, and 'the sanity of the less interesting members of the population' at the opposite end (p.201). In what must be seen as something of a compromise position, Venables suggests that, 'to state that schizophrenia is an appropriate unifying concept is not the same as to suggest that it is a *unitary* concept' (p.200, original emphasis). Whether this compromise makes sense is something which the reader must decide: what is clear is that even this position gives up much that is assumed in the traditional categorical model as described in most psychiatric textbooks.

If the traditional textbook account of schizophrenia does not survive critical scientific scrutiny, then the persisting popularity of this account requires explanation. Moreover, if widely held views about the nature of schizophrenia are so clearly wrong, it is important to identify the historical source of this error. It is therefore worth considering briefly the potential relevance of historical analysis for the understanding of contemporary psychopathology.

THE HISTORICAL PERSPECTIVE

All science is human activity. Despite periods in the history of Western thought in which scientific reasoning has been seen as a pure inductive exercise – the detached extraction of general laws from unbiased observation – it is now quite clear that this model of scientific progress is woefully inadequate (Chalmers 1976). None the less, scientists sometimes express irritation about the way in which critics use historical and sociological arguments to undermine their claims of objectivity. In the case of research into psychopathology, Pilgrim (Chapter 8) has quoted a number of prominent psychiatrists, including Roth, Hamilton, and Clare, all of whom seem to construe such criticism as a kind of left-of-centre anti-scientism. One consequence of this nervousness about arguments from history is the wholesale rewriting of the history of science in order to 'sanitize' it. Thus, Brush (1974), in his rather provocatively titled paper 'Should the history of science be X-rated?', has argued that textbook accounts of crucial developments in physics often bear little resemblance to the historical facts as revealed by the examination of contemporary documents, with the result that subjective and non-empirical components of research – hunches, philosophical convictions, not to say the widespread manipulation of data to yield favoured conclusions – are hidden from the student.

The inductivist model of science can be dismissed on logical, historical, and sociological grounds. On logical grounds it is obvious that there is no such thing as a completely objective observation. The search for data always involves decisions, sometimes conscious but often unconscious, about which kinds of observations are worth making. Moreover, as Popper (1963) among others has pointed out, the hypotheses generated in the physical and other sciences are often little more than loose conjectures which may or may not survive subsequent testing. In other words, there is a fair amount of guesswork in scientific research, often guided by the philosophical presuppositions of scientists. This has been more than confirmed by historians of science, who have shown that even the most important breakthroughs, including Newton's mechanics, the atomic theory in chemistry, and Mendel's genetics, have been achieved at the expense of the selective reporting of observations and sometimes even on the basis of outright fraud (Broad and Wade 1984). (A good example of this is Franklin's (1981) discovery that the physicist Millikan, when conducting his famous oil-drop experiment to measure the charge on the electron, simply crossed out measurements which did not accord with his expectations.)

More generally, as Kuhn (1962) has argued, periods of normal scientific development often involve the acceptance by scientists of sets of assumptions or 'paradigms' that go unquestioned until the widespread reporting of discoveries that cannot be accommodated within a paradigm causes a 'scientific revolution', after which a new set of guiding assumptions becomes widely accepted. Sociologists of science have added to these insights by highlighting the role of science as an institution within society, and by drawing attention to the fact that scientists, like other members of society, have values and ideologies which they cherish, and positions and careers to defend (Barnes 1974; Powers 1982). (It is interesting, in this regard, that even the textbook accounts of science do not portray great scientific discoveries as dispassionate observations. On the contrary, the conventional history of science is populated by great heroes – clearly a self-serving myth.)

Examples that are sometimes given of the sudden change in the organizing principles of a science are the development of relativistic and quantum mechanics in physics, and the widespread acceptance of the theory of continental drift in geology. The important point here is that until a period of scientific revolution, many core concepts in a science – for example, the idea of absolute motion in classical physics – go unquestioned because at the time they seem relatively uncontentious. Sometimes within the history of a discipline, ideas which make perfect sense from a certain perspective – for example, the assumption that burning involves the release of phlogyston or the assumption that there must be a medium, the aether, through which light travels – are completely abandoned at a later stage. It is conceivable that the concept of schizophrenia will prove to be just such an idea.

As already noted, many scientists find these kinds of suggestions uncomfortable, perhaps because they seem to strike a blow against the notion that science involves the pursuit of 'absolute truth'. It is important, therefore, to be quite clear about both the power and the limitations of historical analysis. Practitioners of science, when evaluating a theory or hypothesis, usually refer to current arguments and observations that bear directly on the hypothesis or theory in question. The presence or absence of observations predicted by the theory are usually considered to be of particular importance. In this respect, it may be necessary to draw an important line between arguments pertaining to the development of a theory (historical analysis) and arguments concerning a theory's current value (usually empirical considerations): ideological issues may well have had a considerable role in the development of the Copernican account of planetary motion but we turn to astronomers and not to historians to tell us whether the Earth, in fact, moves around the Sun.

On the other hand, the myth that science is a completely objective enterprise (as if conducted by disinterested robots) remains just that – a *myth*, and historical and sociological analysis, if nothing else, reminds us of the frailness of our convictions. Moreover, when a scientific enterprise is in trouble, perhaps because (as in the case of schizophrenia) its claims, theories, and observations stand in contradiction to each other, historical and sociological analysis may point towards the source of the difficulty. Thus, while it would be wrong to reject the concept of schizophrenia *only* on the observation that early psychiatrists stood to benefit (along with their present-day colleagues) from the idea that madness is a form of illness, this is certainly something to consider when the traditional model looks in danger of collapse. In addition, historical analysis may give us the courage to reject assumptions that look increasingly untenable in the light of modern developments.

The historical arguments of Pilgrim, Boyle, and Marshall (Chapters 8, 1, and 4 respectively) may therefore be of considerable importance. However, one problem with turning to history in order to account for present difficulties is that there may be no consensus about what happened in the past and why. Indeed, as already suggested, histories of science are themselves theories which may be self-serving. In Pilgrim's chapter (Chapter 8), the implications of competing histories of psychiatry are therefore examined. Pilgrim distinguishes between early historical accounts that naïvely portray the development of psychiatry in terms of gradual scientific progress and later, more critical accounts that locate the emergence of the medical approach to madness against a background of an increasing concentration of power in the hands of medical practitioners. More importantly, perhaps, Pilgrim suggests that traditional historical accounts serve to maintain an approach to the treatment of mental disorder that over-emphasizes medical concepts and techniques and which under-emphasizes effective changes at the social and political level.

Boyle (Chapter 1), in an analysis of Kraepelin's original work (somehow unexamined by most contemporary writers on the topic of schizophrenia), shows that he had no clear criteria for the identification syndromes. Indeed, Kraepelin hardly had a method at all. It is not therefore surprising that his work contains certain contradictions. Most important among these was probably his reliance on outcome to justify distinguishing dementia praecox from other disorders when he was simultaneously taking into account the history of the disorder when diagnosing patients. On a separate point, Boyle also proposes an intriguing hypothesis to account for the fact that few latter-day schizophrenics present with the clinical features described by Kraepelin. Historical changes in the form and distribution of psychotic symptoms reported by psychopathologists have been discussed by a number of authors but Boyle suggests that at least part of the problem follows from the fact that the bulk of Kraepelin's schizophrenics would now be diagnosed as suffering from encephalitis lethargica. Although this suggestion, on first acquaintance, seems rather unlikely, Boyle's comparison of the clinical descriptions of Kraepelin and von Economo provides convincing evidence that the hypothesis merits further examination.

Marshall's chapter (Chapter 4) analyses the emergence of the genetic theory of schizophrenia once Kraepelin's diagnostic system had become widely accepted. The idea that a vulnerability to schizophrenia is inherited has become one of the foundation-stones of modern psychiatric theory. However, data manipulation seems to have played an important role in this line of research, so much so that widely cited studies cannot be trusted. Kallmann's research, still often quoted, is an important case in point, but Marshall shows that the much more recent Danish–American adoption studies are equally untrustworthy. Part of the problem seems to be that genetics is not the exact science it is often portrayed as being: a variety of assumptions are made when calculating concordance rates in twin studies, for example, and the results achieved vary widely according to the method used. Researchers have consistently chosen methods which give high estimates of the degree of inheritance involved in schizophrenic behaviour. Marshall suggests that they have done this because the genetic determination of schizophrenia has always been treated as an *axiom* rather than a *hypothesis*. The origins of this axiom, in turn, can be traced to the socio-political conditions in which the early work of Kallmann was carried out (Germany in the Nazi period). As Marshall points out, the implication of this analysis is *not* that genes play no role in psychosis, but that this possibility needs to be examined afresh, once the ideology of biological reductionism has been, as far as possible, stripped away. Unfortunately, recent developments in the genetic investigation of schizophrenia (which will be described briefly in the next section) suggest that currently, this ideology is as strong as ever.

THE AETIOLOGY OF SCHIZOPHRENIA AND BIOLOGICAL SCIENCE

Consideration of the history of genetic research into schizophrenia leads naturally to questions of aetiology. For reasons which Pilgrim and Marshall describe, exclusively biological models of schizophrenia have always enjoyed strong support.

Questions about the biological determination of behaviour raise complex philosophical issues. No one seriously doubts that biological variables influence how we act: observation of the conduct of revellers after an evening of drinking suggests that such variables sometimes have a very powerful effect. What is at issue is the way in which biological and non-biological determinants of behaviour interact. It is important not to fall into an over-simplistic form of biological reductionism: the behaviour of the drunk is influenced by more than alcohol. Similarly, the intentionality of many psychotic symptoms (the fact that psychotic persons are often not just disturbed but disturbed *about* particular events in their lives) suggests that theories of psychotic behaviour should take into account semantic as well as formal aspects of cognition.

The untrustworthiness of much of the genetic research, as detailed by Marshall, has already been mentioned. In the time between Marshall writing his chapter and this book going to press, the genetic theory of schizophrenia has taken a new twist which adds even more strength to Marshall's case. A team of researchers at the Middlesex hospital, London, announced that, using the new techniques of molecular genetics, they had managed to locate the genetic locus of schizophrenia on chromosome five (Sherington et al. 1988). This apparent discovery was announced via the media (the first I heard about it was from a teletext headline which dramatically stated that the genetic cause of schizophrenia had finally been discovered) with the promise that publication in the journal *Nature* would immediately follow. In fact, some time passed before the

290

Middlesex team's paper was finally published, the researchers showing some reluctance to discuss this delay with the interested press (Hill 1988). When the paper finally appeared it was accompanied by a second paper in which a group of US and Swedish researchers announced that they had found strong evidence that a gene for schizophrenia *was not* located on chromosome five (Kennedy et al. 1988). Moreover, a subsequent paper by a group of investigators in Edinburgh reported a further failure to replicate the Middlesex findings (St Clair et al. (1989).

Examination of these reports reveals some intriguing features of the three research projects. Molecular genetics offers a new set of techniques for studying inherited disorders: by studying families in which there appears to be a high prevalence of a disorder, investigators can use sophisticated biochemical techniques to identify genetic differences between those who suffer from the disorder and those who do not. The Middlesex team studied a total of 104 individuals from five Icelandic and two British families, whereas the US–Swedish team studied only one Swedish family with 81 subjects who could be examined. On the other hand, the US–Swedish team used a considerably more powerful method of genetic mapping than the Middlesex team. The Edinburgh group studied a total of 166 subjects from fifteen families using similar methods to the Middlesex researchers. In a review of the two studies published together Lander (1988) outlined a number of technical reasons why the results must be interpreted with caution. However, one reason which is obvious even to the genetically uninitiated concerns diagnosis: the best results from the Middlesex study, for example, were obtained when a small group of 'fringe phenotypes', including individuals diagnosed as suffering from depressive disorders, drug addiction, alcoholism, and phobias, were included in the analysis as cases of schizophrenia. Interestingly, the Edinburgh group explicitly tried to maximize its chances of replicating the Middlesex findings by using a range of diagnostic criteria but no evidence of genetic linkage was found regardless of how broadly or narrowly schizophrenia was defined.

Clearly, molecular genetics offers a promising approach to the study of inherited factors in psychopathology and this approach is only just beginning to be exploited. However, progress is jeopardized when the ideology of biological reductionism leads researchers to make inflated claims for their techniques. Under such circumstances it is difficult for the observer to distinguish science from rhetoric. The publicity given to the Middlesex findings is a case in point. Newspapers reported these findings as if a fundamental breakthrough had been achieved and as if *the* cause of schizophrenia had been found; it seemed that all the researchers had to do next was sit back and wait for a call to Stockholm. Methodological weaknesses of the Middlesex project, such as the way in which the depressives, phobics, drug addicts, and alcoholics were counted as schizophrenic, were not mentioned. Moreover, media discussion of the discrepancy between the Middlesex findings and those of the other groups has been kept to the minimum, yet as Lander (1988) soberly noted, the evidence from the Middlesex and US–Swedish papers, if taken at face value, suggests that schizophrenia is not a unitary disorder. Moreover, 'it would be wrong to conclude that all schizophrenia is entirely "genetically determined"...it is important to remember that the 50 percent discordance rate among identical twins points to powerful non-genetic factors' (ibid.: 106). Indeed, as Lander notes, the study of families in which there is a high prevalence of schizophrenia can be misleading if it leads to an over-emphasis on genetic factors.

Interestingly, Claridge (Chapter 6), who is much less sceptical than Marshall about the results of genetic studies, notes that the available evidence from traditional genetic research points to a multidimensional rather than a categorical model of schizophrenia. Further biological evidence that schizophrenia is not a unitary disorder is described by Jackson (Chapter 5), who reviews the relevant neuropsychological and biochemical data. In a novel approach, Jackson presents this data uncritically in order to show that the very diversity of the findings is strong evidence that schizophrenics form a heterogeneous group.

RESEARCH

The heterogeneity of schizophrenic persons raises important issues about research. The traditional research paradigm in psychopathology involves some form of comparison of one group of individuals with a particular diagnosis with one or more other groups of individuals (including a group deemed 'normal' who lack the diagnosis). Given the conclusion that schizophrenics are a highly diverse group this strategy amounts to *the comparison of one group of people who in all probability have nothing in common with another group of people who also probably have nothing in common.* It is difficult to see how this can hope to succeed yet researchers, all too immobilized in the amber of Kraepelinian doctrine, are extremely reluctant to seek new strategies.

A good example of this resistance to change is a recent document on the future of schizophrenia research published by the Medical Research Council of Great Britain (MRC 1988). The document hardly discusses the problems of diagnosis raised by many of the authors in the current volume but instead recommends that the 10th edition of the International Classification of Diseases and DSM-IIIR be used to differentially categorize the clinical phenomena (i.e. yield diagnoses). Alternative research strategies such as those advocated by the authors in the present volume (for example, the study of symptoms, the study of schizotypal traits in normal individuals, the study of the careers of schizophrenic individuals) are barely mentioned.

Not only are researchers reluctant to pursue research using new strategies, they are also reluctant to investigate non-biological variables. Recent textbooks on schizophrenia (for example, Kerr and Snaith 1986) give almost no weight to psychosocial determinants of symptoms or outcome. Moreover, the Medical Research Council, in its document, makes ten recommendations for future areas of research funding: (1) genetic investigations; (2) neuropathological studies of post-mortem brains; (3) studies of synaptic connections in particular brain regions; (4) brain-imaging studies; (5) clinical trials of preventive medication and other care; (6) clinical studies of abnormalities of thought and intention using EMG and MEG; (7) neuropsychological studies of dopamine pathways; (8) evaluations of services to patients; (9) more epidemiological studies; and (10) studies of symptom identification. The US National Institute for Mental Health, in a comparable exercise (Keith and Matthews 1988), makes recommendations which are marginally less depressing: again, emphasis is placed mainly on neurobiological investigations but the authors acknowledge problems of diagnostic validity, stress the importance of investigating the relationship between schizophrenia and normal variations in behaviour and cognition, and recommend that, 'significant attention be given to the careful study of psychosocial factors that may contribute to the aetiology and modification of vulnerability to illness' (p.430).

HELP FOR PERSONS LABELLED SCHIZOPHRENIC

Finally, it is important to consider how individuals diagnosed as schizophrenic might best be helped by mental health professionals and others. Questions of this sort usually suggest answers in terms of some recommended form of treatment. However, some of the contributors – for example, Barham and Hayward, and Pilgrim (Chapters 3 and 8 respectively) – point out that the mentally disordered within our society typically live an impoverished, marginalized existence, and that their needs therefore extend far beyond treatment. Certainly, when visiting people diagnosed as schizophrenic in their homes it is often difficult not to be shocked by the appalling conditions in which they are forced to live. In such circumstances I have often found myself thinking, *How can any treatment, no matter how effective, hope to overcome this?* None the less, these kinds of needs scarcely merit a mention in most psychiatry or clinical psychology textbooks. Pilgrim suggests that the ideology of biological reductionism has led directly to these wider needs being ignored. Items on his 'shopping list' of political interventions include: better education about mental disorder, improvement in the material conditions of the mentally disordered, a greater availability of appropriate employment opportunities, and the democratization of mental health services.

Despite these concerns, treatment is clearly an important issue to consider and Slade and Tarrier (Chapters 9 and 10 respectively) both review evidence pertaining to the possible role of psychological interventions in helping psychotic persons. There is a widespread pessimism about the usefulness of such interventions (Barham and Hayward quote a leading British psychiatrist to the effect that they are a waste of time), but such pessimism is not justified. Thus, Slade outlines a number of behavioural and cognitive techniques that may be effective in treating specific symptoms. Tarrier in turn describes well-validated family interventions which have been shown to be successful in the prevention of relapse. The problem with these interventions is that hardly anyone is doing them. Perhaps the most shameful consequence of the dominant role that biological psychiatry has gained in mental health care is the almost complete absence of these kinds of services.

Taken together, these conclusions seem like a fairly damning indictment of much of contemporary thinking in psychiatry. The dominant paradigm in psychiatric research, which treats mental disorder as if it can be naturally carved into convenient categories, and which places almost exclusive emphasis on biological explanations of abnormal behaviour, cannot be defended on either scientific or logical grounds. This objection to the current paradigm in psychopathology must not be thought of as anti-scientific or even anti-biological: many of the authors in the present volume (myself, Marshall, Claridge, Jackson) have taken care to emphasize that they favour biological research in the right context and those who have written on the topic of treatment (Slade, Tarrier) have been careful not to deny the value of phenothiazine medication in the treatment of some patients. What is wrong is the assumption that *only* biological variables count, that *only* biological treatments are effective. Such a stance, which can rightly be called the *ideology* of biological reductionism, may perhaps have the trappings of science but is in fact deeply anti-scientific. It is a stance that future generations of schizophrenic individuals are unlikely to thank us for accepting.

REFERENCES

Barnes, B. (1974) *Scientific Knowledge and Sociological Theory*, London: Routledge.

Broad, W. and Wade, N. (1984) *Betrayers of the Truth: Fraud and Deceit in Science*, Oxford: Oxford University Press.

Brush, S.G. (1974) 'Should the history of science by X-rated?', *Science* 183: 1164–72.

Chalmers, A. (1976) *What is This Thing Called Science?*, Milton Keynes: Open University Press.

Franklin, A.D. (1981) 'Millikan's published and unpublished data on oil drops', *Historical Studies in the Physical Sciences* 11: 185–201.

Hill, D. (1988) 'Psychiatric delusions', *New Statesman*, 12 September.

Keith, S.J. and Matthews, S.M. [eds] (1988) 'A national plan for schizophrenia research', *Schizophrenia Bulletin* 14: 343–470.

Kennedy, J.L., Giuffra, L.A., Moises, H.W., Cavalli-Sforza, L.L., Pakstis,

A.J., Kidd J.R., Castiglione, C.M., Sjogren, B., Wetterberg, L., and Kidd, K.K. (1988) 'Evidence against linkage of schizophrenia to markers on chromosome 5 in a northern Swedish pedigree', *Nature* 336: 167–70.

Kerr, A. and Snaith, P. [eds] (1986) *Contemporary Issues in Schizophrenia*, London: Gaskell.

Kuhn, T. (1962) *The Structure of Scientific Revolutions*, Chicago: Chicago University Press.

Lander, E.S. (1988) 'Splitting schizophrenia', *Nature* 336: 105–6.

Medical Research Council (1988) *Research into Schizophrenia: Report of the Schizophrenia and Allied Conditions Committee to the Neurosciences Board*, London: MRC.

Popper, K. (1963) *Conjectures and Refutations: The Growth of Scientific Knowledge*, London: Routledge.

Powers, J. (1982) *Philosophy and the New Physics*, London: Methuen.

St Clair, D., Blackwood, D., Muir, W., Baillie, D., Hubbard, A., Wright, A., and Evans J. (1989) 'No linkage of chromosome 5q11–q13 markers to schizophrenia in Scottish families', *Nature* 339: 305–9.

Sarbin, T.R. and Mancuso, J.C. (1980) *Schizophrenia: Medical Diagnosis or Moral Verdict?*, New York: Pergamon.

Sherington, R., Brynjolfsson, J., Pertursson, H., Potter, M., Dudleston, K., Barraclough, B., Wasmuth, J., Dobbs, M., and Gurling, H. (1988) 'Localization of a susceptibility locus for schizophrenia on chromosome 5', *Nature* 336: 164–7.

AUTHOR INDEX

SUBJECT INDEX